Essential
Visual Studio 2019

Boosting Development Productivity with Containers, Git, and Azure Tools

Bruce Johnson

Apress®

Essential Visual Studio 2019: Boosting Development Productivity with Containers, Git, and Azure Tools

Bruce Johnson
ObjectSharp Consulting
Toronto, ON, Canada

ISBN-13 (pbk): 978-1-4842-5718-0
https://doi.org/10.1007/978-1-4842-5719-7

ISBN-13 (electronic): 978-1-4842-5719-7

Managing Director, Apress Media LLC: Welmoed Spahr
Acquisitions Editor: Joan Murray
Development Editor: Laura Berendson
Coordinating Editor: Jill Balzano

Cover image designed by Freepik (www.freepik.com)

Distributed to the book trade worldwide by Springer Science+Business Media New York, 233 Spring Street, 6th Floor, New York, NY 10013. Phone 1-800-SPRINGER, fax (201) 348-4505, e-mail orders-ny@springer-sbm.com, or visit www.springeronline.com. Apress Media, LLC is a California LLC and the sole member (owner) is Springer Science + Business Media Finance Inc (SSBM Finance Inc). SSBM Finance Inc is a **Delaware** corporation.

For information on translations, please e-mail rights@apress.com, or visit http://www.apress.com/rights-permissions.

Apress titles may be purchased in bulk for academic, corporate, or promotional use. eBook versions and licenses are also available for most titles. For more information, reference our Print and eBook Bulk Sales web page at http://www.apress.com/bulk-sales.

Any source code or other supplementary material referenced by the author in this book is available to readers on GitHub via the book's product page, located at www.apress.com/9781484257180. For more detailed information, please visit http://www.apress.com/source-code.

Printed on acid-free paper

I'd like to dedicate this book to the most important people in my life – my four children, Kyle, Cameron, Gillian, and Curtis, and my partner in life, Rachel. The kids are all adultlike now, so giving me space to write came naturally. And getting space from Rachel is not something I ever want to experience.

Table of Contents

About the Author

Bruce Johnson is cofounder and partner at ObjectSharp Consulting. He has more than three decades of experience, starting in UNIX, but then moved into the Windows development. Over the course of his career, he gained expertise in rich client applications, web applications, and APIs, with a dash of database, microservices, and front-end development thrown in. After 20 years it's almost impossible not to become a full-stack developer.

Formerly a Microsoft MVP and MCT, Bruce enjoys teaching and presenting within the developer community. He has spoken hundreds of times at conferences and user groups throughout North America and Europe. As well, he is the author of many books, articles, and columns. He can be reached on Twitter at @LACanuck and LinkedIn at `www.linkedin.com/in/bruce-johnson-95b468`.

About the Technical Reviewer

Jort Rodenburg is a software engineer and author specializing in C#. He has worked on software in a variety of fields such as financial compliance and reporting, inkjet printing, and medical imaging. Originally from the Netherlands, Jort has lived in a random array of places such as Vermont and Arizona over the years with his wife and two cats. Jort is the author of *"Code Like a Pro in C#"*.

Acknowledgments

Writing a book is by no means an individual effort. Not by a long shot. If all you had to read was the first draft, well, I would suggest that you would be disappointed. It takes the efforts and assistance of a large number of people to make a project like this a success. The fact that the text is clear, accurate, and coherent is because of the incredible contributions of my editor, my technical editor, my copy editor, and the proof reader. And I haven't even gotten to those who are responsible for the production of the graphics, the people who do the production work, and any other members of the team I have forgotten to mention. I'm immensely grateful for the help and have enjoyed working with a very talented and diligent group of people. The process is much more enjoyable because of them.

I would especially like to thank everyone at Apress who has helped me through this process. In particular, thanks go out to Jill Balzano. This is our first book together and I'm not always the easiest author to work with. Her patience is very much appreciated.

Thanks also go to Jort Rodenburg, who did a fantastic job ensuring that any of the numerous technical mistakes in the original draft were cleaned up before publication. And he made many great suggestions that helped me clarify my writing. Beyond that, he appreciated that I used the word "triumvirate" in a sentence that was both grammatically correct and meaningful. That in itself is enough for me to bow down before him.

The efforts of all these individuals and then some are what made this book possible and, hopefully, a success.

Introduction

Visual Studio is an integral part of the daily life of millions of developers around the world. And, even as it approaches the age of 20 years old, it hasn't stopped innovating ways to make developers' work life more productive. This is a laudable achievement and is one of the reasons for Visual Studio's success.

The challenge, however, is keeping up with the innovations. With each new edition, there are changes made to the user interface, new features that get added, and existing functionality that is improved. And the cadence of the editions has been every 2 years. Knowing what these modifications are and when they can be used is critical to taking full advantage of the power of Visual Studio. The goal of this book is to bring the developer up to speed on Visual Studio 2019. It will not be focused just on functionality added in Visual Studio 2019, but on taking a deep dive into the areas where Visual Studio 2019 made changes. That way, even if you're coming from much earlier versions of Visual Studio, you can see where and when upgrading to Visual Studio 2019 could make you more productive.

Who This Book Is For

Essential Visual Studio 2019 is targeted at developers who are not new to Visual Studio. It doesn't cover the basics of creating projects, editing files, and debugging your applications. Instead, the focus is on the features that you might not be familiar with. This includes not just those capabilities added with Visual Studio 2019, but also talks about the areas that have been the focus of the Microsoft development team over the last couple of years.

This is not to say that developers new to Visual Studio can't benefit from the book. The depth of coverage is more than you will find in many larger books. And the relentless focus is on features that are used. The content goes deeper than how to create a "Hello World" project. It touches on areas that real-world developers will find useful every day.

To use this book effectively, you'll need only one additional item – Microsoft Visual Studio 2019 Professional Edition. While there are a couple of features that are available only with the Visual Studio 2019 Enterprise Edition (and this limitation is mentioned when it comes up), the vast majority of the book deals with the Professional version. And in fact, a majority of the book content equally applies to the Community edition also.

While there are some coding samples in the book, they are not particularly extensive or complicated. The samples are only used to illustrate the Visual Studio features being discussed. But as a result, this book assumes that you have some familiarity with C#.

How This Book Is Structured

This book is divided into ten chapters, each focusing on a different aspect of Visual Studio 2019.

Installation and IDE Differences – With every version of Visual Studio, there are some minor changes to the user experience. This chapter covers the installation process, options, and limitations. As well, it describes the fundamental changes and additions to the IDE itself.

Assisted Coding – Writing code is a relatively crucial function when it comes to Visual Studio. Part of the productivity promise is to help you write code, find code, and navigate through code. This chapter looks at the features Visual Studio offers to help you do all of these things, including coverage of both CodeLens and Code Cleanup.

Unit Testing – The modern flow for software development is red/green/refactor. To support the developer, Visual Studio provides both a framework and functionality to enable the red/green portion of that process. And in some cases, Visual Studio can help you generate tests automatically.

Refactoring Code – To complete that trifecta of development flow, Visual Studio 2019 provides a decent number of refactoring actions. This chapter describes the different refactoring options that Visual Studio exposes.

Using Git in Visual Studio 2019 - Git has become the source control of choice for most developers. In this chapter, the support that is provided by Visual Studio 2019 for using Git and some of its most frequently used concepts are covered.

Collaboration – One of the up and coming ideas for developing is collaboration. And in a world of distributed development, collaboration across the Internet is an interesting one. This chapter looks at the different ways that Visual Studio supports distributed coding, including how you can use Live Share to perform distributed pair programming and debugging.

Debugging and Profiling – Bugs are an inevitable part of software development. A good IDE finds different ways to support a developer's efforts to identify and correct problems. This chapter looks at the different ways that Visual Studio 2019 helps, including data breakpoints and time travel debugging.

Language-Specific Improvements – Each new version of Visual Studio provides different sets of improvements depending on the language that you're working with. This chapter looks at the additions for different languages from across the .NET spectrum.

Azure Tooling – Azure is a big part of the Microsoft ecosystem. So it shouldn't come as a surprise that Visual Studio 2019 includes a large number of tools for working with various parts of Azure directly from the environment. This chapter looks at some of the more recent additions and how they are integrated with Visual Studio.

Containers and Orchestration – There is a strong move toward using containers when it comes to deploying applications. And Visual Studio 2019 includes support for the most popular container, Docker, but also one of the leading orchestration tools in Kubernetes. This chapter looks at how you can work with these tools directly without leaving your Visual Studio environment.

CHAPTER 1

Installation and IDE Differences

Visual Studio has an interesting heritage. It has been around in different forms for more than 15 years. And if you trace its heritage back to Visual Basic, Microsoft has been providing development environments for almost 30 years. That experience makes it understandable that Visual Studio is one of the most used (and most loved) tools by developers, regardless of the kinds of applications they are trying to create.

One of the strengths that Visual Studio has, particularly over the last five versions, is a high degree of consistency. If you're familiar with earlier versions of Visual Studio, you can easily navigate your way through Visual Studio 2019. Such is the power of stability and familiarity.

But that having been said, just knowing that Visual Studio 2019 is similar to earlier versions doesn't tell the whole story. With each version, new features have been added and existing functionality enhanced. This is not surprising given that the Microsoft ecosystem continues to evolve – and quite rapidly at that: Azure; DevOps; Docker; Xamarin; web frameworks like Angular, React, and Vue; and big data.

Not all of these might be of interest to you. But odds are pretty good that some of them are. What it means, though, is that if all you're doing is continuing to use Visual Studio the way you used to, you're missing out. And that's the point of this book – to keep you from missing out, ensuring that you know how and where Visual Studio 2019 has evolved. By identifying new areas that might be of use for you, you can become more efficient in your day-to-day work. And that, ultimately, is the goal of this book.

To start, before getting into some of the advanced features, let's talk about the basics. No question that the interface has not changed significantly. But there are still things that have been added or tweaked. And sometimes the small times are the most useful.

1

© Bruce Johnson 2020
B. Johnson, *Essential Visual Studio 2019*, https://doi.org/10.1007/978-1-4842-5719-7_1

Installing Visual Studio 2019

The starting point for this chapter will be the installation process. It is also one of the more volatile functions over the past few versions. Seemingly each new release comes with a new installer interface. And Visual Studio 2019 is not breaking that trend.

Visual Studio 2019 can be installed side-by-side with earlier versions of Visual Studio. In fact, you can run Visual Studio 2019 independently of every version from Visual Studio 2012 to Visual Studio 2017. This gives you the ability to support older applications using components that might not be readily available in Visual Studio 2019 (e.g., Crystal Reports).

What this also means, pragmatically, is that you're not upgrading from Visual Studio 2017 to Visual Studio 2019. You are installing a brand-new instance of Visual Studio 2019. There is no upgrade process, per se. Just installation.

This is not to say that projects created and opened in Visual Studio 2017 don't work in Visual Studio 2019. They do. More importantly, opening a project in Visual Studio 2019 doesn't mean that you can't open it in earlier versions. The format of the project and solution are backward compatible between Visual Studio 2019 and Visual Studio 2013. The exception, naturally, is that if your Visual Studio 2019 solution includes a project template with functionality that doesn't exist in the earlier versions. For instance, you're not going to be able to open a Docker project in Visual Studio 2015. But a Windows Forms or ASP.NET project created in Visual Studio 2013 will open in Visual Studio 2019 just fine and vice versa.

The installation of Visual Studio 2019 is driven through the Visual Studio Installer. You can download the most recent installer from `https://visualstudio.microsoft.com/downloads/`. On this page, you have three editions of Visual Studio to choose from: Community, Professional, and Enterprise. The difference between these editions is, in some ways, minor and, in other ways, important.

Each edition gives you the ability to develop applications in every language supported by Visual Studio. And you can install the necessary workloads to develop web applications, Universal Windows Platform (UWP) applications, cross-platform applications, and data science functionality, where you start to see significant differences in some of the productivity and testing tools. Neither Community nor Professional editions include IntelliTest, Code Cloning, live dependency validation, live unit testing, snapshot debugging, or time travel debugging. These are all features that will be discussed in this book, if only so that you can better choose whether Enterprise is a more appropriate option for your development habits.

Once you have downloaded the installer and executed it, you will be presented with the dialog seen in Figure 1-1.

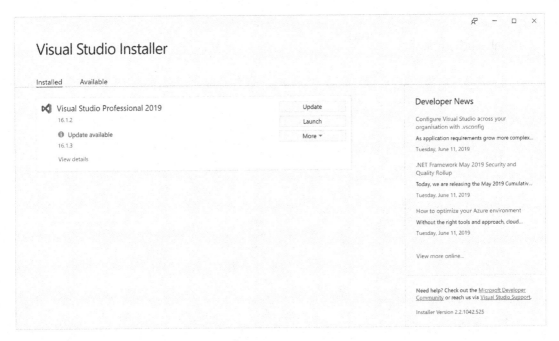

Figure 1-1. *Installed tab in Visual Studio Installer*

This is the starting point for both installing Visual Studio 2019 from scratch or for adding and removing the installed workloads and components after you've started using it. There are two tabs visible in the dialog. The Installed tab shows all of the Visual Studio versions that are currently installed on your computer. The Available tab shows the editions and versions of Visual Studio that are available to be installed. As you can see, the Installed tab shows that there is a version of Visual Studio 2019 ready to be updated. Figure 1-2 illustrates the Available tab.

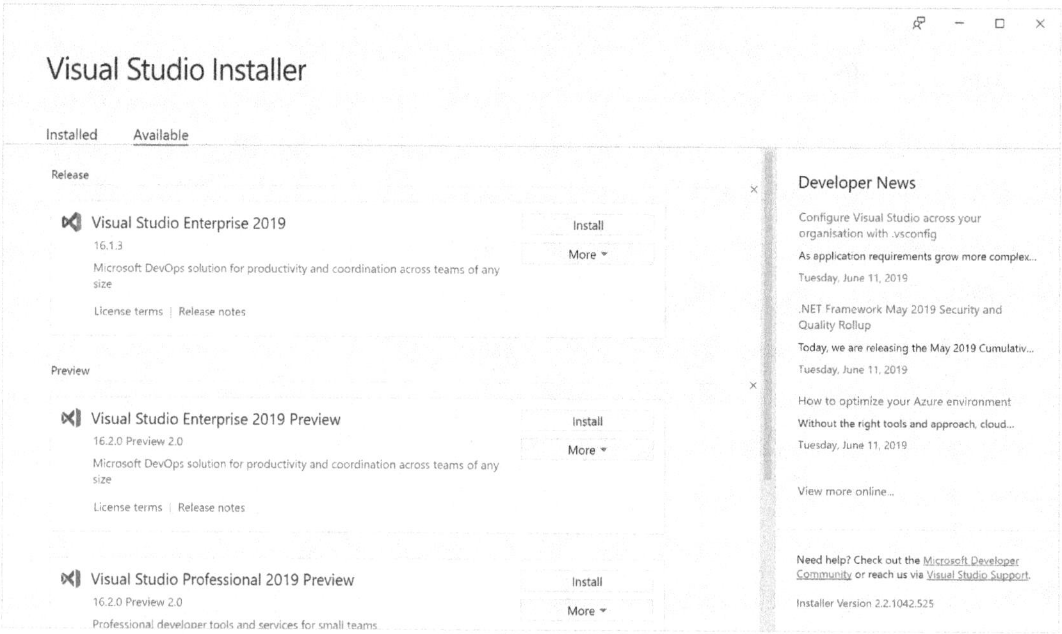

Figure 1-2. *Available tab in Visual Studio Installer*

Here you can see that there are two editions of Visual Studio 2019 that can be installed. While all versions of Visual Studio that you have installed on your machine appear on the Installed tab, the Available tab only shows the most recent version. And note that there are two groups of available versions. Visual Studio Enterprise 2019 is in the Release section. That means that you would have installed the currently released version. The Preview section contains two editions which are still in preview mode. This means that they have features and tooling that are going through the testing process. Don't take this to mean that the quality of preview versions is not high... it is. But it's possible that changes in supported functionality or configuration can take place between preview mode and when it gets released.

To launch the installation process, locate the desired version and click the Install button. Similarly, to update an existing instance, find it on the Installed tab and click the Update button. Both actions launch the same dialog, shown in Figure 1-3.

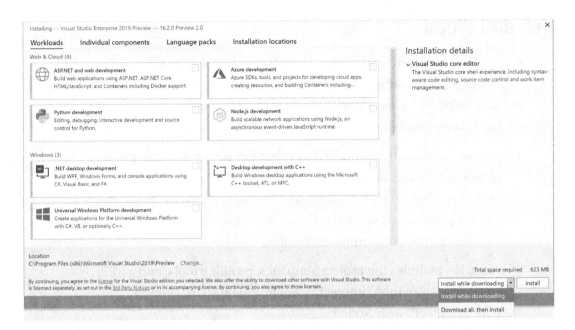

Figure 1-3. *Visual Studio installation dialog*

One of the recent innovations in the Visual Studio installation process is the concept of a workload. There was a realization at Microsoft that not every developer required the same components to be installed with Visual Studio. Installation speed could be improved by allowing the developer to choose what they required and then installing only those pieces. But there are dozens of available components and how could any developer know which were required. Certainly the naming of the components didn't provide any useful indication. So the concept of a workload was introduced.

A workload is a predefined set of components that have been identified as being part of a common type of development. Figure 1-3 contains the workloads that are available. For example, there is a workload for web developer. It contains all of the components that are required to code, debug, and deploy web applications using ASP.NET or ASP. NET Core. If that's the kind of development you do, you would choose the workload and start the process. The same is true for the other workloads that are available. Identify the type of development you plan on doing, select the appropriate workloads, and start the installation.

The available workloads are broken into different categories based on common usage patterns. The list of categories, and the workloads found in each one, can be found in the next sections.

Web and Cloud

- ASP.NET and web development – Includes the components used to build web applications using ASP.NET Core, ASP.NET, and HTML/JavaScript. In a bow to one of the major trends today, it also includes the tooling needed to work with Docker components.

- Azure – Includes the Azure SDK, project templates, and other tooling to help you create and manipulate the different Azure resources. You can create Azure-based web applications, virtual machines, and like the preceding ASP.NET and web development workload, it also includes the Docker component tooling.

- Node.js – Includes the project templates, profiling tools, and a REPL (read-eval-print loop) interactive environment so that you can effectively work with Node.js.

- Python – Includes support for building Python-based web applications using frameworks like Flask and Django. This workload is also useful for creating data science applications based on Python, as it comes with built-in support for Conda and IPython.

Windows

- Desktop development with C++ – Used to build traditional Windows apps using C++. Some of the supported tools include CMake, Clang, and MSBuild.

- .NET desktop development – Also used to build traditional Windows apps, but now the technologies of choice include Windows Forms and WPF (Windows Presentation Foundation), while the supported languages are Visual Basic, C#, and F#.

- UWP development – The Universal Windows Platform (UWP) workload allows you to target a wide range of platforms, including Xbox, HoloLens, Surface Hub, and the typical desktop. This is also a workload that might be of interest if you're working in Windows 10 IoT (Internet of Things).

Mobile and Gaming

- Game development with C++ – This workload includes the components used to create games using C++. Included is the ability to support engines like DirectX and Unreal.

- Game development with Unity – Unity is a cross-platform game development environment that can be used to create 2D and 3D games. This workload supports the Unity game development framework, with its ability to publish to mobile platforms, Mac, desktop, web applications, and game consoles.

- Mobile development with .NET – While the name includes .NET, this workload could easily be called Xamarin. With Xamarin, you can create native applications for iOS, Android, and UWP using C# and XAML and the underlying technologies.

- Mobile development with C++ – This workload also allows you to develop applications for iOS and Android, using C++ as the language of choice.

Other Toolsets

- .NET Core cross-platform development – .NET Core is a development platform that Microsoft has placed into open source for all to see (and even contribute to). This workload adds the components necessary to create .NET Core applications, including ASP.NET Core.

- Data science and analytics – Being able to perform complex queries against data warehouses is a compelling application that has come to the forefront in the past decade. This workload includes tools and support for languages like Python, F#, and R, allowing you to build applications that extract, cleanse, and query data.

- Data storage and processing – Over the past view years, there have been several additions to Azure (such as Azure Data Lake and support for Hadoop) and additions to SQL Server to support large quantities of data. This workload includes the components that are used to work with big data, both from a storage and querying perspective.

- Linux development with C++ – This workload includes the components that are used to create applications for a Linux environment. While this might seem surprising to long-time Windows developers, it is less unusual than you might think. Windows 10 includes options to install an Ubuntu-based Bash shell and includes a Windows Subsystem for Linux that allows Linux applications to be run from within Windows.

- Office/SharePoint development – The development approach for both Office and SharePoint has changed a great deal in recent years. This workload adds the components that are used to create applications for the most recent version of both Office and SharePoint. This includes add-ins for Word, Excel, and Outlook, as well as the different SharePoint solutions that are available.

- Visual Studio extension development – Visual Studio boasts an incredible set of extensibility points. You can, with relative ease, create code analyzers or tool windows that are deeply integrated into Visual Studio. This workload adds the components and project templates to get you started.

Behind each definition is a collection of components that get installed with the workload. Choosing a workload is the same as saying you want to install the corresponding components, but without needing to know which components you require. Choosing workloads is not the only means of identifying the components you want to install. You can select the individual components yourself.

Near the top of the dialog, select the Individual components link. The list of components, seen in Figure 1-4, appears. Here you can choose any of the individual components from the list. And, as you would expect, the selected components will be installed on your machine.

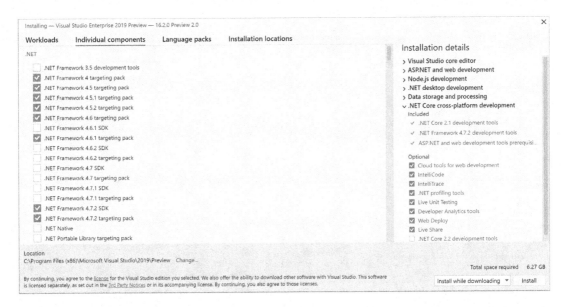

Figure 1-4. *Individual Components*

Naturally, there is a relationship between workloads and the individual components. After all, the entire point of the workload is to give you prepackaged sets of components based on the kind of development you are doing. If you select a workload from the installation page, a list of the components that are included can be seen in the pane on the right side of the dialog. And they are checked off in the list of all of the components that appears on the left. If you want to add or remove components from the installation, check or uncheck the corresponding item.

There is a third way to impact the installation of Visual Studio 2019. Clicking the Language packs link, also at the top of the dialog, displays a list of the available language packs (shown in Figure 1-5).

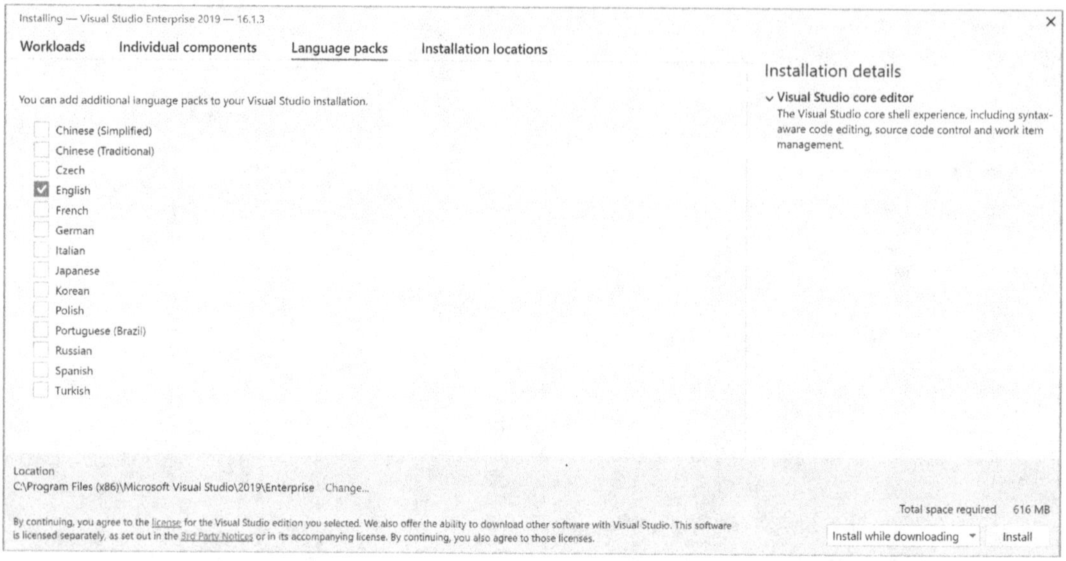

Figure 1-5. *Language packs*

The installation of the language packs is independent of the installation of components, which means that you can choose a collection of components, then go to the list of language packs, and choose a number of them as well. There is no correlation between workloads and language packs, nor between individual components and language packs. Regardless of the combination, all of the selected items will be installed.

Once you have selected your components and language packs, the installation is ready to begin. There is a default location for the installation, or you can choose a different location, if you want. An alternate location is identified by clicking the Installation locations link at the top, revealing the screen shown in Figure 1-6.

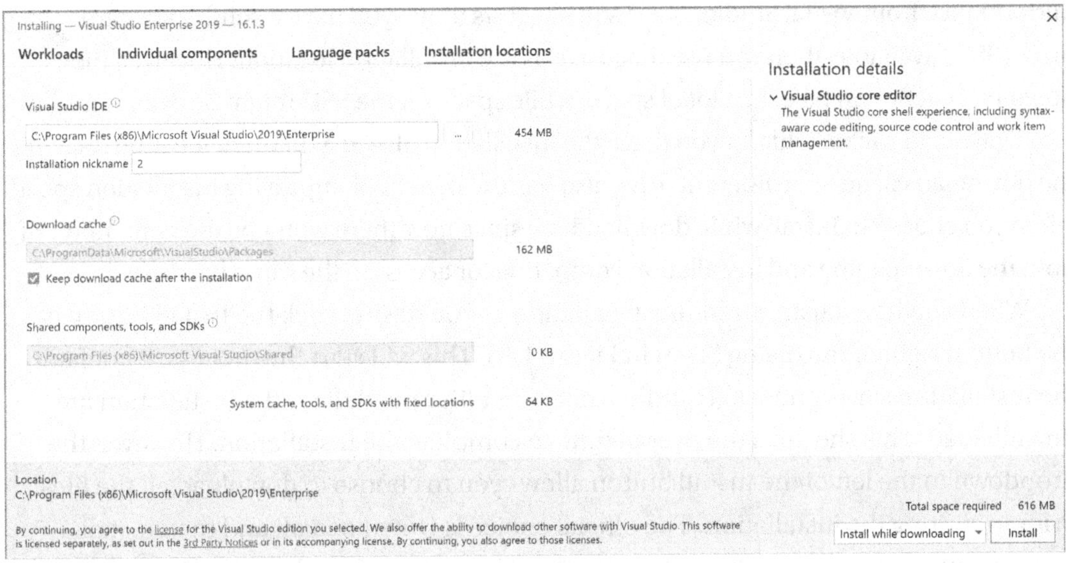

Figure 1-6. *Installation locations*

There are three locations that are available on this screen, which might be two more than you expect. At the top, the Visual Studio IDE field defines the main location for the installation. This is typical for installing any product. But the second field is where there is divergence from "normal."

The Download cache field lets you know where the files downloaded as part of the installation will be placed. There is also a check box that allows these files to be kept after the installation is complete (because they normally would be deleted when you're done).

The Shared components, tools, and SDKs field is also informational. This is the directory where the component files will be placed. This location is used by the different versions of Visual Studio that you installed on your machine, which is why the location can't be changed. However, if you do have earlier versions of Visual Studio installed, make sure that the path matches the path that those versions are using. Otherwise, you will be adding the shared component files to your system twice, once for the earlier versions and once for Visual Studio 2019.

You might wonder why Microsoft felt the need to let you specify a different place for the download cache. The rationale has to do with a recommendation that Microsoft has regarding the installation location.

Visual Studio has a lot of files associated with it – not just for the core development environment but also for the different components that get installed. When you are running the application, there is a lot of disk I/O activity going on. To get the best

11

performance from Visual Studio, Microsoft suggests that if you have a solid-state hard drive (SSD) available, then you use that drive as the installation location. However, the download cache can take up a lot of space, while space on the SSD might be at a premium. The Download cache fields let you place the installation files in a different location. Placing the download cache on a different drive also has the benefit of improving installation speed when you choose to Install while downloading, since now there won't be the contention of both the downloading and installation competing for access to the same hard drive.

When you have customized the installation as you desire, click the Install button at the bottom right of the dialog (seen in Figure 1-3). This will start the process. By default, the installation starts on Visual Studio while other files needed for the installation are downloaded. This shortens the overall time to complete the installation. However, the dropdown to the left of the Install button allows you to choose to download all the files prior to starting the installation. The official choice is Download all and then install.

Why might you choose this option? Well, if you install while downloading, then you need to stay connected to the Internet for the entire installation process. If you are running across a slow or limited Internet connection, this can be annoying. However, if you download all of the files before starting the installation, you can disconnect as soon as the installation is ready to start.

Note   If, for whatever reason, installing Visual Studio isn't an option to you, Microsoft has placed virtual machines containing Visual Studio into the Azure Marketplace. You can go into your Microsoft Azure account and create virtual machines containing the Enterprise or Community edition of Visual Studio 2015 through 2019. All the workloads have been installed and the images are updated monthly, so that they are consistently up to date.

Updating Visual Studio 2019

There is a regular cadence that Microsoft has for releasing updates to Visual Studio. Expect you'll have the opportunity to install updates on a regular basis. The Visual Studio Installer is ultimately how updates are installed, but Visual Studio notifies you when updates are available not just to Visual Studio but also to the various components that you have installed.

The starting point is a notifier that appears at the right side of the status bar, seen in Figure 1-7.

Figure 1-7. *Status bar notifier*

This notifier has a badge containing the number of notifications that are available. Not all notifications relate to updates. You might get notified if your license key is getting close to expiration, for example, or if there were issues connecting to your source control provider. And other components can produce notifications, including both Microsoft-provided and third-party developed. When you click the notifier, the notification messages appear in a pane of their own (Figure 1-8).

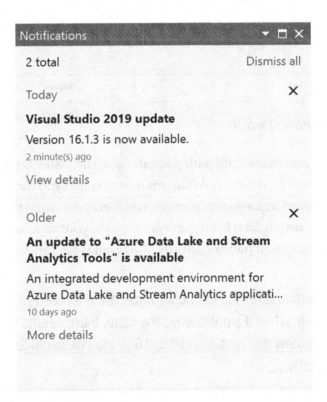

Figure 1-8. *Notification pane*

You can see two notifications that are currently visible, including one for an update to Visual Studio 2019. This is your cue that an update is available. Because, well, that's pretty much what the notification message says. At this point, there are two paths you can take to install the update. First, the Show Details link at the bottom left of the message is used to open information about the update. Figure 1-9 shows a typical dialog that appears when you click the link. If you click the Update button, the Visual Studio Installer will launch.

Figure 1-9. *Notification Details*

This leads neatly into the second path you can take. The Visual Studio Installer is a separate application within Windows. What this means is that you can execute it as you would any other application on your computer. You can find it listed within the list of installed programs or search for it from the search area in your task bar. Whether you launch it from the notification pane or directly, the result is the same.

Note   It is quite common for the Launcher application to need to update itself when you run it. While it's not always the case, there seems to be a high correlation between new dot versions (16.1, 16.2, etc.) of Visual Studio and new versions of the Installer.

The Installer is used to manage all the Visual Studio instances you have on your computer. In Figure 1-1, you can see that Visual Studio 2019 Professional has been installed. If you had Visual Studio 2017 installed, that instance would also appear. To the right of each instance description is a number of buttons whose labels depend on the state of the instance. Unsupported preview editions of earlier versions would have the top button labeled as Uninstall.

For Visual Studio 2019, the top button reads either Update or Modify, depending on whether a Visual Studio update is available. Clicking Update will start the process of updating to the current version of Visual Studio. Clicking Modify allows you to add or remove workloads from your existing instance.

There are two other buttons available. The middle button, labeled Launch, is used to launch the instance. Below that is a More button that displays additional functionality. This functionality includes options to repair or uninstall Visual Studio. If there is an update available, you can run the update using the Download and then Install button. And finally, there is the ability to Import or Export configurations. In this case, the configuration that is being imported or exported is a collection of workloads, components, and language packs. If you choose the Export option, then the collection for your current installation is placed into a config file. This file can then be imported by someone else, so that the set of features can be synchronized between the two of you. This makes it easier to work on the same project without later discovering that some critical component hasn't been installed.

Launching Your Code

Another area of high volatility, at least in terms of user experience, is the startup flow for Visual Studio. When you launch Visual Studio, the screen shown in Figure 1-10 appears.

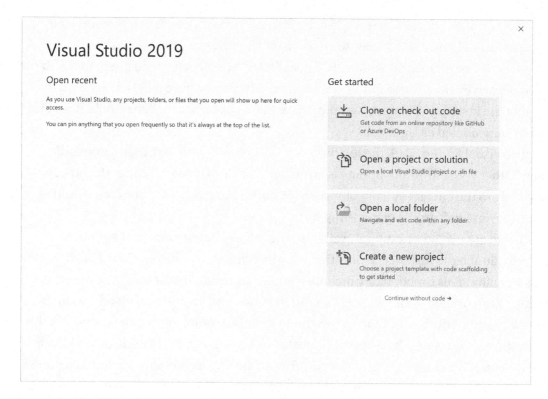

Figure 1-10. *Visual Studio 2019 startup screen*

There are two main parts to the startup screen. On the left is a list of the most recently opened projects, solutions, or files. This gives you quick access to your most recently used artifacts. Clicking the project/solution/file causes them to be opened. On the right is a collection of buttons that let you perform some very common activities related to creating a new project.

As you open different items, the list on the left will grow. And it does remember a large number of projects, which is to say that you are not likely to exceed whatever maximum does exist. To help you navigate through the list, there are a couple of options available to you. Figure 1-11 shows a typical entry, along with a context menu.

Figure 1-11. *Recently opened project item*

You can see options in the context menu to both pin the item to the Recent Projects list and remove it from the list. This way you can ensure both that regularly opened artifacts stay at the top of the list, regardless of any intervening projects that get opened, and that the list can be decluttered of projects that are no longer needed. While it's not visible when the context menu is active, there is a pin icon at the right of the item so that you can easily pin and unpin the item.

The buttons on the right surface are the most common options if you're not going to be working with a previously opened project. A description of each of the buttons follows.

Clone or check out code – When clicked, you are presented with a couple of options for how to proceed. The dialog is seen in Figure 1-12.

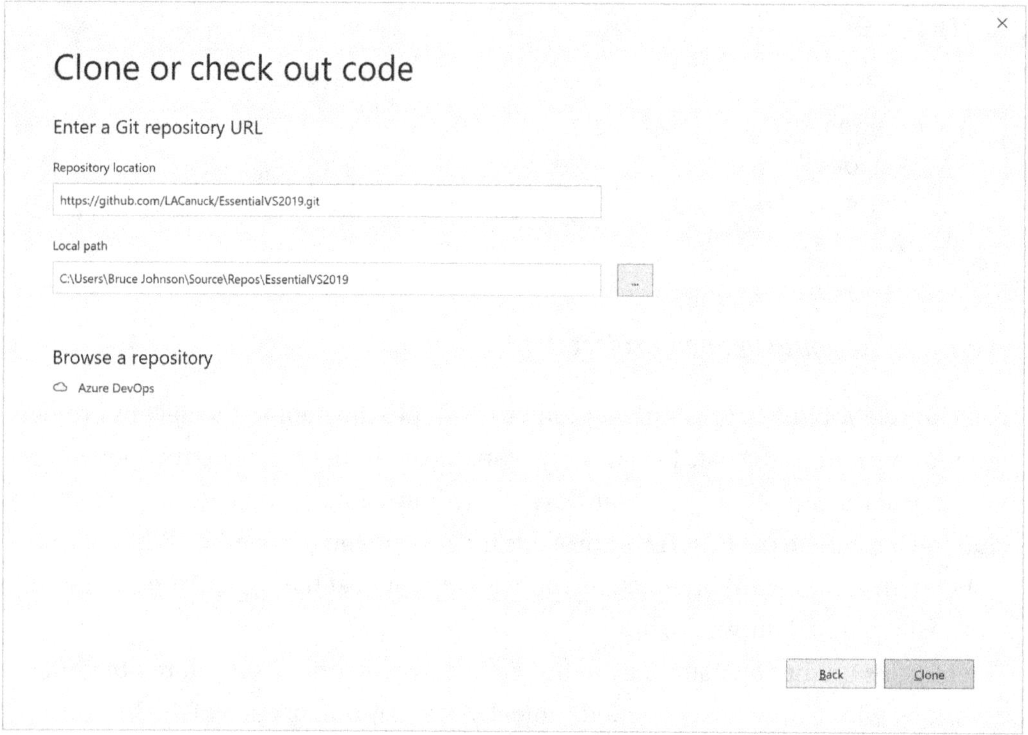

Figure 1-12. *Clone or check out code dialog*

The first option is to enter the URL for the Git repository that you would like to clone. In this case, you will provide the URL in the Repository location field and the location on your machine for the repository in the Local path field.

The second option is to Browse a repository, such as Azure DevOps or a local Team Foundation System (TFS) server. The list of configured repositories can be seen under the Browse a repository label. When you click the desired repository, what happens next depends on the repositories host. For example, if you have an Azure DevOps account configured, you would see a dialog like Figure 1-13 appear.

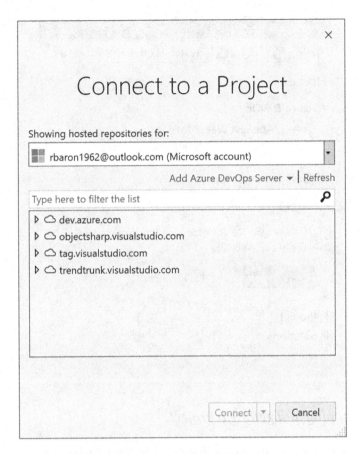

Figure 1-13. *Dialog to connect to an Azure DevOps project*

A slightly different dialog appears for a TFS server. But the outcome is the same. Locate the project that you would like to clone and connect to it. Once you have connected, the Team Explorer pane in Visual Studio will appear, seen in Figure 1-14.

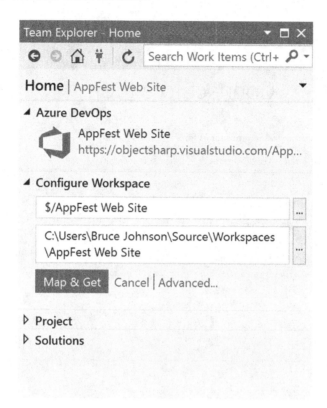

Figure 1-14. *Mapping and getting a project*

In this dialog, you can specify the local directory into which the project code is placed. When you have done that, click the Map & Get button. This downloads the code into the directory and establishes the mapping between the files and the project in TFS.

Open a project or solution – This option allows you to navigate through the drives that are available to your location machine to find a local project or solution. The flow is straightforward. A standard Open File dialog opens up. You navigate as normal looking for the project or solution file you desire. When you find it, click Open and Visual Studio opens it. The only truly different thing about this dialog is the number of different types of project files that are supported. If you click the dropdown list, the results look like Figure 1-15.

```
All Project Files (*.sln;*.dsw;*.vcw;*.slnf;*.csproj;*.csp
All Project Files (*.sln;*.dsw;*.vcw;*.slnf;*.csproj;*.csp
Solution Files (*.sln)
Compatible Workspace Files (*.dsw,*.vcw)
Solution Filter Files (*.slnf)
C# Project Files (*.csproj)
U-SQL CSharp Project Files (*.csproj)
F# Project Files (*.fsproj)
VB Project Files (*.vbproj)
Azure Stream Analytics Project Files (*.asaproj)
Docker Compose Project Files (*.dcproj)
Shared Projects (*.shproj)
Cloud Computing Project Files (*.ccproj)
Fabric Application Project Files (*.sfproj)
U-SQL Script UnitTest Project Files (*.usqlutproj)
Exe Project Files (*.exe)
.NET Core 2015 Project Files (*.xproj)
Hive Project Files (*.hiveproj)
Pig Project Files (*.pigproj)
Visual Basic Project Files (*.vbproj)
Azure Stream Analytics Project Files (*.edgeproj)
U-SQL C# UDO UnitTest Project Files (*.csproj)
U-SQL Project Files (*.usqlproj)
U-SQL UnitTest Project Files (*.csproj)
Deployment Project Files (*.deployproj)
Common Project System Files (*.msbuildproj)
Storm Project Files (*.csproj)
U-SQL Database Project Files (*.usqldbproj)
SQL Project Files (*.sqlproj)
Database Project Files (*.dbproj)
```

Figure 1-15. *List of supported project types*

Open a local folder – Conceptually similar to the previous button, except that instead of searching for a project file, you're searching for a folder. Oh, and the list of extensions isn't there, because you're looking for a folder, not a file.

This option is used for the type of projects that don't have a separate manifest describing the contents of a project (like the .csproj file in C# does, for instance), but instead just presumes that the contents of a particular folder (at least the contents that are not ignored by using one of the .ignore files that are commonly available) are part of a project.

Create a new project – If you don't have an existing project or folder to work with, this option will display a list of the project templates that have been installed on your system and allow you to create a new project based on it. The actual list of available templates depends on the workloads that have been installed. And this is a part of Visual Studio that hasn't changed significantly over the past few versions. The New Project dialog can be seen in Figure 1-16.

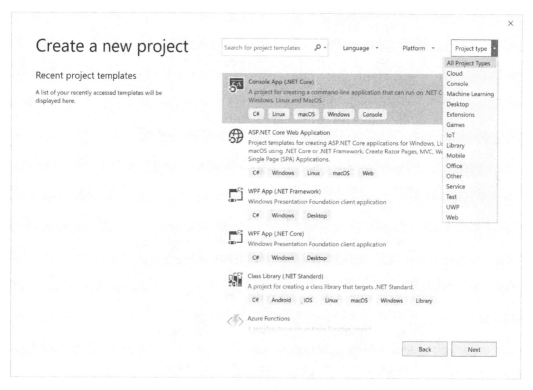

Figure 1-16. *New Project dialog*

The organization of project templates has changed significantly from earlier versions of Visual Studio. Now, the focus is on the template types, as opposed to the earlier versions where you started by choosing the project type and language before you got to see the available templates.

On the right of the dialog, you can see a list of the available templates. For each template, there are labels that indicate the languages and platforms that are supported by the template. You can search for a template using the search box at the top of the list. Or you can filter the list of templates by language, platform, or project type. The list of project types is visible in Figure 1-16.

Once you find the template, click Next to reveal the dialog seen in Figure 1-17.

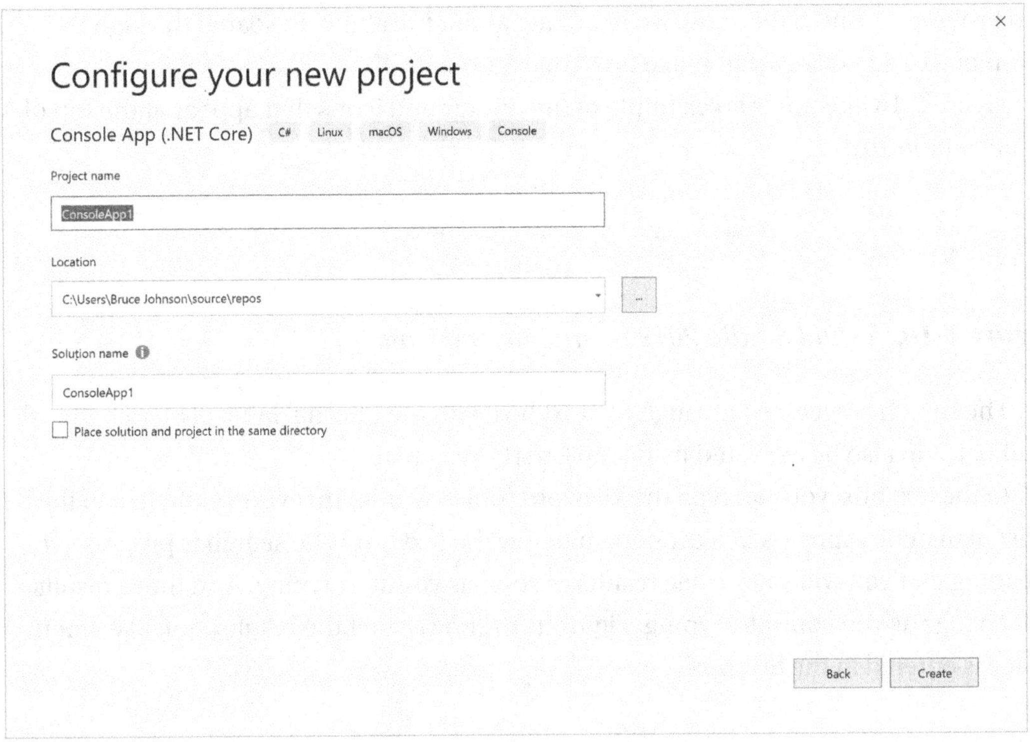

Figure 1-17. *Configure your new project dialog*

In this dialog, you provide a location and name for the new project, as well as the name for the solution. When you are ready, click Create. At this point, the specifics of what happens next depend on the template. Some templates take you through a wizard, giving you the ability to choose different customizations. Other templates will just create a new project, based on the requirements of the template. Regardless, once the process is finished, Visual Studio will have the new project open and you're ready to start writing code.

Searching Visual Studio

Now that we've looked at the basic installation of Visual Studio 2019, as well as the new way to open or create a project, if you have been working with Visual Studio 2017 or 2015, you'll find that not much has changed. The menu, the toolbar, and the various windows are pretty much exactly as you'd expect. One of the areas of improvement is the search functionality.

There is a search that checks for matches within your code base. And there is a search that looks within the current executing debug context (see Chapter 7, "Debugging and Profiling"). But in this case, we're talking about the ability to search through the commands and settings that make up Visual Studio itself.

Figure 1-18 illustrates an example of the menus and icons that appear at the top of Visual Studio 2019.

Figure 1-18. *Visual Studio 2019 menu bar and icons*

The search is accessed through the text box with the internal label of Search Visual Studio. It can also be activated using the Ctrl+Q keystroke.

In the text box, you can type the keyword (or keywords) that you would like to find. A list of matches appears in a dropdown below the text box. The search is progressive, meaning that you will start to see results as soon as you start typing. And those results will change as you continue typing. Figure 1-19 shows what the results look like when space is entered in the text box.

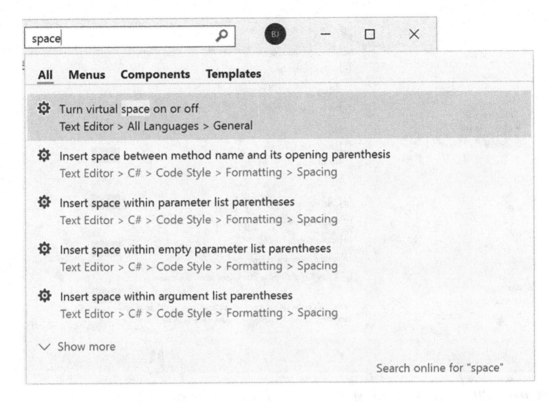

Figure 1-19. *Search results*

The results are divided into three categories: Menus, Components, and Templates. By default, all of the results are visible, but by clicking the headers at the top of the list, only the results for that category are displayed.

What happens when you click a search result depends on the type for the result. A Menu result triggers either the command to be executed (if the result is a menu command) or the Options dialog to be displayed, with the screen that contains the option visible. For example, clicking the Turn virtual space on or off result displays the Options dialog as seen in Figure 1-20.

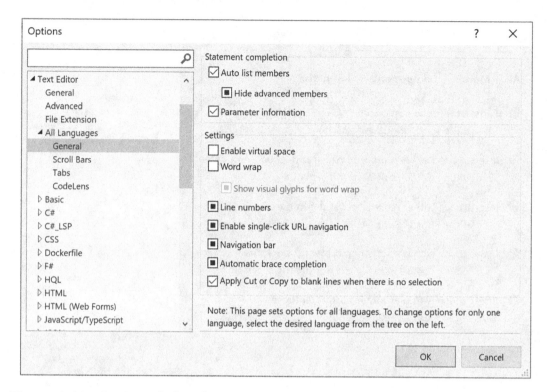

Figure 1-20. *Options dialog showing Enable virtual space*

Here, the desired option, Enable virtual space, is visible in the middle of the dialog, under the Settings header.

A Component result contains components that are known to be available, but have not yet been installed on your machine. If you go back to the installation process, it was possible to select Individual Components to install (Figure 1-4). Selecting a Component result triggers the installation of that component, which is to say that it launches the Visual Studio Installer and selects the corresponding component as one to be installed.

A Template result is used to create either a new element (such as a class or a web page) for the current project or a brand-new project. In both cases, a dialog appears that takes you through the steps to name the element or project, as well as make any choices that the template requires.

At the bottom right of the dialog shown in Figure 1-19, there is a link that allows you to search online for the term that you entered into the text box. This allows you to find components and templates that are not part of the Visual Studio installation. This includes items that have been contributed to the Visual Studio Marketplace.

Sharing and Synchronizing Settings

Configuring Visual Studio can be a personal thing. Like any IDE (integrated development environment), people like what they like. And they get used to certain key combinations launching certain functionality. As well, it can sometimes be useful to get all members of a team using the same set of keyboard shortcuts. This helps with communication between the members, and it's quite likely that what is going to be efficient for one team member will be efficient for all of them.

There are two settings that can help drive this functionality. First, it is possible to define the location for your settings file. This is available through the Environment ➤ Import and Export Settings tab in the Options dialog (accessible through the Tools ➤ Options menu item). Figure 1-21 shows the Options dialog.

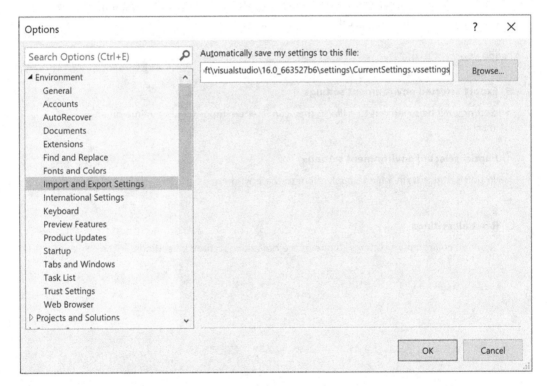

Figure 1-21. *Import and Export Settings in Options dialog*

This is the location used to store your settings when you modify them. And the contents of the file are read when you launch Visual Studio. What makes this useful for a team is that the file can be on a network share. That way everyone on a team can use the same settings file. The only caveat is that if people make changes to their settings, then everyone on the team will pick up those changes. Not overly dangerous, but something to be aware of if some expected functionality disappears overnight.

On a more personal level, you can export your current settings to a separate file for backup and then import them at a later time. This is accomplished through the Import and Export Settings Wizard, which can be launched through the Tools ➤ Import and Export Settings menu option. The initial screen for the wizard can be seen in Figure 1-22.

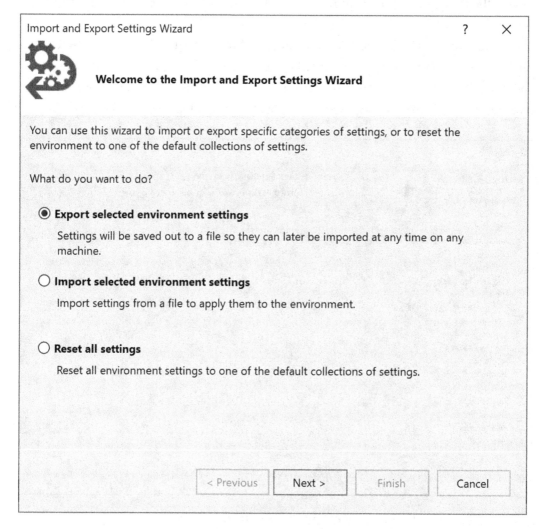

Figure 1-22. *Import and Export Settings Wizard*

Choose the Export selected environment settings and click Next to start the export process. The next step in the wizard, seen in Figure 1-23, lets you choose which settings are to be exported.

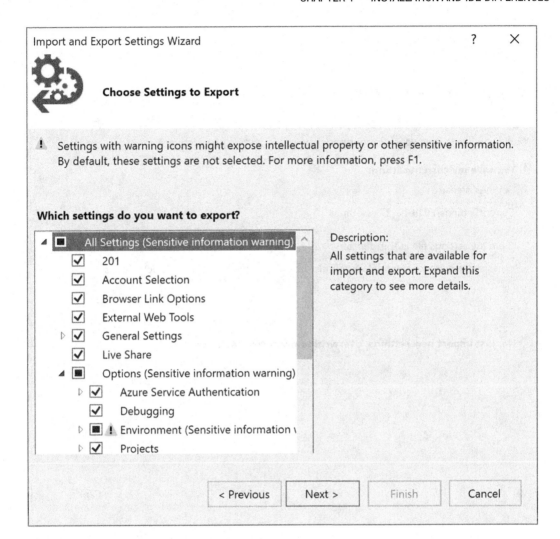

Figure 1-23. *Choose settings to export*

There are a large number of settings to choose from. By default, all of the settings are selected, with the exception of those that might contain sensitive information. Those settings are marked with a yellow warning triangle, such as the one seen next to Environment in Figure 1-23. Those settings are not exported by default, so if you want to include them, you'll need to add them manually.

The last of the dialogs in this wizard allows you to specify the name of the saved file and the directory in which it will be placed. When you click Finish on the final dialog, the settings are saved.

The import process for settings is a little simpler. If you choose the Import selected environment settings seen in Figure 1-22, the dialog shown in Figure 1-24 appears.

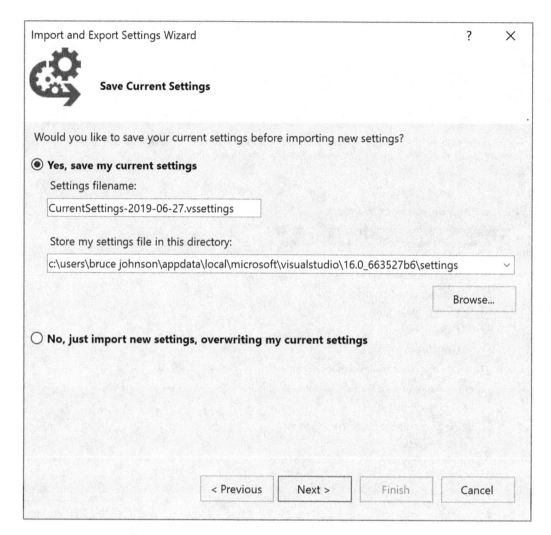

Figure 1-24. *Save Current Settings while importing settings*

You are given the option to save your current settings prior to importing a new set. Or you can just overwrite your current settings. Clicking Next gives you a dialog (Figure 1-25) where you can choose the settings to import.

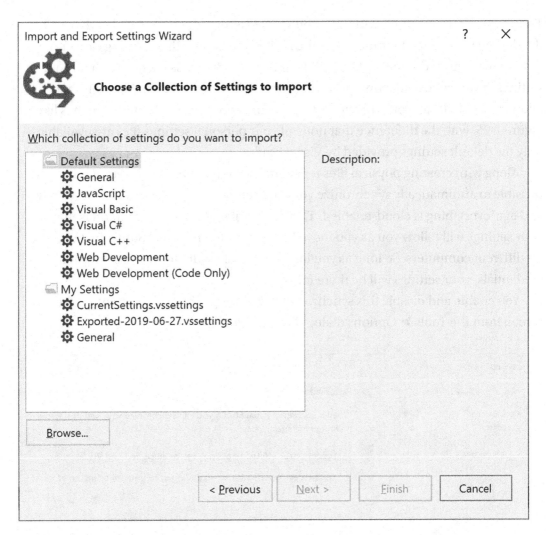

Figure 1-25. *Choose the settings to import*

At this point, you select the settings to import. There are two categories for your choices. You can pick one of the default settings. There are settings, defined by Microsoft and targeting a particular subset of developers. The premise is that the settings used by Visual Basic developers, for example, are different than the settings used by Visual C++ developers. The differences are based on the environments that the developers for the different categories have come from historically, or the different parts of Visual Studio that they are expected to use more frequently.

Along with the default settings are also the settings that you have previously saved, either explicitly or automatically. These are the settings files found in the default directory.

There is also a Browse option that lets you identify a settings file stored elsewhere. Choose the desired collection of settings, click the Finish button, and those settings are imported.

There is one additional option visible in Figure 1-22 that is used to reset all your settings. If you choose that option, you go next to the screen seen in Figure 1-24 that allows you to back up your current settings before continuing. The next screen is like Figure 1-25, with the difference that none of your personal settings files are available – only the default settings provided by Visual Studio.

Along with creating physical files that contain your Visual Studio settings, it's also possible to automatically synchronize your settings to the cloud, because, in this day and age, everything is cloud-enabled. The benefit of cloud synchronization is that your settings will follow you as you move between different Visual Studio instances on different computers. So long as you log into Visual Studio using the same cloud credentials, your settings will be there for you.

You enable and disable this synchronization through the Environment ➤ Account screen from the Tools ➤ Options dialog (Figure 1-26).

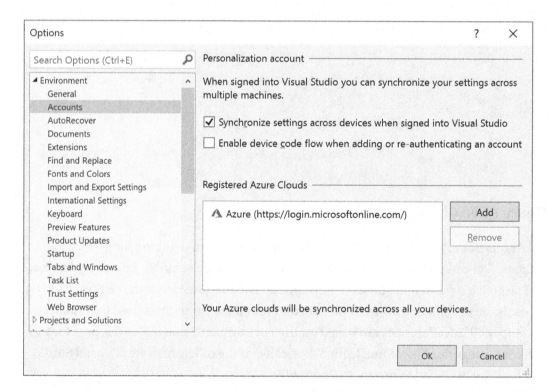

Figure 1-26. *Personalization account settings*

There is a check box that enables the cross-device synchronization. As well, there is a list of cloud accounts (the Registered Azure Clouds) that are the accounts that are recognized as sharing settings. For most people, there will only be one item in the list, that being their Azure account. However, if you have multiple Azure accounts available to you, you can add them to this list by using the Add button.

Summary

In this chapter, we covered the process of installing and updating Visual Studio 2019 and what it looks like when you launch the application. This includes having access to previously opened projects and solutions, as well as the process of creating an application from scratch or cloning it from a repository. As well, we examine some of the features of the IDE that are useful to team development, or if you're just trying to find that one setting buried deeply in the Options dialog.

In the next chapter, we start to take a look at how Visual Studio 2019 helps you write code more effectively. Because when you get right down to it, helping you write code is what Visual Studio is all about.

CHAPTER 2

Assisted Coding

As an integrated development environment, one of the strengths of Visual Studio is to help you write code more effectively and efficiently. It is a focus of the Visual Studio Team at Microsoft, and every version has several features, both big and small, aimed at improving the programming process. In this chapter, we'll cover the features added in Visual Studio 2019, as well as improvements that have been made to features that were introduced in earlier versions. In every instance, the goal is to reduce the effort involved in coding.

There are three areas that are going to be the focus of this chapter:

- Finding code – Being able to quickly search for the piece of code you want to see next, as well as identify who has worked on the code historically.

- Writing code – Assistance in the process of writing code.

- Keeping code clean – Also known as static analysis, we'll cover the steps involved in identifying and cleaning up code that doesn't meet a defined set of standards. Code analyzers are used to help identify problematic code. And Code Cleanup helps to "correct" code.

Finding Code

The ability to search your code base for a string or symbol is most definitely not new in Visual Studio 2019. The basic search functionality, including searching within the current document or across all of the files in the solution, is the same as in Visual Studio 2017. The only enhancements to speak of can be found in the Find in Files dialog, as seen in Figure 2-1, and the search results pane, shown in Figure 2-2.

© Bruce Johnson 2020
B. Johnson, *Essential Visual Studio 2019*, https://doi.org/10.1007/978-1-4842-5719-7_2

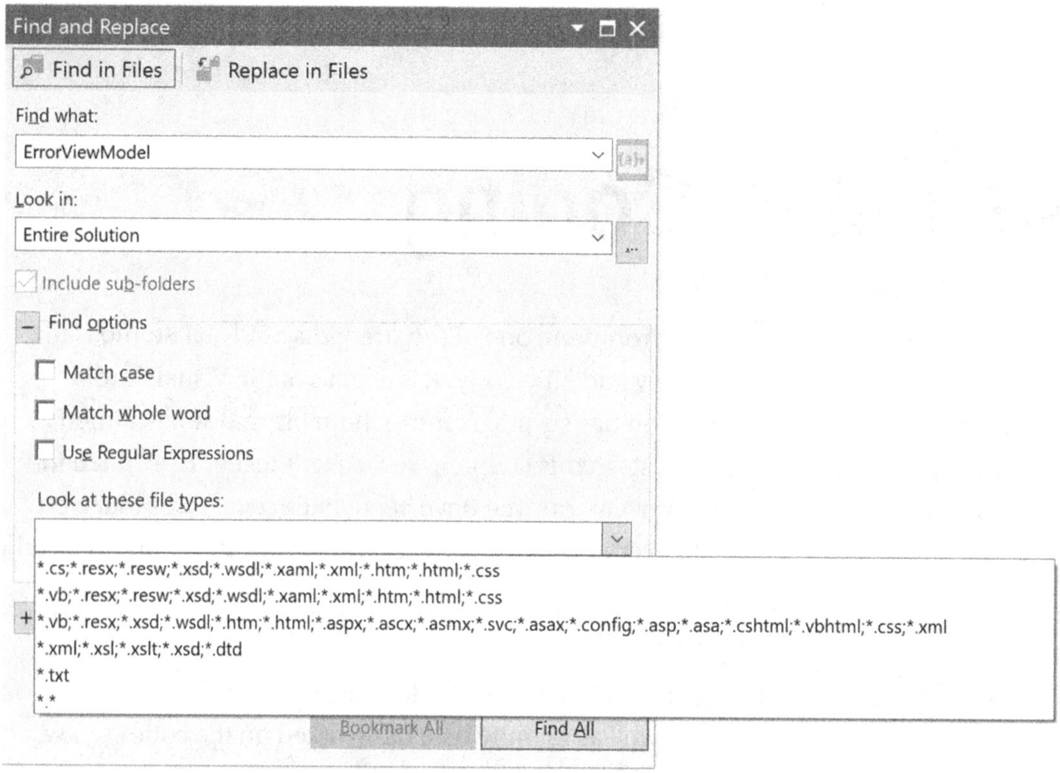

Figure 2-1. *Find in Files dialog*

The additional functionality for the Find in Files dialog is found in the dropdown. Previously, it wasn't possible to identify a set of files across which the search would be performed. However, using this dropdown, you can restrict the files that are searched.

By choosing one of the options from the dropdown, only files with extensions in the list will be searched. This can greatly reduce the number of results found. But the functionality goes a little further. You can modify the list of extensions manually or even enter your own list. And, when you change or create a new list, it is remembered and appears in the dropdown as one of the options going forward.

The search results pane (Figure 2-2) has been significantly changed in Visual Studio 2019.

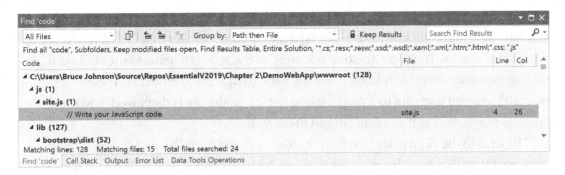

Figure 2-2. *Search results pane*

This pane has gone through a significant redesign, starting with the name on the tab. Instead of Find Result 1, the name on the tab now includes the string that was the target of the search. This makes it much easier when you start to have multiple search result panes active simultaneously.

By default, the results are grouped by path, then by file. In Figure 2-2, this means that the log directory path has 128 matches. Within that directory, there is a js folder that has a single match. That single match is found in the site.js file. The same is true as you move down the results, with the matches grouped by folder before identifying the file and the actual matches.

As for the match itself, the line where the match was found is displayed, along with the file, the line number, and the column number. If you click the match, the file will be opened into the editor, with the cursor set to the line and column for that match.

The toolbar across the top of the pane contains ways to manipulate and use the results. The first dropdown lets you modify the scope of the search. The choices are as follows:

- All Files – The search is across all files, with any file types constrained by the dropdown described earlier in this section.

- Open Documents – The search is limited to all the files that are currently open in the editor.

- Current Document – The search is limited to only the current document.

- Changed Documents – The search is limited to those files which are marked as being changed by source control.

Immediately to the right of the dropdown is a copy icon. This is enabled once you have selected one of the results. The names of the column, along with the information in the selected result, are copied to the clipboard. You can select multiple results using the standard Ctrl+(right-click) and Ctrl+Shift+(right-click) keystrokes or a Ctrl+A to select the entire set of results. The copy function will copy all the selected items to the clipboard.

The next two icons are related. They are used to move to the next and previous match. When you navigate to a match using the icons, the file is displayed, and the cursor is positioned as if you had clicked the match.

The icon to the right of the navigation icons is disabled in Figure 2-2. It is used to clear any filters that have been set for the search results and is enabled once at least one filter has been defined. For instance, if you have selected Open Documents from the first dropdown, the Clear Filters icon would have become enabled. Then clicking it would have reverted the value for the dropdown back to its default setting of All Files.

The dropdown to the right of Click Filters is used to control the grouping of the results. As was just mentioned, the default is to sort the results by path then by file. However, there are two additional grouping options available in this list. If you select Path only, then the matches are only grouped by the folder in which they are found and not by the file as well. The name of the file appears in the File column (visible in Figure 2-2), and they are sorted by file. It's just that the file name is not part of the result hierarchy.

The other grouping option is No Grouping. In this case, the results just appear as a list. As before, file name appears in the list, but there is no reference to the path, at least not in the default view. It is possible to add the path column by right-clicking the results list and choosing the Column Options ➤ Path item from the context menu. This view is the closest result to what the default settings in Visual Studio 2017 are.

The next icon, the Keep Results icon, does pretty much what the label says. It keeps these results as a separate tab. If the icon has not been selected, then a new Find in Files function will reuse the same tab, which is to say that your previous results would be lost. If you click Keep Results, then the next Find in Files will create a new tab for those results, allowing you to work with multiple search result sets.

Finally, the text box on the right is used to further refine the search results. Any keywords entered here are used to reduce the result set. Only those matches which also contain the keywords will continue to be displayed.

Aside from Find in Files, the other mechanisms used to find symbols within your code that have been introduced in the last couple of Visual Studio versions are still available. For example, if you right-click a class or variable name, the context menu includes the options seen in Figure 2-3.

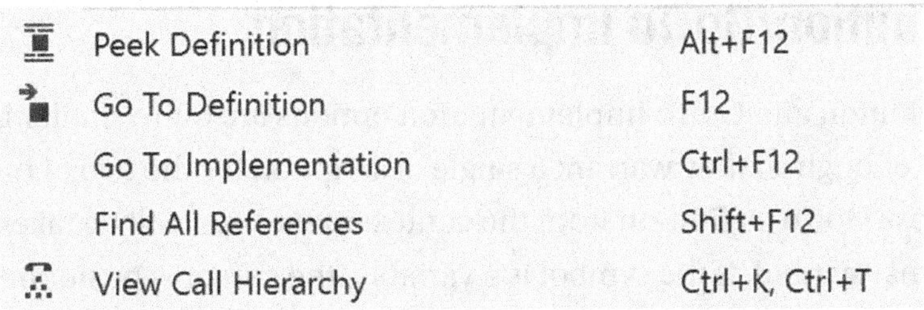

	Peek Definition	Alt+F12
	Go To Definition	F12
	Go To Implementation	Ctrl+F12
	Find All References	Shift+F12
	View Call Hierarchy	Ctrl+K, Ctrl+T

Figure 2-3. Part of the editor context menu

These features are not new to Visual Studio 2019, but from personal experience, they are not used as frequently as they could be. In particular, Peek Definition, Find All References, and View Call Hierarchy seem to be lacking in love and attention from developers.

Peek Definition

The idea behind Peek Definition is ingenious in its simplicity. When you select Peek Definition from the context menu, the definition of the symbol is displayed in the editor, in line with the rest of the code. Figure 2-4 provides an illustration.

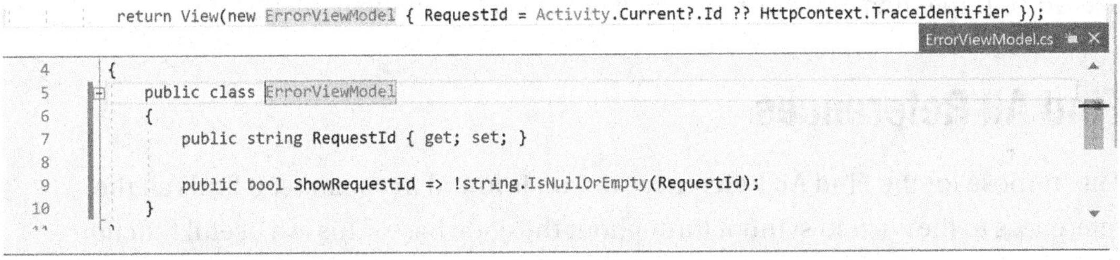

```
        return View(new ErrorViewModel { RequestId = Activity.Current?.Id ?? HttpContext.TraceIdentifier });
                                                                              ErrorViewModel.cs
  4        {
  5            public class ErrorViewModel
  6            {
  7                public string RequestId { get; set; }
  8
  9                public bool ShowRequestId => !string.IsNullOrEmpty(RequestId);
 10            }
```

Figure 2-4. Peek Definition

Now you can see the definition without needing to switch to a different editor pane. This is incredibly convenient, as it allows you to stay in your current context. And it's possible to nest peeks. So from within a Peek display, you can right-click a symbol and choose Peek Definition from that context menu. This will display the definition in the same inline window. Two dots appear in the tab indicator that allow you to navigate between the two (or more) Peek displays.

Go To Definition/Go To Implementation

The Go To Definition and Go To Implementation options are quite similar in their functionality – enough so they warrant a single description for the two of them.

If you choose Go To Definition from the context menu, you will be taken to the definition for that symbol. If the symbol is a variable, the cursor is positioned on the declaration. If the symbol is a method, the cursor is positioned at the method declaration. This is fairly straightforward.

The catch occurs if the method or property is part of an interface. In that case, the declaration is considered to be the definition of the element within the interface. But in many cases, that's not really what you're looking for. You really want to find an implementation of that method. This is where the Go To Implementation option is used.

If you choose Go To Implementation and the symbol is part of an interface, the cursor is positioned on corresponding method, property, or even within a class that implements the interface. If there is more than one class available in the solution that implements the interface, you are given the option to select the implementation that you would like to navigate to.

As it turns out, if you use Go To Implementation, and the symbol is not part of an interface, then it works exactly the same as Go To Definition. For that reason, I'll typically use Go To Implementation as my default choice between the two.

Find All References

The purpose for the Find All References option is found in its name. It finds all the references to the current symbol throughout the code base. This is a useful function if you're trying to identify where a symbol is referenced while trying to figure out the impact that a change might have.

While the functionality offered by Find All References hasn't changed in Visual Studio 2019, the user interface for viewing and manipulating the results has – to the point where it is almost identical to the Find in Files result pane. Figure 2-5 contains an example.

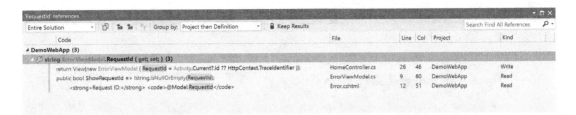

Figure 2-5. *Find All References result pane*

By comparing this pane with Figure 2-2, the similarities are quite apparent. The dropdowns and icons across the top perform the same functions in both case. The differences are that there is an extra option (Current Project) in the first dropdown. And the options available for grouping are completely different. They are Project then Definition (the default), Definition only, Definition then Project, Definition then Path, Definition, Project then Path, and No Grouping.

As well as the toolbar changes, there is an additional column, Kind, that doesn't exist in the search result. The Kind value represents the type of usage. In Figure 2-5, the values are Read and Write because the target symbol is a property. Method calls also have a Kind value of Read. The other possibility is Constructor, for when the constructor of a method is invoked.

View Call Hierarchy

A Call Hierarchy is the set of all calls into a method. Be aware of earlier versions of Visual Studio and even some online documentation that says that all calls made from that method to other methods are also shown. That is not the case for all languages. The option to see outgoing calls was removed at Visual Studio 2015 for C# in order to cut down on the clutter of the results page. Not to mention that, in most cases, you should be able to easily tell which methods are being called by looking at the code. If the method is too big to see that information quickly, it could be a sign that you need to do some refactoring. But that's the topic for Chapter 4, "Refactoring Code."

Figure 2-6 illustrates the results from clicking the View Call Hierarchy option from the context menu.

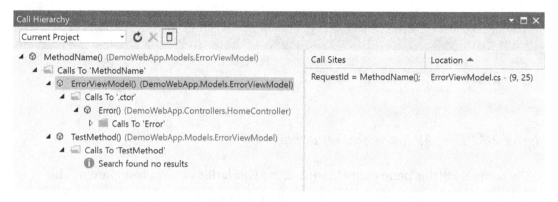

Figure 2-6. *View Call Hierarchy results*

The results are displayed in a cascading tree. There is a single root node that contains the target method name. This is followed by a single Calls To node, followed by one child for each instance where the method is being called. If you click an instance, information about the call site appears on the details pane. Specifically, you can see the line of code that makes the call and the name of the file containing the call, along with the row and column. Double-clicking the detail line opens the file in the editor, with the cursor positioned on the line of code.

Each instance also contains a Calls To of its own. This allows you to find out the places from which the call site is invoked. And you can continue to cascade Calls To nodes until you reach a point where no calls are being made. That is visualized through a message, seen at the bottom of Figure 2-6.

You can limit the scope for the call hierarchy by using the dropdown list at the top left of the dialog. Here you can select the current project, the current document, or the entire solution.

CodeLens

While the options mentioned to this point are incredibly useful, many developers have found that the functionality available through CodeLens to be a significant performance enhancer when it comes to navigating through both the present and history of the code base. The design concept behind CodeLens was to allow you to determine what has happened to your code without leaving the editor. In other words, you get to stay in the flow of coding while still finding out useful information about the code. This useful information includes changes that have been made, bugs that have been linked, code reviews, and unit tests.

Note   Not all CodeLens functionality is available in the Community edition of Visual Studio 2019. Specifically, the information related to source control is not visible.

To get a sense of what CodeLens looks like, consider the example in Figure 2-7, which shows the heads-up display.

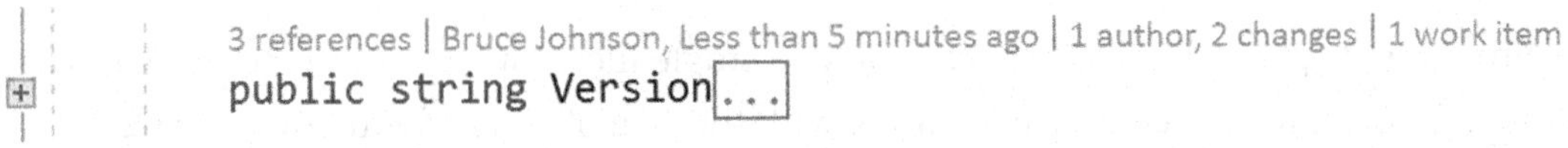

```
3 references | Bruce Johnson, Less than 5 minutes ago | 1 author, 2 changes | 1 work item
public string Version...
```

Figure 2-7. *Code with CodeLens heads-up display*

This is a property within a class after a number of changes have been made over the course of time. Well, not a lot of time, as the Less than 5 minutes ago suggestions. But it's enough that changes were made.

There are four pieces of information available in the CodeLens heads-up display:

- References – Indicates the places in code that reference this property. This is similar to the Find All References functionality.

- Last modification – The name of the person who last touched this line of code and the relative time when it happened.

- Authors – The number of people who have made changes to this property or method, as well as the number of changes that have been made in total.

- Work items – The work items that are related to the property or method.

Each of the items in the heads-up display is a link. Let's examine the available information in more detail.

References

The References link displays information about where the property or method is used. Figure 2-8 contains an example.

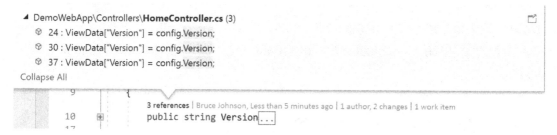

Figure 2-8. *References display*

From the display, all the references are in a single file, HomeController.cs. The line number for each reference is visible, along with the line of code. If you double-click a reference, then the editor for the file opens and the cursor is positioned on the variable. If the code is referenced in more than one file, you will see multiple nodes like the one seen in Figure 2-8. By default, the pane opens with the references visible, but that can seem cluttered if there are a lot of references. Clicking the Collapse All link at the bottom left closes the references so that only the file names appear.

Because of the heads-up nature of CodeLens, the References pane (and, in fact, all the CodeLens panes) is transitory. When you click the link, it appears. When you click elsewhere, the pane goes away. If you want to keep the pane around longer, click the Dock Popup icon in the top-right corner of the pane. This moves the Reference information to its own floatable and dockable pane. All the information and functionality remains, with the addition of a Refresh link which updates the list of references.

Last Modification

The last modification information indicates the person who most recently made a change to the property or method and when they did it – not specifically when they made the change, but instead a relative time. The relative time is descriptive, based on the most appropriate unit. It could read "5 minutes ago," as seen in Figure 2-7. It could read "3 months ago," if it has been a while since the line was modified. The purpose is to give you a sense of when the change took place. If you want to find out exactly when it happened, right-click the method and select Source Control ➤ Blame (Annotate). The output from this option includes the exact date, time, and commit ID for the most recent change.

Clicking the link displays a color-coded timeline of the changes, an example of which is visible in Figure 2-9.

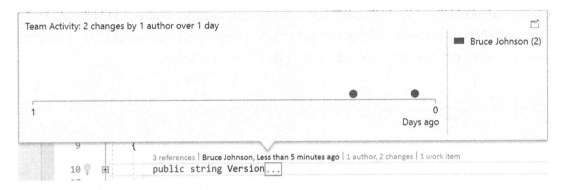

Figure 2-9. *Last modification timeline*

The timeline uses relative time as the scale. Each dot represents a change that was made to the method or property. Quite specifically, it's the time that the change was committed to source control. On the right is a list of the authors involved in making a change, with a color code that ties an author to a particular change on the timeline.

Hovering over a dot causes details about the change to be displayed as a tool tip, seen in Figure 2-10.

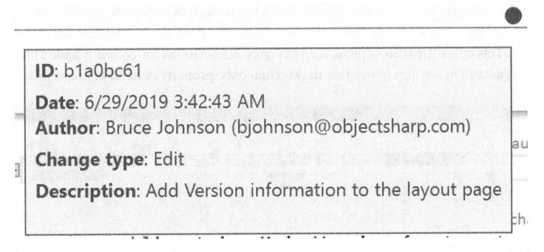

Figure 2-10. *Last modification timeline details*

In the details, the exact date of the change is visible, along with the person who made the change, the type of change (Edit or Add), and information about the commit associated with the change. Specifically, the commit ID and the description are included.

45

Authors

While the last modification information did include some details about the people who made the change, the authors information goes a little bit deeper. In the heads-up display, only the number of authors and changes appear. It's when you click the link that a wealth of information appears. Figure 2-11 contains an example.

Figure 2-11. *Authors detailed information*

From the heads-up display, you could see that one author made two changes. With the details, you can see the actual commits that accounted for those two changes. For each commit, the commit ID, description, author, and date are available easily. If you hover over the commit, even more information appears in the tool tip.

At the bottom of the details pane, there are a couple of controls that impact how many changes are visible. By default, it only shows the commits for the past 12 months. On the right, that value is in a text box that can be changed as you desire. If you want to see all of the commits, then click the Show All File Changes link at the bottom left of the pane. This opens the History pane, seen in Figure 2-12. Now all the commits for the file are displayed, regardless of whether they included the property or method in question.

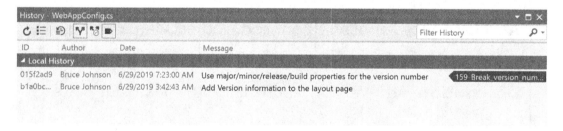

Figure 2-12. *History pane*

You'll notice that for the first commit, you can expand the node and see the work items that have been associated with the commit. And, as with the commit itself, hovering over the work item displayed additional details.

Tip   You'll notice in the commit details shown in Figure 2-11, part of the description includes the text "Related Work Items: #158." If you are using a Git repository, this is important text to include in the description. It is used to associate the commit with a specific work item. In this case, it associates the work item with an ID of 158 with the commit. Without it, the work item is not included as a child of the commit in the display. And it's not included as a work item when it comes to the next component in the heads-up display. If a particular commit includes more than one work item, you need to include the hashtag (number sign) in front of each ID. In other words, the description would include a link like "Related Work Items: #158, #159."

In the details pane, the author is also a link. In general, the purpose of clicking the link is to put you in touch with the author of the commit. The idea is that you have a question about the commit that you would like the author to address. What actually happens when you click the link depends on the environment in which you are working.

At a minimum, clicking the link opens an email form for your default mail program. The email address for the author is included in the To field. The subject and body of the email includes information about the repository and commit in question, allowing the recipient to quickly establish the context for the question. The rest of the question is up to you.

However, if both you and the author use Skype for Business, all kind of additional magic is available to you. Included in the Author column is a presence indicator for the author. And by clicking the link, you have the option of sending an email or even Skyping directly with the author.

Work Items

The information available in the Work Items detail pane is similar to that available in the Authors detail pane. The difference is that the focus is slightly different. Figure 2-13 contains an example.

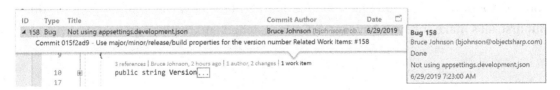

Figure 2-13. *Work Items detail pane*

Instead of starting with a commit and displaying child work items, this view displays the work items associated with the method or property and has the commits nested underneath. The information when you hover over a commit is the same information seen in Figure 2-11. And when you hover over a work item, you see details (author, status, description, and date/time) about the work item, exactly as if you hovered over the work item in the Authors detail pane. And the same functionality found in the Authors detail pane exists when you click the author link. Either an email is begun or you have access to Skype for Business functionality, depending on the environment in which you work.

There is an additional piece of information available in the heads-up display when unit tests have been written that cover the targeted property or method. That will be covered in Chapter 3, "Unit Testing."

Writing Code

Helping to speed up the code writing process has always been at the heard of Visual Studio. As an example, consider how integral a feature like IntelliSense has been to you. Once you get used to it, it's difficult to write code without the assistance that it offers. Some might argue that it reduces the knowledge of developers, by not forcing them to learn how to write code with the correct syntax and parameters manually. That feels much like the same argument against calculators three decades ago, and against smartphones today. In all cases, the arguments presume that using the tool effectively isn't a better way to perform the desired task. And I'd argue that it is. Fortunately for developers, Microsoft agrees.

For Visual Studio 2019, the code writing feature of greatest note is IntelliCode, although, to be fair, IntelliCode is actually an extension to Visual Studio. And it provides support not only for all versions of Visual Studio 2019 but also recent versions of both Visual Studio 2017 and Visual Studio Code.

When it comes to the question of what exactly is IntelliCode, the one-line answer feels a little vague: IntelliCode uses artificial intelligence techniques to enhance your coding experience. Let's pull that sentence apart and see how it actually applies to you. But first, let's make sure you have IntelliCode installed and ready to go.

Installing IntelliCode

There are two ways to get IntelliCode onto your system. The first, and possibly the easiest, is to choose one of the workloads that includes it by default. That would be any workload that supports C#, C++, TypeScript/JavaScript, or XAML. Also, you need to be running version 16.1 of Visual Studio 2019 or later.

Alternatively, you can download it from the Visual Studio Marketplace. The link is `https://marketplace.visualstudio.com/items?itemName=VisualStudioExptTeam.VSIntelliCode`. This will download a VSIX (Visual Studio Extension Installer) file which, when executed, will install IntelliCode into all of the Visual Studio instances on your machine that supports it.

Once IntelliCode has been installed, the features need to be enabled before it can be used. This is done through the Tools ➤ Options menu item, followed by navigating to the IntelliCode section. The dialog looks like Figure 2-14.

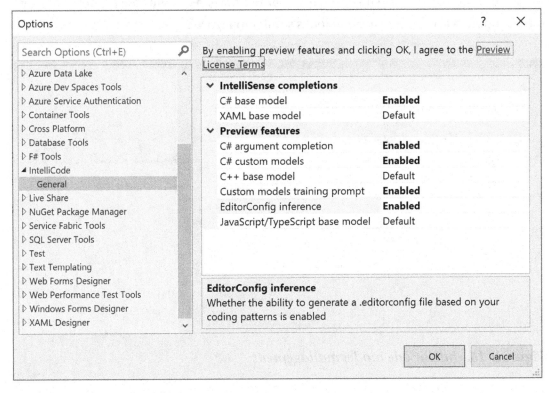

Figure 2-14. *Configure IntelliCode features*

By default, the properties you see marked as "Enabled" were set to "Default" – which, since IntelliCode has been in Preview, is to be expected. As of this writing, some of the features were on the verge of being released as Live, but to be certain, simply enable the features you want to use, which, for the purposes of this book, are the C#, custom training, and EditorConfig features.

Now that you have IntelliCode available for use, let's pull apart that one-line description. First, the artificial intelligence part. Yes, it's true that this is a bit of a buzzword for new features and products. In this particular case, however, Microsoft has utilized machine learning to generate the heuristic used to make "intelligent" suggestion from within IntelliSense. As its initial body of knowledge, thousands of highly regarded (more than 100 stars), open source GitHub projects were used. Based on this, IntelliCode established a base of common practices and likely suggestions. However, IntelliCode also uses your existing code to tweak the suggestions even more in your favor. And to do that, you must train it on your code base to create a custom model.

To start this process, use the View ➤ Other Windows ➤ IntelliCode Model Manager menu option. A screen appears that looks similar to Figure 2-15.

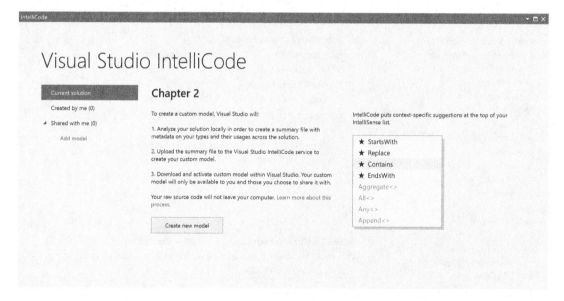

Figure 2-15. *IntelliCode model management*

This page lets you manage the various IntelliCode models you have throughout your environment. It's possible to use multiple models (not simultaneously, but for different solutions). But if you read the description on the page closely, there is something in the process that might give you pause.

First, IntelliCode analyzes your project, looking for usage patterns. That information is bundled into a summary file. This file contains metadata about the types that are declared and how those types are being used. That summary file is then uploaded to the Visual Studio IntelliCode service, where it is combined with the current IntelliCode model. That result, a custom model specific to your solution, is then downloaded and activated for your use. The download model can actually be shared with anyone you choose – others on your team, for example.

The part of this process that might give pause has to do with the uploading of the summary file to the cloud. Microsoft states explicitly that your source code is not being uploaded. It's only summary information. But while this won't be an issue for many, there are certain organizations that will be leery of moving what seems like it's part of their intellectual property to the cloud. Unfortunately, doing so is a requirement for being able to use IntelliCode.

If you are interested to see what is being shared, the files are located in the %TEMP%\Visual Studio IntelliCode folder. The names of the folders are randomized, so open the one for your more recent training session by sorting the folders by descending date.

Inside the folder is the entire set of files that are sent to Microsoft. The UsageOutput subfolder contains a JSON file that has the information that was extracted by IntelliCode. This is the information used to train the model with your custom data. The UsageOutput_ErrorStats file contains any errors found when trying to build the extracted file. It is used by Microsoft if they need to debug any issues with the summary file generation process.

To begin the training process, click the Start a New Model button. Almost immediately a summary file is created, uploaded, and processed. When finished, the result is something like what's shown in Figure 2-16.

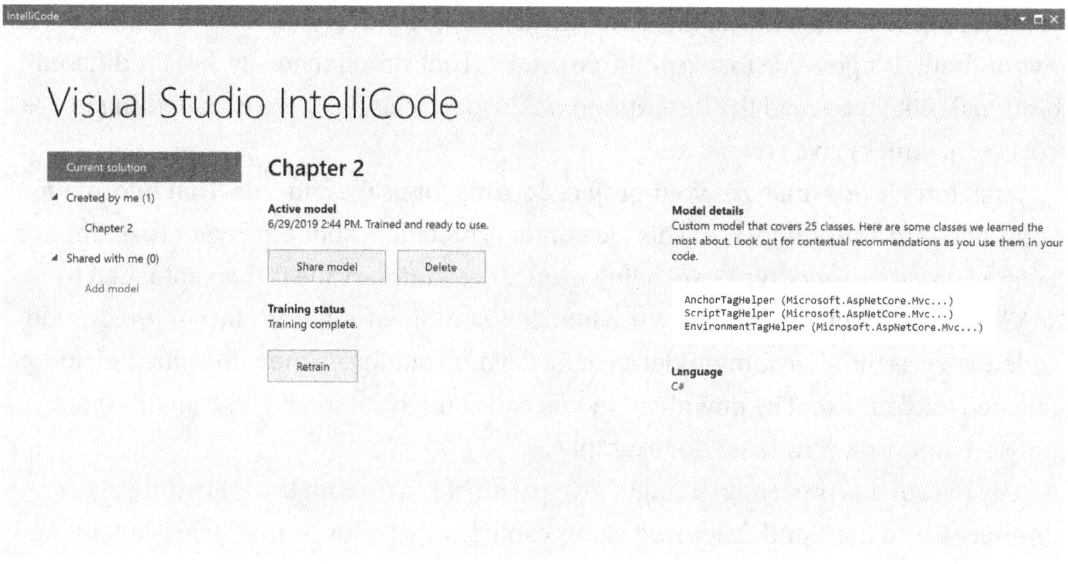

Figure 2-16. *Results from training the IntelliCode model*

You have a couple of options at this point. First though, understand that your model is ready to use. You don't need to do anything more at this point to take advantage of IntelliCode. The choices on this page are about managing the models that you have.

First, underneath the Active model label, there are two buttons. The second is the easiest to understand. The Delete button is used to delete the current model. That means that IntelliCode functionality won't be available for that solution. The first button, Share model, is used to share this model with other people. A URL is generated and added to your clipboard. That way you can send the URL to anyone with whom you would like to share the model. They use the Add model link that appears on the left side of the page. Clicking the link launches the dialog seen in Figure 2-17.

Figure 2-17. *Adding a shared IntelliCode model*

Paste in the link that has been shared with you, click Add, and that model becomes the active model for the solution.

Note   Yes, the fact that someone else can access your model using a URL means that a copy of the model is kept in the cloud. It also means that you should treat the URL as if it were source code and not share it with people who you don't trust.

The other button seen in Figure 2-16 is used to rerun the model training process. This is not something that you need to do regularly. It is only after code has been added and you're not getting the type of results from IntelliCode (in terms of the suggested completed or parameter overloads) that you expect. But when you click Retrain, the entire process is redone. A new summary file is generated and a new model created and downloaded. And if you want to share that with people, a new URL is required.

IntelliCode Features

Now that IntelliCode is ready, what does it do? Well, there are several features that are part of IntelliCode, but more are being added regularly. One of the reasons why it's installed separately from Visual Studio 2019 is so that it can have an upgrade cycle that is not linked to Visual Studio itself. So new features can be previewed or released without a need for a corresponding update to Visual Studio.

Context-Aware Code Completion

As a starting point, let's consider one of the features that is most visible in IntelliCode. By now, most developers are aware of IntelliSense. In fact, a high percentage of them live and die by how good it is. The Context-Aware Code Complete feature utilized the machine learning to provide better suggestions. Consider the following figures. Figure 2-18 is the IntelliSense before IntelliCode is added.

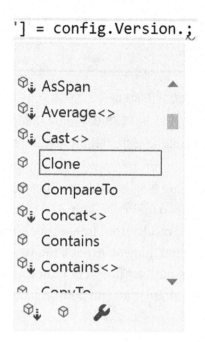

Figure 2-18. *Pre-IntelliCode IntelliSense*

The properties and methods are in alphabetical order. It's easy to select the correct property, but it usually requires typing extra characters or using the mouse to do so. Figure 2-19 is at the same point in the code, but with IntelliCode enabled.

Figure 2-19. *Post-IntelliCode IntelliSense*

While most of the methods are still in alphabetical order, there are five that have been moved to the top of the list. The items with the star to the left of the name are the ones that IntelliCode has suggested for you. While it doesn't cover all possible cases, if you think about it, it's likely that those five functions cover a very high percentage of the functions you use for strings. And they are now only a cursor or two away. That is the goal of the Context-Aware Code Completion feature.

Generating EditorConfig Files

A detailed discussion of EditorConfig takes place later in this chapter, but in brief, an EditorConfig file is used to help ensure that written code adheres to certain standards – standards like capitalization of variables and method names, minimal variable length, and other rules that help keep code consistent across a large code base.

While it's possible to build the EditorConfig file by hand, IntelliCode will look at your code base and generate one for you. In the Solution Explorer, right-click either the solution or a project and choose Add ➤ New EditorConfig (IntelliCode) from the context menu. This examines the code in the solution or just the project, creates a `.editorconfig` file, and adds it to the solution or project.

Information on how EditorConfig files are used can be found in the "Code Cleanup" section later in this chapter.

Keeping Code Clean

For a long time, FxCop was the standard tool to ensure that .NET code met certain standards and specifications for style. It performed static code analysis on the files in a project or solution and reported on the results, typically as errors or warnings. However, over the past few years, the introduction of the .NET Compiler Platform (otherwise known as Roslyn) has supplanted the need for static analysis. Instead, you are immediately faced with the familiar green and red squiggles when your code isn't up to a defined standard. In this section, we look at how Visual Studio 2019 helps to ensure that your code meets a common standard, that your code is free of green and red squiggles.

Visual Studio 2019 includes a set of built-in code analyzers. These analyzers evaluate your code as you type. If there is a violation detected by an analyzer, it is reported in the Error List window, as well as in the code editor. The report in the code editor consists of the squiggly underline that all developers know well.

A power feature of the dynamic analysis process is that many rules have one or more code fixes defined. The idea being that if you apply the code fix, the problem is corrected, and the squiggle goes away. Code fixes are shown in the light bulb icon menu as one of the Quick Actions.

Configuring Analyzers

Most projects come with their own set of built-in analyzers. You can find them in the Solution Explorer under the Dependencies node. Figure 2-20 illustrates the analyzers for an ASP.NET Core project.

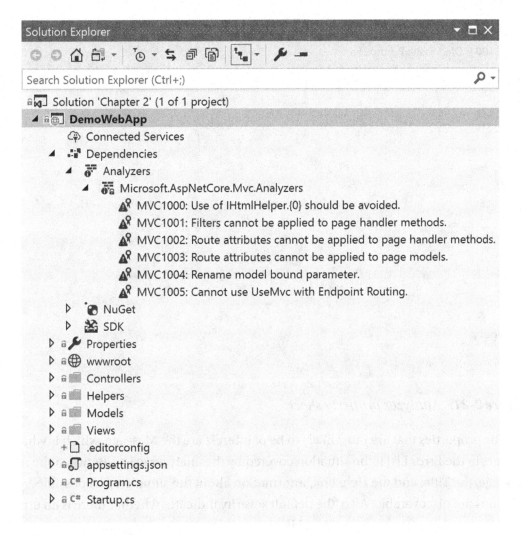

Figure 2-20. Built-in analyzers in Solution Explorer

These are just the built-in analyzers. It's possible to add analyzers to your project, typically through NuGet packages or as Visual Studio extensions. Also, be aware that depending on the analyzer, sometimes the list might appear under the References node, as opposed to the Dependencies node in Figure 2-20.

For any of the installed analyzers, you can view the properties and modify one of the settings. The properties are visible through the property sheet. This is accessed by right-clicking the analyzer and selecting Properties from the context menu. An example of the properties for an analyzer is seen in Figure 2-21.

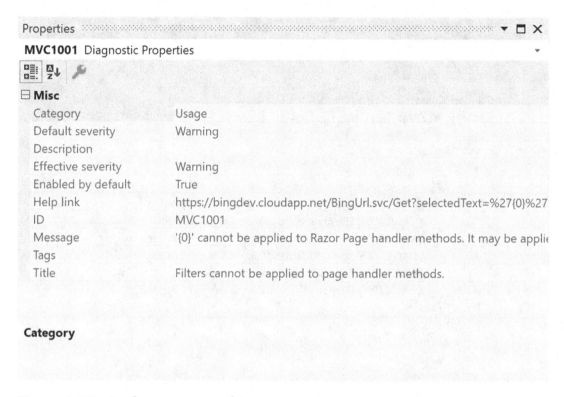

Figure 2-21. *Analyzer property sheet*

The properties that are most likely to be of interest are the Message, which is what appears in the Error List if the situation covered by the analyzer exists. Between the Message, the Title, and the Help link, information about the situation and possible solutions are discoverable. Also, the default severity indicates whether there is an error or a warning that appears in the Error List.

While it might not be apparent from Figure 2-21, all of the values in the property sheet are disabled, which means that you can't modify any of the values for the analyzer. This makes sense, when you think about it. However, there are times when you might want to modify the default severity. This is actually not done through the property sheet, but through the Solution Explorer.

Right-click the analyzer in the Solution Explorer, and then choose the Set Rule Set Severity option from the context menu. This displays a set of choices as seen in Figure 2-22.

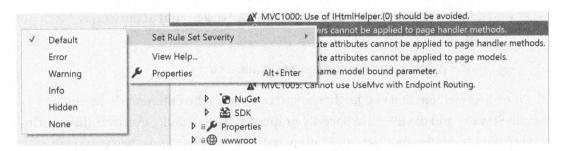

Figure 2-22. *Setting Rule Set Severity for an analyzer*

The choices available are as follows:

- Default – Use the default severity that is specified with the analyzer.

- Error – Display the message as an error. Typically, the difference between Error and the other severity is how other tools regard it. First, the squiggle is in red. Second, other tools frequently look at error messages as being a termination of further pipeline process. So, for example, it would keep a compile from being successful.

- Warning – Display the message as an error. The squiggle is green, and it only impacts pipeline process if the pipeline has been configured to stop on warnings.

- Info – The message appears as informational and the squiggle is gray. There is no impact on any pipeline processing.

- Hidden – There is no display for the developer to see. The violation is reported to the IDE diagnostics engine. As a result, it might appear in some logs or be counted among rule violations.

- None – All messages or indications related to the rule set are suppressed.

The icon that appears to the left of the Analyzer name in the Solution Explorer provides a visual indication of the current rule set severity.

- Error – An "x" inside a circle

- Warning – An "!" inside a circle

- Info – An "i" inside a circle

- Hidden – Also an "i" inside a circle, but the background of the icon is light

- None – A downward pointing arrow inside a circle

One other element that you might want to consider is the difference between the Default Severity and the Effective Severity properties. The Default Severity is the severity that is defined with the analyzer installation. It doesn't change, and when you set the Rule Set Severity as the Default, this is the value that is used.

However, there are other elements that determine the actual or effective severity for an analyzer. For instance, changing the Rule Set Severity impacts the Effective Security process. As well, project-level settings, such as treating warnings as errors, also come into play to determine the Effective Security.

Customizing Rule Sets

To this point, we have been using the term rule set in the abstract. But it's worthwhile drilling a little deeper into details, especially since it's possible to customize the rule sets that are included with the built-in analyzers, but also to create rule sets from scratch.

At its heart, a rule set is just an XML file. Included in the XML file is the analyzer identifier and a collection of rule identifiers. For each rule, the severity is included, if it's different than the default. The reason for this minimalist approach is that every analyzer comes with its own set of rules and the default severity for each. The XML file contains just the changes from those defaults.

Because editing XML is no fun, there is an editor for the ruleset files. To launch the editor, right-click the Analyzer node in the Solution Explorer and choose the Open Active Rule Set option. This opens the ruleset editor for the current rule set, an example of which is seen in Figure 2-23. This is the same editor that would appear if you manually create a ruleset file.

Note   This option on the context menu is not available for .NET Core projects. There is no ability to open the active rule set through the Solution Explorer for those types of projects. Instead, a ruleset file would be created manually and then added to the project. But along with that, the project file needs to be edited manually. More specifically, a Project Group like the following needs to be added:

```
<PropertyGroup>
    <CodeAnalysisRuleSet>
        $(MSBuildThisFileDirectory)MyCustom.ruleset
    </CodeAnalysisRuleSet>
</PropertyGroup>
```

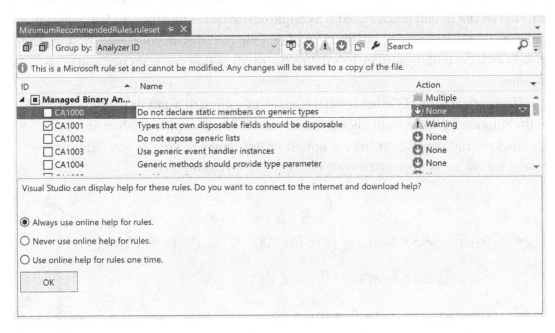

Figure 2-23. *Ruleset editor*

Each of the related analyzers gets their own node. Within the analyzer, there is a collection of rules. Then, for each rule, there is an ID, a Name, and an Action, which is actually the severity. You use the check box at the front of the rule ID to indicate if the rule should be active or not. Then you specify the severity for the rules by modifying the action.

For the ruleset, there is one additional option that is available to you. At the bottom, there is a radio button that determines whether the help links that are part of the individual rules will be used. The third option might seem a little weird. After all, why would you want to use online help one time. But it relates to how the help is displayed. In this case, it prompts you for whether you want to use the online help and then remembers your choice.

Since this ruleset file was taken from the active rule set, it can be saved directly. If you make any changes and save them, you will automatically be prompted to provide a new file name. That file becomes part of your project and will be the active ruleset going forward.

Code Cleanup

New for Visual Studio 2019 is a feature called Code Cleanup. The premise is taken from the Format Document function. With a couple of keystrokes or a mouse click, you can run a process that performs a defined set of cleanup routines on your code. To start, and to help with the understanding, let's define the routines that you want performed on cleanup.

The configuration of Code Cleanup is accessible through a couple of methods. First, in the Solution Explorer, right-click a project, and then choose the Analyze and Code Cleanup ➤ Configure Code Cleanup option – a little cuter, but not as accessible as the broom icon at the bottom of the code editor (seen in Figure 2-24).

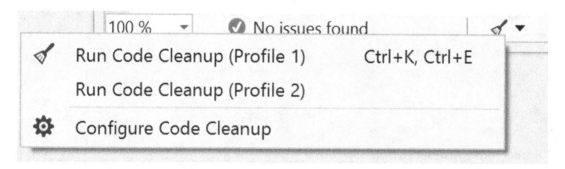

Figure 2-24. *Configuring Code Cleanup from the editor*

Clicking the dropdown to the right of the icon displays a menu which includes the Configure Code Cleanup option. The downside of this approach is that the icon is only available for editors which are supported by Code Cleanup. Regardless of how you get there, Figure 2-25 displays the dialog used to configure Code Cleanup.

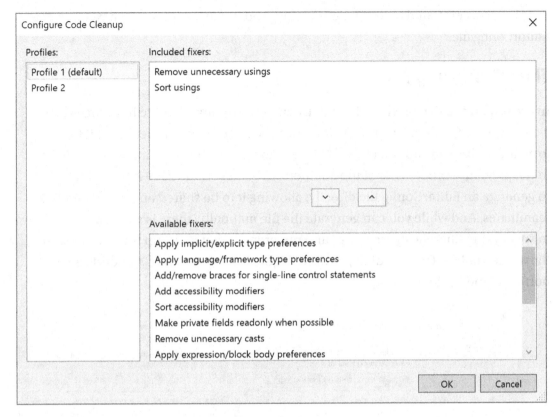

Figure 2-25. *Code Cleanup configuration dialog*

Conceptually, the configuration is pretty straightforward. There are two profiles available to you. For each profile, you can choose the filters that you want to apply. By default, the profiles have a couple of filters already added (Remove unnecessary usings and Sort usings). At the bottom of the right side is a list of other filters. To add them to a profile, select them from the bottom list, and then click the up arrow. To remove filters from the profile, select the filter in the top list and click the down arrow. Once you have the profiles configured as you wish, click OK to save them.

To run a Code Cleanup for a profile, either use the Solution Explorer option (right-click a project, and select the Analyze and Code Cleanup option) or the broom icon. In both cases, choose the Run Code Cleanup item with the desired profile in the name.

That seems simple and painless. And, for the most part, it is. Most of the filters are pretty easy to understand. However, there are a number of filters that include the word "preference" in them, such as Apply "this" qualification preferences and Apply implicit/explicit type preferences, where can you specify your preferences.

The answer is found in the Options dialog. And it also leads into the next topic, the EditorConfig file.

The EditorConfig File

In the past, when you used the Format Document command, there has always been a collection of filters that were performed on the document in order to get it to be formatted. The same approach is also true of the Code Cleanup function described in the previous section. One of the additions to Visual Studio 2019 is the ability to generate an EditorConfig file directly, allowing it to be shared among different teammates. And while you can generate the file manually, there is still a matter of how to specify the different style settings and preferences that make up the file. To define those, the Tools ➤ Options dialog is used. Figure 2-26 shows the C# ➤ Code Style portion of the Options dialog.

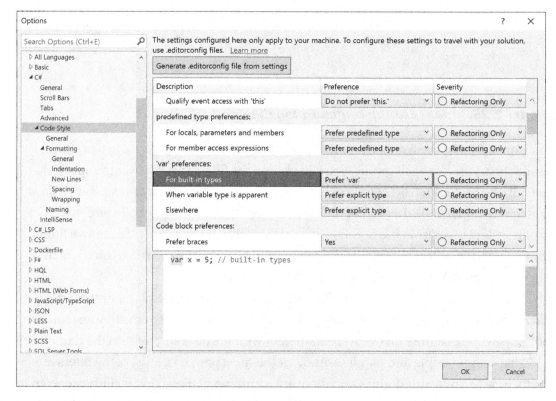

Figure 2-26. *C# Code Style screen in the Options dialog*

You'll notice that there are a fair number of style settings available to tweak. And if you go back to the question at the end of the last section, here are the places where you can specify your preferences. In Figure 2-26, the preference is that implicit declarations be used for built-in types, but explicit declarations otherwise. When Code Cleanup is run, with Apply implicit/explicit type preferences set as one of the filters, then those choices are applied to the code.

In order to share the style preferences among your team members, they need to be exported into a `.editorconfig` file. At the top of the settings section in Figure 2-26, there is a button that generates the file based on the current settings. When you click the button, you'll be prompted to give the file a name. When you save the file, it will also be added to the project. It's a good idea to save the file within your project structure so that it becomes part of your repository.

Alternatively, you can send the `.editorconfig` file through any other methods. It's a physical file. And once you add the file to your project, the settings contained therein become the settings used to perform Code Cleanup.

Summary

In this chapter, you've learned about the different ways that Visual Studio 2019 is able to help with functions that are intrinsic to your day-to-day development flow. Finding code and writing code are pretty basic developer tasks. And keeping code clean and consistent pays off dividends in the unlikely chance that you'll ever have to look at code you wrote 2 years ago, or 2 months ago. Having a tool to ensure that your code (and everyone else's) adheres to a common standard makes reading the entire code base a lot easier.

The next chapter continues the theme of making your code better. It contains a discussion of unit testing and the support that Visual Studio 2019 has to help you write and run unit tests.

CHAPTER 3

Unit Testing

For the modern application developer, a typical workflow involves a series of steps repeated over and over again. These steps are colloquially known as red/green/refactor. You create a unit test for the functionality under development that fails. This causes a red to appear in the unit test results. Next you write enough code to make the unit test pass, and then rerun all your tests. If all has gone well, you should have a green (all tests pass). The final step is to refactor the code you wrote. Neatening it up. Locate duplicated code and convert it into separate methods. Ensure that coding standards have been adhered to. And when you're finished, run the tests once more to ensure that they are still green. At this point, the cycle is done... red, then green, then refactor. And this cycle is repeated until development on the current task is complete.

Visual Studio 2019 helps you through this cycle with a number of related features. It has the ability to create and run unit tests using a number of different frameworks. And there are tools to help you with the refactoring step. But beyond helping out with the basics, Visual Studio 2019 provides the ability to automatically generate unit tests and determine how much of your code is being tested. And if you have the Enterprise edition of Visual Studio 2019, Live Unit Testing, it allows you to keep track of the status of your unit tests ever while you're typing. But let's start with the basics... creating unit tests in Visual Studio 2019.

Writing and Running Unit Tests

Visual Studio 2019 includes a built-in framework for unit testing. It's called MSTest. However, not every team is using MSTest. Frameworks like NUnit and xUnit are in common use among professional development teams. They too are supported by Visual Studio. What's nice is that while some of the details change, the basic structure and flow of writing a unit test is the same regardless of the testing framework. For the examples in this section, we'll be using MSTest, because it is included with Visual Studio. But for the other frameworks, it's pretty much only the syntax and attribute names that change. The flow is close to identical.

67

© Bruce Johnson 2020
B. Johnson, *Essential Visual Studio 2019*, https://doi.org/10.1007/978-1-4842-5719-7_3

The starting point for the example will be a web application. While the application is a simple sales order system, the functionality that you'll be creating test cases for is in the Order class, specifically a method that adds an OrderLine object to the collection of lines in the Order class.

To get started, use Visual Studio to open the Chapter 3.sln file from the Starting folder. There are a number of projects in the solution (and you're welcome to run it to see it in action), but the one that we care about is called OrderWebApp.Library. That is the project that contains the class that is to be tested.

There are testing project templates that are part of most of the workloads available for Visual Studio. For ASP.NET Core Web applications (the sample application is ASP. NET Core), there are three different types. If you right-click the solution within Solution Explorer, then choose Add ➤ New Project, the Add a new project dialog appears. Type test into the search box at the top to display only the templates for different types of tests. Figure 3-1 is what you will see.

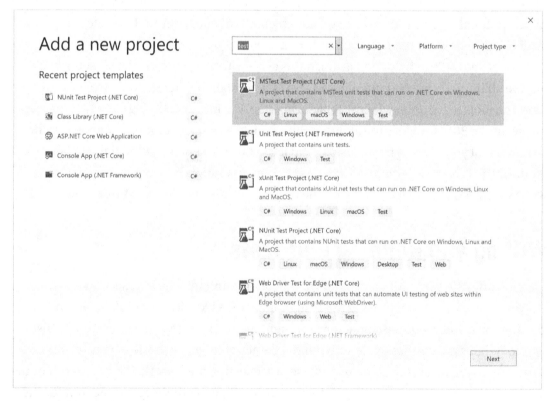

Figure 3-1. *Add a new project dialog for test templates*

Three of the top four templates are the projects for MSTest, NUnit, and xUnit testing for .NET Core applications. Choose the MSTest Test Project (.NET Core) and click Next. Enter a project name of OrderWebApp.Library.Test and click Create to create the project.

The newly created project is not much to see. Figure 3-2 shows the project's structure.

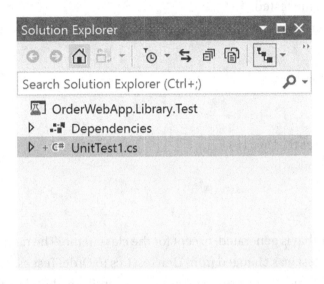

Figure 3-2. *Unit test project structure*

Not much at all. Just a single file containing placeholders for a test method and a test setup method. But before anything else, what does need to be added is a reference to the library being tested. Otherwise, it won't be possible to invoke the methods that will be tested. Right-click the project and choose Add ➤ Reference from the context menu. In the dialog that appears, choose the OrderWebApp.Library project, because that is where the class that we want to test is implemented.

Before getting into the code, just a brief digression into the naming both of unit test classes and test methods. First, one of the more generally accepted approaches to method names is to use the following format: UnitOfWork_StateBeingTested_ExpectedResult. The UnitOfWork can be small, like a single method, although it's more common to group tests together at a class level. The StateBeingTested represents the state within the unit of work that is the subject of the test. The ExpectedResult indicates the expected outcome from running the test. Possible values would indicate the type of success or a specific exception that is encountered.

For organizational purposes, the test methods are placed into different classes. The naming of these classes should be based solely on how you want to display the tests in the Test Explorer, as the class name is part of the hierarchy used to display the test results. In general, and as will be used in this example, each class gets its own unit test class. Also consider that the name of the class and the unit of work really don't need to be duplicated. Creating an OrderTest class and then having the unit of work be Order is duplicating information. Use the unit of work to represent the property or method in the Order class that's being tested.

Putting all of that together, let's look at the code for a simple unit test:

```
[TestClass]
public class OrderTest
{
    [TestMethod]
    public void TestMethod1()
    {
    }
}
```

This is the code that is generated, except for the class name. The name of the file containing the unit test was changed from UnitTest1.cs to OrderTest.cs, resulting in the change to the class name. There are two elements that indicate this class is to be used in unit tests. The TestClass attribute on the class indicates that the class will contain tests. And the TestMethod attribute that decorates the method declaration marks the method as a test. The TestMethod attribute is required because not every method in a class is a test method. It's possible, and frequently desirable, to have different helper methods within the test class that are used within the test methods. When you choose to run unit tests, the Test Runner (the process that performs the tests) looks at the test classes in the test project and finds all the methods that have the TestMethod attribute. Those are the tests that will be executed.

For this example, we're going to write a test for the AddOrderLine method in the Order class. The success criteria for the test will be that the Lines property on the Order object will have a count of 1 when the order line has been added. To run this test, the following method should replace the TestMethod1 method in the OrderTest class:

```
[TestMethod]
public void Lines_AddOrderLine_LinesCountIsCorrect()
{
    Order target = new Order();

    target.AddOrderLine();

    Assert.AreEqual(1, target.Lines.Count,
        "The order line was not added");
}
```

As it sits, this application shouldn't compile successfully. Although you can't see it without looking at the code for the Order class, the AddOrderLine method is not yet defined. This is part of the "red" process for unit testing. But being unable to compile isn't helpful. An AddOrderLine method needs to be added to the Order class. You could do this manually by editing the Order class and adding a method called AddOrderLine. Or you could use Quick Actions to accomplish the same goal without switching from your current editing context. Use the Ctrl+. keystroke to open the Quick Actions menu (it can also be opened by clicking the light bulb at the left of the target.AddOrderLine() line of code), and choose the Generate method "Order.AddOrderLine" option from the context menu. If you use the Quick Action, the method looks like the following:

```
public void AddOrderLine()
{
    throw new NotImplementedException();
}
```

This method doesn't do anything, other than throwing an exception when it's invoked, which is exactly where you want to start from. It's what helps turn the test "red." But to confirm that it is red, we need to run the test.

There are a couple of options to run tests. From the code within the unit test class itself, the simplest approach is to right-click anywhere within the editor and choose Run Tests. This builds the project and runs the test, displaying the results in the Test Explorer. A second way is to use that same Test Explorer dialog. To get to the Test Explorer, use the Test ➤ Test Explorer menu option. The Test Explorer will look like Figure 3-3. At least it will after you've expanded all the nodes in the tree.

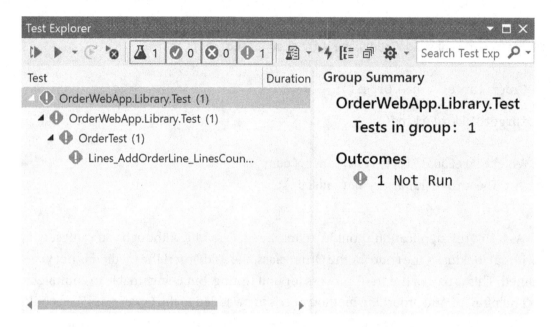

Figure 3-3.   *Test Explorer*

The Test Explorer gives you lots of ways to run tests. But for this first execution, click the Run All Test toolbar button (first one on the left). After a build and run, the results look like Figure 3-4.

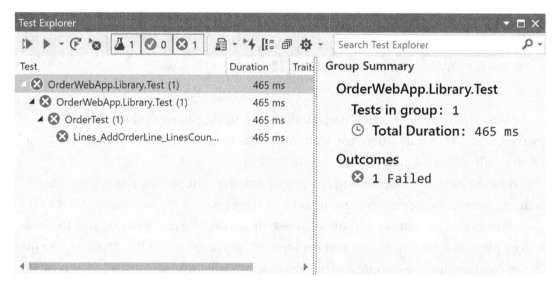

Figure 3-4.   *Test Explorer with a failed test*

It's not apparent, given that the image is black and white, but there is red all over the tree. All of the icons along the tree indicate that there was a failed test. As well, in the toolbar, there is a red icon with an X. Next to that icon is the number of failed tests. And having all of these different indicators is the idea. The "red" of red/green/refactor has been achieved.

The next step in the process is to fix the test by writing the minimal amount of code necessary to make the test pass. Changing the AddOrderLine method to look like Figure 3-5 accomplishes this.

```
1 reference | ⊗ 0/1 passing | 0 changes | 0 authors, 0 changes
public void AddOrderLine()
{
    Lines.Add(new OrderLine());
}
```

Figure 3-5. *Making the method pass the test*

First, note that only a single line is added in order to make the test pass. That's the minimal aspect of the process. Second, there is an addition to the heads-up display for the method that was described in Chapter 2, "Assisted Coding." The second element in the display indicates that the method is covered by 1 unit test, and that 0/1 of the tests are passing. The functionality of the testing element in the heads-up display is covered in more detail later in this section.

Back to making the test green. Once the code has been changed, in the Test Explorer pane, click the Run All link again. The project builds, the test runs, and the results can be seen in Figure 3-6.

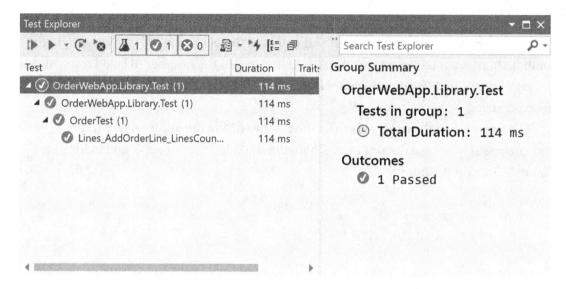

Figure 3-6. *Test Explorer with passing tests*

What used to be red is now green. And the green icon in the toolbar (with the check mark) now has a 1 next to it (for one successful test), while the red icon has a 0 next to it. Step two of the red/green/refactor process is complete. Step three is covered in Chapter 4, "Refactoring Code."

Test Explorer

Test Explorer is the heart of unit testing with Visual Studio 2019. And it contains several features aimed at streamlining the running of unit tests.

You have already been using the Run All Test toolbar button at the top to execute all the tests within the solution, which is fine when there are just a few tests (or when you really need to run all the tests). But immediately to the right is a Run toolbar button that opens a dropdown when clicked. The contents of the dropdown are visible in Figure 3-7.

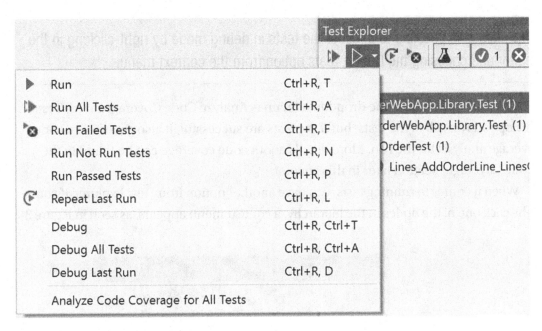

Figure 3-7. Run... dropdown

The first option, Run, runs all of the tests contained within the selected node in the tree. If a class is selected, then all of the test in that class are executed. If a single test is selected, then just that test runs. The second option, Run All Tests, does exactly that. All of the test in the current solution are executed.

The next three options in the context menu run different sets of tests, based on the state of a test. A test can be in one of three states: passed, failed, and not yet run. A passed test would be considered "green," a failed test would be considered "red," and a not yet run test is one that has not been run within the current working session. The available options let you execute one of those subsets of tests. The Repeat Last Test option is used to re-execute the previous test run, regardless of the set of tests that were included.

The three options in the second section of the dropdown menu from Figure 3-7 are used to debug different sets of tests. From the set of tests executed, Debug, Debug All Tests, and Debug Last Run are the same as Run, Run All Tests, and Repeat Last Test. The difference is that if there are breakpoints set within the tests or the application, the execution is paused when a breakpoint is hit. This functionality is very useful if you're trying to figure out why a test is failing.

Tip   It's also possible to execute the tests in debug mode by right-clicking in the editor and choosing the Debug Tests option from the context menu.

The final option from the dropdown menu is Analyze Code Coverage for All Tests. This option runs all of the tests, but if the tests are successful, it also generates a code coverage analysis for the run. More details about code coverage can be found in the "Code Coverage" section later in this chapter.

When it comes to running tests, you have another option from Test Explorer. If you right-click one of the nodes in the hierarchy, a context menu appears, as seen in Figure 3-8.

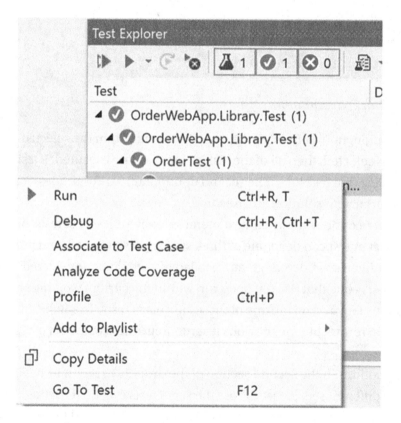

Figure 3-8. *Test Explorer context menu*

The top two options in the context menu run the tests. The tests that are included depend on the node that was selected, but ultimately all of the tests at or under the selected node. In other words, if you right-click OrderTest, and select Run, all the tests in OrderTest are executed. The same applies to Debug, with the exception that the tests are executed in debug mode.

At the bottom of the context menu, there is a Go To Test option. Only enabled when a single test is selected, this option opens the file in which the selected test is located and sets the cursor at the corresponding method.

There are four other options in the context menu: Associate to Test Case, Analyze Code Coverage, Profile, and Add to Playlist. The Associate to Test Case and Add to Playlist options are covered in their own section later in this chapter. The Analyze Code Coverage option runs the tests for the selected node, with the twist that after a successful test run (i.e., no failures), code coverage analysis is performed. The details of Code Coverage are covered in its own section later in this chapter. The Profile option is used to initiate the performance profiling for the code that is exercised by the test. Details on profiling can be found in Chapter 7, "Debugging and Profiling."

To see some of the additional functionality available in Test Explorer, let's add another unit test to the OrderTest class. In particular, add the following method:

```
[TestMethod]
public void Lines_AddOrderLineWithProduct_ProductIsCorrect()
{
    Order target = new Order();
    Product product = new Product()
    {
        Id = 1,
        Number = "A-123"
    };

    target.AddOrderLine();

    Assert.AreEqual(1, target.Lines.Count,
        "The order line was not added");
    Assert.IsNotNull(target.Lines[0].Product ,
        "No product was added to the order line");
    Assert.AreEqual(product.Id,
        target.Lines[0].Product.Id,
        "The product was not added to the order line");
}
```

The idea behind this unit test is that a product object is passed into the AddOrderLine method and that product should then be found on the added order line. At this moment, the unit test should fail, which is exactly what we want. And the Test Explorer looks like the following (Figure 3-9) when all the tests are run.

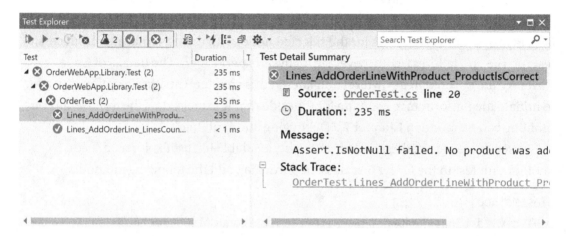

Figure 3-9. *Test Explorer with multiple failed tests*

You'll notice that one of the tests passed and one of them failed. If you select a failed test, then details about the failure appear on the right side. The useful pieces are the message, which is included in the call to the Assert methods and the stack trace. The stack trace contains a list of the calls made to get to the exception. Although there is only one in the example, there can be more items in the stack trace. Each item is a link that, when click, opens up the editor to the corresponding file and sets the cursor to the method that was executing when the exception took place. All of this is very useful when trying to identify the source for a bug.

Earlier in this chapter, the heads-up display in the code was mentioned. Figure 3-10 includes the current view for the AddOrderLine method.

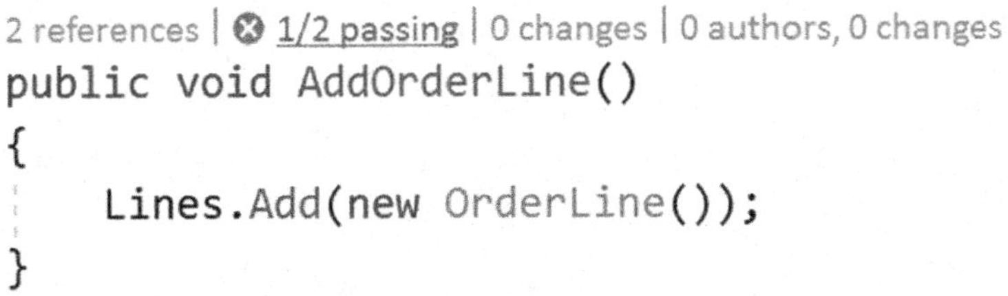

2 references | 1/2 passing | 0 changes | 0 authors, 0 changes
public void AddOrderLine()
{
Lines.Add(new OrderLine());
}

Figure 3-10. *AddOrderLine method heads-up display*

The heads-up display element related to testing shows that 1/2 tests are passing. If you click the link, the information seen in Figure 3-11 is shown.

Test
Duration
Lines_AddOrderLineWithProduct_ProductIsCorrect
108 ms
Lines_AddOrderLine_LinesCountIsCorrect
61 ms
Run All | Run
2 references | 1/2 passing | 0 changes | 0 authors, 0 changes
public void AddOrderLine()

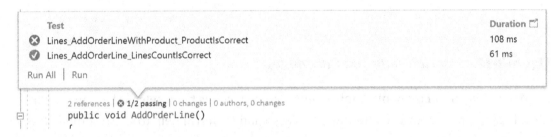

Figure 3-11. *Testing head-up display information*

The heads-up display mentioned that there were two tests, one of which was passing. The information display includes the list of the tests, with the icons on the left indicating the status (passing or failing) of the tests. From the information display, you can navigate to a test by double-clicking the test. Also, at the bottom left, there are links to run all the tests or just to run the selected tests.

Associating with Test Cases

The Associate to Test Case option is used to link a unit test to a test case in TFS (Team Foundation Server) or Team Services. Figure 3-12 shows the dialog that appears when the option is selected.

Note If the Associate to Test Case option isn't visible, it is likely that the account you signed in to Visual Studio with is not associated with TFS or Team Services.

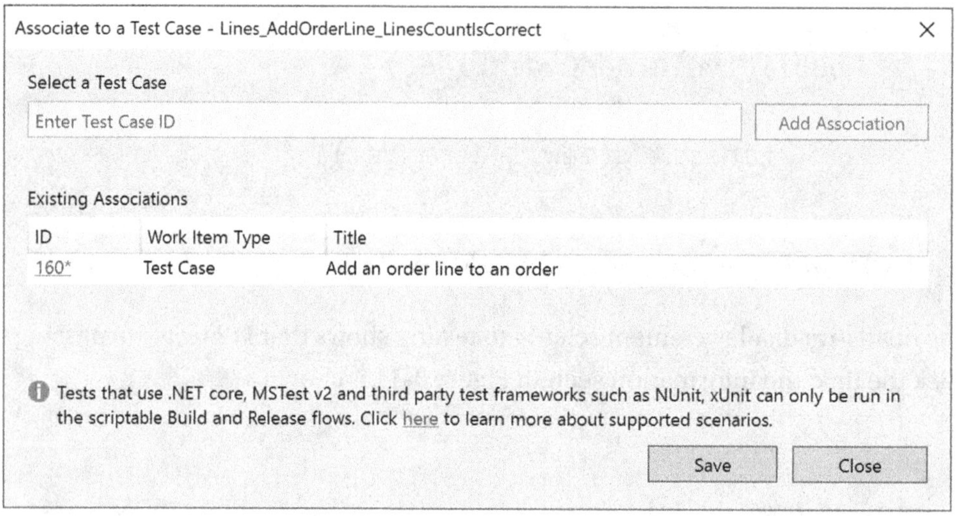

Figure 3-12. *Associate with Test Case dialog*

While this option is enabled only when a single test has been selected, it's important to understand the context surrounding this association. It will help to grasp some of the limitations by associating a unit test with a test case.

A test case in Team Services/TFS is a description of a set of steps that need to be executed in order to test a piece of functionality. For example, a test case might be to create an order for a customer that includes product "A-123." It includes a detailed list of the steps that a user would take in order to add the order, including the menu options selected, data entered, and buttons clicked. In the past, this might have been roughly the equivalent of a manual test.

When you associate a test with a test case, you are saying that the test covers the functionality that is described in the test case. That means that successful completion of the test has the same weight as if a user had manually gone through all the steps in the test case and they all passed.

The true gain for associating a test with a test case comes when executing the tests is automated. If the project and tests are part of a build pipeline, it's possible to configure the tests to run automatically. When this happens, and the test associated with a test case is executed as part of the build, the result from that test run is also associated with the test case. If the test passes, the test case is marked as completed. If the test fails, the test case is considered a failure as well. For complex systems that have lots of moving pieces in development, the association of tests with test cases and the subsequent inclusions in a build pipeline can be a powerful addition to a development workflow.

However, as a result of the context related to test cases, there are some limitations as to which types of tests can be associated with a test case. After all, it doesn't really make sense to link a simple unit test of the type built in this chapter with a multistep, manually executed test case. The following types of tests can be associated with a test case:

- Coded UI tests (although be warned that support for Coded UI is being deprecated after Visual Studio 2019)

- Selenium tests

- Unit tests written using version 1 of the MSTest framework

- MSTest version 2, NUnit, and xUnit tests (however if they are built using a TFS pipeline, it cannot be one of the older XAML builds)

- .NET Core Framework tests (however, they cannot use the older XAML builds)

Tests that use a JavaScript testing framework, such as Chutzpah or Jest, cannot be associated with a test case.

Note   While the same test can be associated with more than one test case, each test case can only be associated with one test.

If you do have a test that qualifies, the flow for associating a test with a test case is straightforward. Get the identifier for the test case, using the TFS portal, for instance. Enter the identifier into the text box and click Add Association. The list at the bottom of the dialog shows all of the existing associations for the selected test.

Playlists

Also visible in the context menu seen in Figure 3-8 is an Add to Playlist option. A playlist is a mechanism for creating groups of tests that can be executed together. To this point, the only categorization of tests has been based on status (passed, failed, not run) or by the physical location of the code (the class or the project). A playlist provides a customizable way of grouping tests.

To create a playlist, start by selecting one or more nodes in Test Explorer. Then right-click and select the Add to Playlist ➤ New Playlist option from the context menu. A new instance of the Test Explorer appears, with the tree of tests rooted at the node you had selected originally. The only difference between the two Test Explorers is that the new created one has a Save icon immediate to the right of the message type icons. If you want to persist the playlist between Visual Studio sessions, clicking the Save icon will prompt you for the file name (with the .playlist extension). Once you have created the playlist, it becomes possible to use it in different places throughout Test Explorer. For example, you can open the playlist to see the test using the Playlist icon at the top (see Figure 3-13).

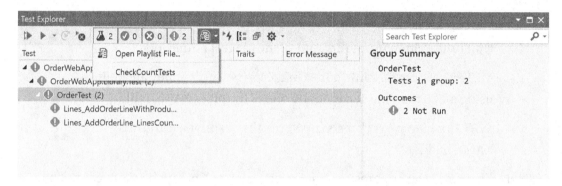

Figure 3-13. *Opening an existing playlist*

Or you can add tests to an open playlist. Go through the same process as when you created the playlist by selecting Add to Playlist from the context menu. Then choose the name of the playlist to which you'd like to add the test(s). If you're feeling particularly adventurous, you can even edit the .playlist file directly. The playlist information is stored as an XML document where each test in the playlist is a node. One of the attributes of the node is the fully qualified name of the test method.

Every time you open or create a playlist, a new instance of the Test Explorer is opening, showing only tests contained in the playlist. The functionality in that new instance is the same as for the original Test Explorer, which is to say that you can run tests, debug tests, and view the results for any test.

IntelliTest

Writing unit tests is an interesting mental exercise. Following the red/green/refactor pattern generates some unit tests, but those unit tests are designed to cover functionality. They might not necessarily cover all the edge cases, particularly in terms of the range of values for the parameters that are passed in. It's up to the developer to think about all the different possibilities for the parameters and then write unit tests for each scenario. Not technically challenging, but necessary. And tedious.

It's into this gap that IntelliTest fits. It started as a Microsoft Research project (code-named Pex) that targeted the generation of unit types by performing dynamic analysis on the code, which means that it examines the code being tested and identifies unit tests that should be created. It tries to ensure that all paths through the code are covered by tests. It ensures that extreme values for the parameters (such as passing a null for an object) are included in the tests.

Over time, the functionality that came from that project was released into production in the form of IntelliTest. IntelliTest examines your code looking for the following items:

- Conditional branches – For each switch or if statement, parameter values are identified to have execution pass through each branch.

- Assertions – Parameter values necessary to both pass and fail the assertion are determined.

- Out-of-range – For certain types of parameters, tests that include null value are found.

This information is used to create a suite of unit tests. And, if you choose, those unit tests can be added to your project, either in an existing project or a separate one.

The process of initiating IntelliTest is simple. Right-click anywhere in the method that you want to process and choose IntelliTest ➤ Run IntelliTest from the context menu (Figure 3-14).

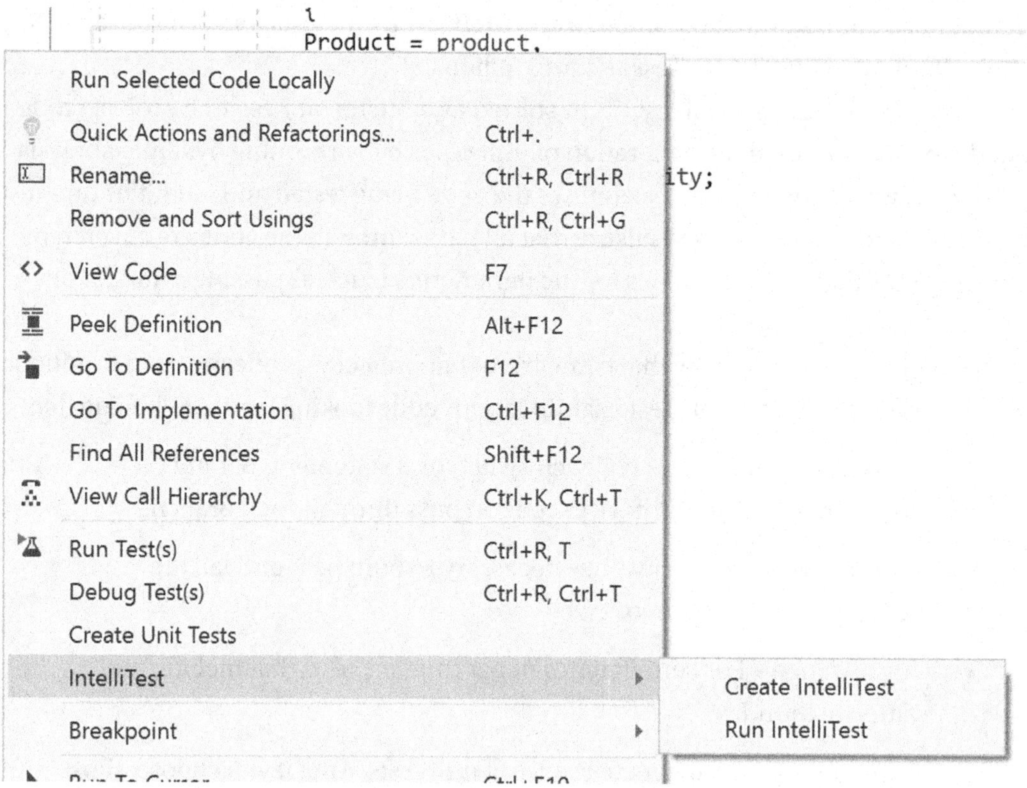

Figure 3-14. *IntelliTest context menu*

Note   There are a couple of conditions that need to be met before the IntelliTest menu option is visible. First, IntelliTest is a feature for the Enterprise edition of Visual Studio 2019. The Professional and Community editions won't show the menu item. Also, depending on the version number, IntelliTest does not support .NET Core applications. The most recent word from Microsoft is that support for IntelliTest and .NET Core will be included in bits and pieces starting with version 16.3, but there is no current timeline for complete support.

When you run IntelliTest, the project is built and then the dynamic analysis on the method takes place. The results are shown in its own pane, as seen in Figure 3-15.

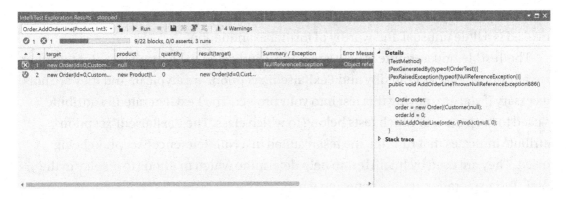

Figure 3-15. *IntelliTest exploration results pane*

From the results of the IntelliTest run, there were two unit tests that were generated. The first column in the output includes the constructor for the object being tested (in this case, an Order object). The method being tested (AddOrderLine) has two parameters, a product and a quantity. There is one column in the display for each of those parameters (labeled product and quantity), and you can see the values that were passed in as part of the test. The next three columns deal with the result of running the test. In the first row, there was an exception generated (NullReferenceException) when the test was run. There is also an error message containing the message associated with the exception. In the second row, the test passed and the column labeled result(target) show the state of the target object after the successful execution.

Running IntelliTest in this manner does not generate the code for the unit test and add it to a project. Instead the tests are generated and executed completely in memory. If you select a row, the section on the right side of the pane in Figure 3-15 shows the code for the generated unit test. It can also be found as follows:

```
[TestMethod]
[PexGeneratedBy(typeof(OrderTest))]
[PexRaisedException(typeof(NullReferenceException))]
public void AddOrderLineThrowsNullReferenceException886()
{
    Order order;
    order = new Order((Customer)null);
    order.Id = 0;
    this.AddOrderLine(order, (Product)null, 0);
}
```

Some of what you see looks completely normal for unit tests. But how the method is invoked is a little unusual and worthy of further examination.

The TestMethod attribute is how a method is indicated to be a unit test. But the other two attributes, PexGeneratedBy and PexRaisedException, are atypical. And they are not necessary if you are moving this test into your project. The PexGeneratedBy attribute is used to keep track of which tests belong to which class. The PexRaisedException attribute indicates that running the test resulted in a NullReferenceException being raised. They are used by IntelliTest to help determine which methods to display in the IntelliTest exploration results pane and when.

Inside the method itself, the target object is created and the properties set to the appropriate values. Then a call is made to a private method called AddOrderLine. Notice that the target object, along with the parameters for AddOrderLine, is passed.

The AddOrderLine method is an internally generated method. The code follows:

```
[PexMethod]
public void AddOrderLine(
    [PexAssumeUnderTest]Order target,
    Product product,
    int quantity
)
{
    target.AddOrderLine(product, quantity);
}
```

This method doesn't seem on its face to add much value. And in this scenario, it is probably unnecessary. Aside from the attributes (PexMethod and PexAssumeUnderTest) that are used to help the IntelliTest exploration results pane, display the appropriate information that is. However, as a good practice, placing the call to the method under test in a separate method can be useful. For instance, it is quite likely that there will be a number of calls to AddOrderLine. And each one of those will involve checking to see if the call resulted an OrderLine being added to the Order object (represented by the target variable). An assertion could be added to this method below the call to AddOrderLine, and now all calls to AddOrderLine contain that assertion. The number of duplicated assertions that need to appear in each unit test is reduced. This type of refactoring of unit tests would also be performed when the tests are written manually. IntelliTest just gets there from the initial code generation.

Across the top of Figure 3-15 is a toolbar that helps you perform common functions within the results pane. The dropdown at the left includes a list of all of the methods that were included in the IntelliTest run. While in the example described earlier, IntelliTest was executed by right-clicking within a method, if you had right-clicked in the class instead, then IntelliTest would have generated tests for all of the public methods in the class, including the constructors. Choosing a method from the dropdown shows the tests generated for that method.

Immediately to the right of the dropdown is an icon (a square with an arrow) that takes you to the definition for the method under test. This is followed by an icon that runs the exploration (a green triangle) and stops the exploration while it's ongoing (a red square).

The next four icons are used to perform functionality with selected tests from the generated results. If you select one or more of the tests, then at a minimum the first icon is enabled. This icon (which looks like a floppy disk) is used to save the tests into a project. The details of the naming for that project are based on the Create IntelliTest settings described shortly.

The other three icons are enabled quite selectively. For the view seen in Figure 3-15, there is only one possibility and that is the Allow icon (the third of the four). If you select the unit test that failed due to the null reference exception, the Allow icon is enabled. When you click the icon, you are indicating that having the method raise the exception is an acceptable result. This would add the PexExceptedException to the AddOrderLines method described earlier in this section (the one that is part of the test and not the method under test). Now when the exception is raised, it is considered a passing test.

To get to the other two icons requires a slight detour on the toolbar. On the right, there is Warning icon. Visually, it describes how many warnings were found while running the exploration process. But when you click it, you change the contents of the IntelliTest pane to look something like Figure 3-16.

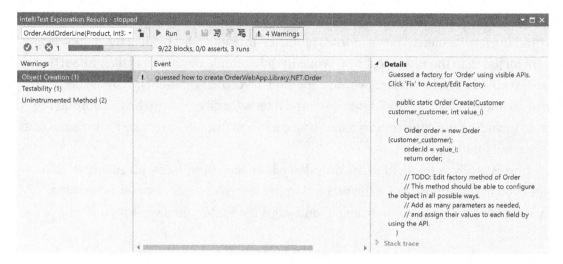

Figure 3-16. *Warnings from IntelliTest*

As part of the exploration process, IntelliTest does an exhaustive walk through each method. But that walk does more than follow any branches or loops that might exist. It looks at the data types for the different variables to determine edge cases. It also considers how instances of objects are created, passing different ranges of parameters into the constructor, if appropriate. If the method has parameters that have an interface as the data type, it looks at any concrete implementation in the project. There are all manner of things that IntelliTest might consider, and if there are questions or even opportunities to improve the testing process, a warning is generated.

In Figure 3-16, there are three categories of warnings visible. If you click the first one, you can see the detail for the that specific warning. In this instance, IntelliTest couldn't find a factory for the Order object. On the right, in the Details sections, is the factory that is proposed by IntelliTest. And it's at this point where the other two icons come into play.

Once you have selected the warning, the two previously disabled icons are enabled. The second icon is used to Fix the warning. In this instance, it would create a test project for the unit tests that it has discovered and add the proposed factory to the execution flow. The second icon is used to Suppress the warning. In that case, no fix is added and the warning will not appear in future explorations.

One thing to consider with the Fix option is that, once the factory has been added to the test project, you're able to adjust it to fit the specifics of your classes. And "adjust" in this case means changing the implementation. Add parameters to the factory. Initialize properties to different values. All options are open as the factory is just a method in the test class and any changes you make will be integrated into the unit test execution flow.

Test Project Settings

To this point in the discussion about IntelliTest, there have been a number of functions that took the generated unit tests and surfaced them in an actual project. For example, fixing a warning from the end of the last section would create a unit test project (if it didn't already exist) and add an appropriately named class that contained the factory method. It is because the code is generated that you can customize to fit your needs.

The trick with generated code, however, is to get it to fit nicely into your projects with a minimum of effort. Have your test project name fit your standards for project names. Create classes that are the same as the unit test classes used in the red/green/refactor process. Fortunately, Visual Studio 2019 provides a mechanism to define the naming pattern for various parts of the generated tests.

The screen that is used to customize the naming is accessed through the IntelliTest ➤ Create IntelliTest menu item in the context menu seen in Figure 3-14. The result is the dialog shown in Figure 3-17.

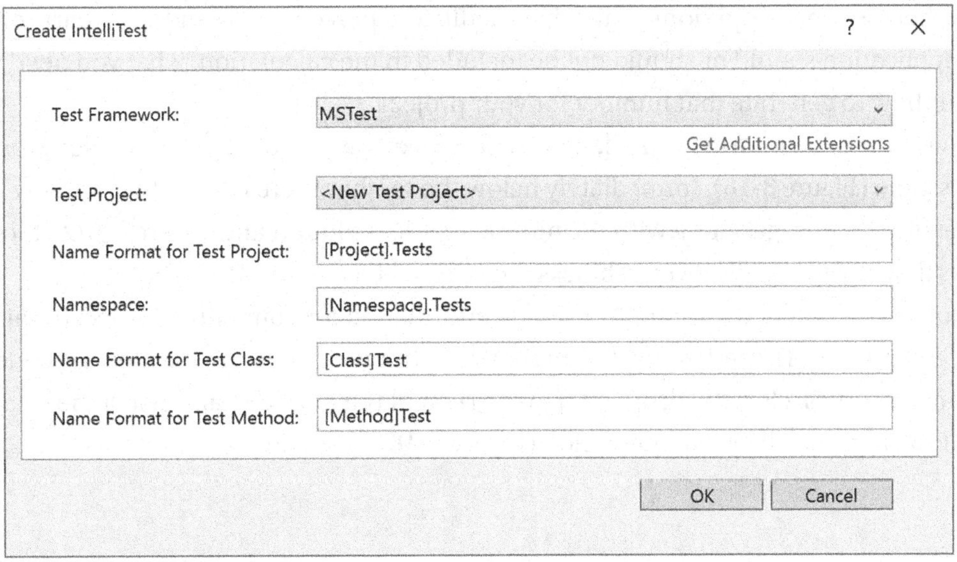

Figure 3-17. *Create IntelliTest dialog*

The starting point is to choose the Test Framework that you are using. The only options delivered with Visual Studio 2019 are two versions of MSTest. If you are using another testing framework, you can find extensions from the Visual Studio Marketplace that support xUnit and NUnit. If you have one (or more) of the extensions installed, you can choose the framework you want to target from the dropdown list.

The next field, the Test Project, is used to specify if you want to create a new project or add the tests to an existing one. The only projects that you'll see in the dropdown list are those that match the selected test framework.

The remaining four fields are used to define the pattern used to name the test project, namespace, test class, and test method. You'll notice that there are four place holders: Project, Namespace, Class, and Method. These are set off from the static portion of the name by surrounding the placeholder with square brackets. You can use any of the placeholders in any of the fields. When you have configured the framework and names as you desire, click OK. This generates the test project (if you haven't selected an existing) and add the scaffolding code to run the tests created when you use the Save function in the IntelliTest exploration results pane.

Code Coverage

One of the more common metrics for unit testing is code coverage. The goal of code coverage is to describe what percentage of your code is being covered by a unit test. While there are many opinions as to what a sufficient percentage is and what parts of your application should or should not be included in the calculation, what you need to know is how to generate that number for your project.

You start to see information related to code coverage in the IntelliTest exploration results pane (Figure 3-16). Immediately below the toolbar there is a bar that roughly indicates the coverage, along with the number of blocks found and covered (9/22 blocks means that 9 of the 22 discovered blocks are covered by unit tests).

However, to generate the code coverage information for your entire project (or at a more granular level), the Test Explorer is used. To run your tests while collecting code coverage statistics, click the dropdown to the right of the Run icon and select the Analyze Code Coverage for All Test menu option (Figure 3-18).

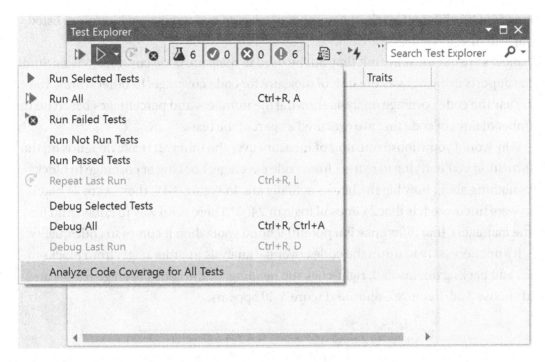

Figure 3-18. *Generating Code Coverage statistics*

At this point, the process is pretty much the same as running tests. The project builds and the tests are executed. The difference is that, once the test run is complete, a different pane appears – one that contains code coverage information and not test results. An example can be found in Figure 3-19.

Hierarchy	Not Covered (Blocks)	Not Covered (% Blocks)	Covered (Blocks)	Covered (% Blocks)
▲ Bruce Johnson_DESKTOP-3U...	24	23.53%	78	76.47%
▲ orderwebapp.library.dll	24	48.98%	25	51.02%
▲ {} OrderWebApp.Library	24	48.98%	25	51.02%
▷ Customer	6	100.00%	0	0.00%
▷ Order	8	32.00%	17	68.00%
▷ OrderLine	3	50.00%	3	50.00%
▷ Product	7	58.33%	5	41.67%
▷ orderwebapp.library.tests.....	0	0.00%	53	100.00%

Figure 3-19. *Code Coverage Results pane*

The code coverage information shown in Figure 3-19 is a hierarchical breakdown of the code coverage by assembly, namespace, class, and (not visible in the figure) method.

For each of the different levels, the number of covered and uncovered blocks are listed, along with the percentage for each.

Blocks are not the only unit that can be used to measure code coverage. Visual Studio also supports using lines as the unit of measure for code coverage. In other words, you can view the code coverage analysis showing the numbers and percentages based on the number of lines of code that are executed as part of the tests.

Why would you choose one unit of measure over the other? It really depends on the information you're trying to extract from code coverage. Looking at coverage in block says nothing about how big the blocks actually are. In Figure 3-19, there were 24 blocks that were uncovered. Is that 24 lines of logic or 2400? There is no way to know. And for some managers, that difference is a potential blind spot when it comes to code quality.

It's not necessary to rerun the code coverage analysis in order to get from blocks to lines and back again. Instead, right-click the heading for the code coverage results area and choose Add/Remove Columns. Figure 3-20 appears.

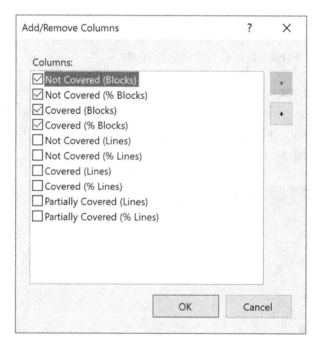

Figure 3-20. *Add and Remove Code Coverage Columns*

You can see that the four columns that appear in Figure 3-19 are all checked. If you want to display the code coverage in lines, then check any or all of the columns that have (Lines) at the end. When you click OK, they will now appear in the Code Coverage results.

While the code coverage numbers are nice to be able to get a sense of the areas of your code base where more testing might be needed, for some developers, the numbers themselves don't really provide enough granularity to determine which tests need to be written. To help with that, Code Coverage in Visual Studio 2019 has the ability to color the lines of code based on whether they were executed as part of a unit test or not.

To toggle the coloring of the lines on and off, click the Show Code Coverage Coloring button immediately to the left of the Remove button on the toolbar in the Code Coverage Results pane. When coloring is turned on, the individual code files have their lines shaded as seen in Figure 3-21.

```
4 references | ● 3/3 passing | 0 changes | 0 authors, 0 changes
public Order()
{
    Lines = new List<OrderLine>();
    OrderDate = DateTimeOffset.Now;
}

0 references | 0 changes | 0 authors, 0 changes
public Order(Customer customer) : this()
{
    Customer = customer;
}

0 references | 0 changes | 0 authors, 0 changes
public int Id { get; set; }
1 reference | 0 changes | 0 authors, 0 changes
public Customer Customer { get; set; }
1 reference | 0 changes | 0 authors, 0 changes
public DateTimeOffset OrderDate { get; set; }
```

Figure 3-21. *Code-colored source code*

While the actual colors aren't apparent in a black and white image, the lines of code that are covered by a unit test are in pale blue, while the lines that are not covered are in light red. This allows you to target your tests against the code that hasn't already been addressed. It's not a perfect way to go (after all, having code covered by a single test doesn't mean that the code doesn't contain a bug), but it's a convenient way of seeing where your testing might be falling short.

Merging Results

The Code Coverage Results pane only shows the results for the more current run of the code coverage analysis process. However, that might not be sufficient if you're trying to determine the coverage being provided by all of your testing. It's possible that some unit tests required multiple runs (with, e.g., configuration information varying between each one) in order to cover all the code.

Within the Code Coverage Results pane, you can combine the results from multiple test runs into a single set of code coverage results. First, if you want to view the results from a previous analysis, they are available in the dropdown list on the left side of the toolbar. Figure 3-22 illustrates the dropdown containing a couple of previously executed tests.

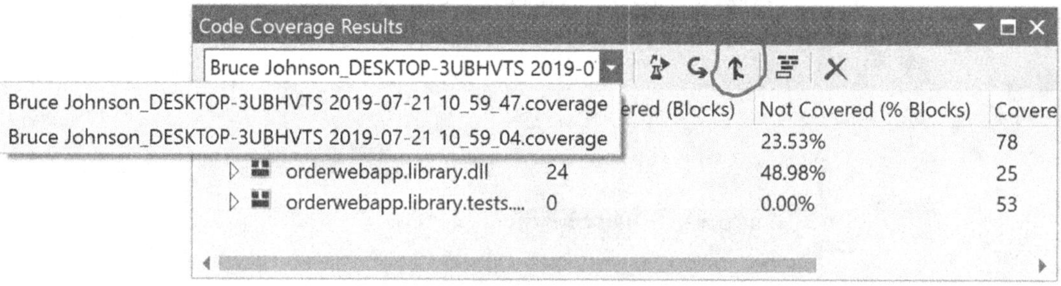

Figure 3-22. *Merging code coverage analysis results*

When you choose any of the items that appear, the results for that analysis are available in the pane. Be aware, however, that this list only includes the analysis runs that have happened since Visual Studio started. If you want to include results from prior to that, you'll need to import the results, a process described in the next section.

But we were considering the ability to merge the results from different analysis into a single report. To do this, you click the Merge Results icon in the toolbar (circled in Figure 3-22). This launches the dialog seen in Figure 3-23.

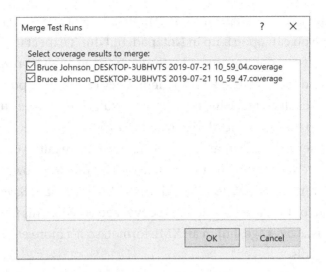

Figure 3-23. *Merge Test Runs dialog*

Choose the different runs that you want to merge into a single report, and when you click OK, they are combined with the results visible in the Code Coverage Results pane.

The main limitation with merging the results from different runs is that they all needed to be executed against the same version of the code. If you think about it, this makes sense. There is information in the results that match a test execution with the lines of code that are executed. If you have made changes to the code being tested, the previous results might no longer be able to match up against the code. So any analysis would no longer be valid for determining code coverage. If you do merge results from different version, it doesn't keep the information from being displayed. They will just be shown independently under two different top-level nodes, rather than combined into a single hierarchy.

Managing Results

The results, whether merged or not, can be exported and sent to others as desired. First, the analysis results themselves are stored in a folder called TestResults at the same level as your solution file. Within the TestResults folder, there is a separate folder for each run. The folder names are annoyingly GUIDs (Globally Unique Identifiers), so there is no way to get a sense of where the run is from based on the name. Only the date is available to guide you.

Inside that folder is a `.coverage` file that contains the test results in a binary format. Which is to say that you can open it up in Notepad, but don't expect to gain any useful information from it. If you need to share the results from an analysis run with someone else, you can just send the `.coverage` file to them. They can then import the results into the Code Coverage Results pane using the Import Results button (the curved arrow icon, seen in Figure 3-22 to the left of the Merge Results icon).

If you would prefer a more human-readable form of the results, you can use the Export Results button (the icon to the immediate right of the dropdown, with the flask as part of it) to accomplish this. When clicked, you get the standard Save File dialog, with the sole format for the saved file being a `.coveragexml` file. This file contains the same information as `.coverage`, but in an XML format, so it's more easily digestible by humans and other tools.

Customization

To this point, the code coverage has been using the default settings. What this means from a practical perspective is that the analysis process considers all the assemblies that are part of the solution. For many situations, this default behavior is more than adequate. However, if you want to get more specific about the artifacts that are included or excluded, Visual Studio 2019 provides a mechanism you can use.

The custom information is kept in a `.runsettings` file. This is just an XML file with an extension of `.runsettings`. To create a file, add a new item to your solution. The item is an XML file with the name set to whatever you want, so long as the extension is `.runsettings`. There is no template for this file available in Visual Studio 2019. If you want a basic layout, consider the following:

```xml
<?xml version="1.0" encoding="utf-8"?>
<RunSettings>
  <RunConfiguration>
    <MaxCpuCount>1</MaxCpuCount>
    <ResultsDirectory>.\TestResults</ResultsDirectory>
    <TargetPlatform>x86</TargetPlatform>
    <TargetFrameworkVersion>Framework45
    </TargetFrameworkVersion>
    <TestSessionTimeout>10000</TestSessionTimeout>
  </RunConfiguration>
```

```xml
<DataCollectionRunSettings>
  <DataCollectors>
    <DataCollector friendlyName="Code Coverage"
        uri="datacollector://Microsoft/CodeCoverage/2.0"
        assemblyQualifiedName=
"Microsoft.VisualStudio.Coverage.DynamicCoverageDataCollector, Microsoft.
VisualStudio.TraceCollector, Version=11.0.0.0, Culture=neutral, PublicKeyTo
ken=b03f5f7f11d50a3a">
      <Configuration>
        <CodeCoverage>
          <ModulePaths>
            <Exclude>
              <ModulePath>.*MyUnitTestFramework.*
              </ModulePath>
            </Exclude>
          </ModulePaths>
        </CodeCoverage>
      </Configuration>
    </DataCollector>
  </DataCollectors>
</DataCollectionRunSettings>
<TestRunParameters>
  <Parameter name="testUserId" value="Admin" />
  <Parameter name="testPassword" value="P@ssw0rd" />
</TestRunParameters>
</RunSettings>
```

Most of the values here are default settings for the code coverage analysis, so that can be removed without changing the behavior. Probably the two most frequently customized elements are ModulePaths and TestRunParameters.

The ModulePaths element optionally includes an Exclude and Include subelement. The Exclude element is a collection of ModulePath elements where the content is a regular expression used to specify assemblies which are not to be included in the code coverage analysis. The Include element is a collection of ModulePath elements where the content is a regular expression used to specify assemblies which are to be included in the analysis.

The ModulePath element is not the only way to specify the elements that are included or excluded from processing. Also available are

- CompanyName – Uses the company attribute of the assembly.

- PublicKeyToken – Uses the public key token of the assembly. This presumes that the assembly has been signed.

- Source – Finds assemblies by the path of the source file.

- Attribute – Looks for elements which have been decorated with a particular attribute. The full name of the attribute, including the "Attribute" portion of the class name, must be used.

- Function – Finds specific methods. The contents of this element are a regular expression that must match the fully qualified name of the function. Fully qualified in this instance includes the namespace, the class name, the method name, and the parameter list. As an example, a method with a signature of `public void Lines_AddOrderLine_LinesCountIsCorrect(int orderNumber)` in the class `OrderTest` and in the namespace `OrderWebApp.Library.Test` would need a regular expression that matches the following string:

```
OrderWebApp.Library.Test.OrderTest.Lines_AddOrderLine_
LinesCountIsCorrect(int)
```

The TestRunParameters element is a collection of Parameter elements. Each Parameter is a name/value pair used to provide parameter information that can be used within the test execution. In this regard, the collection looks like many other name/value pairs, like AppSettings, used to parameterize execution. The trick is now to retrieve the current value and use it in your tests. For TestRunParameters, the values are surfaced through the Properties list in the TestContext object. The following sample in MSTest provides an illustration:

```
private string _testCompanyName;
private string _testEmployeeName;

[ClassInitialize]
```

```
public static void TestClassInitialize(TestContext context)
{
    _testCompanyName =
        context.Properties["testCompanyName"].ToString();
    _testEmployeeName =
        context.Properties["testEmployeeName"].ToString();
}
```

The TestContext is available as a parameter in the method used to initialize the class. It's the ClassInitialize attribute that indicates which method is called at class initialization. In the sample, the values are extracted from the Properties property using the name of the parameter as the index. That value is then stored in class-level variables, so that all of the methods can use them.

You can have multiple .runsettings files available in your project and choose the one used for during test execution. To select the desired file, click the dropdown button next to the gear in the Test Explorer. Figure 3-24 shows the options that appear.

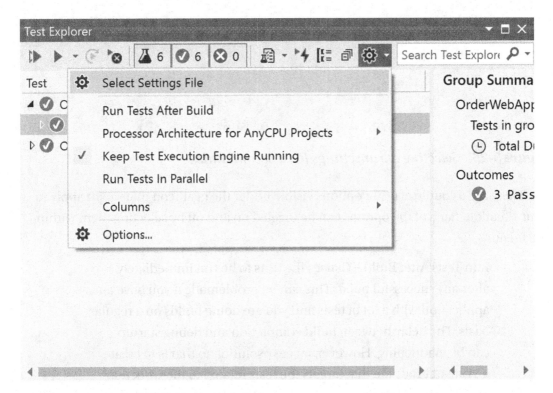

Figure 3-24. Selecting a runsettings file

The Select Settings File option launches the Open File dialog, allowing you to choose the desired settings file. Once you have used a particular file, it gets added to the list of options associated with the gear icon, making it easier to use the next time you need it. Figure 3-25 shows the same menu, but with a settings file having been selected previously.

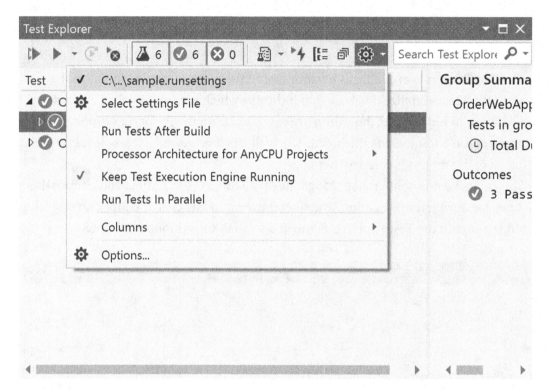

Figure 3-25. *Selecting a .runsettings file a second time*

There are a couple of other options visible under the gear icon that might apply to your situation. Each of the options can be toggled on and off by selecting them within the menu.

> Run Tests After Build – Causes the tests to be run immediately after any successful build. This can be problematic if you have an application with a lot of tests and you are doing builds on a regular basis. The delay between build completion and debug startup can be maddening. However, an easy solution to that is to create a `.runsettings` file that targets the tests related to the work that you're doing. Now the delay is lessened, and if any tests fail, they are directly relevant to the work you're doing.

Processor Architecture for AnyCPU Projects – Allows you to set whether the processor architecture for projects which are marked as being "Any CPU" will be run using x86 or x64. This is different than the setting in the Configuration Manager, in that this value only affects the tests, not the entire project or solution.

Keep Test Execution Engine Running – When Visual Studio runs unit tests, they are actually executed in a separate process. This allows Visual Studio to remain both interactive and stable during unit test execution. This option is used to determine whether you want to keep that separate process running once the test execution is finished. This is a trade-off between speed (the next time you run unit tests, you don't incur the admittedly small time it takes to spin up the separate process) and resources (the test execution process uses memory while it's running). The default for Visual Studio 2019 is to have this setting turned on.

Run Tests in Parallel – This option provides an opportunity to speed up the overall execution of your test by running tests in parallel. First, in order for this to be an advantage, you need to be running on a machine that has multiple cores. Once that requirement has been met, if this option has been turned on, then a separate test execution process will be started on each core. Each process will then be given a testing artifact to work on. In general, the testing artifact is an assembly that contains unit tests. It will be up to the process to run those tests and pass the results back to Visual Studio.

There are a couple of considerations and caveats to understand when it comes to parallel tests. You can configure how many cores are being used in testing and therefore what the degree of parallelization is. This is done through the RunConfiguration element in the .runsettings file. The following element makes sure that no more than two cores are being used:

```
<RunConfiguration>
    <MaxCpuCount>2</MaxCpuCount>
</RunConfiguration>
```

The caveat comes in the form of how you've structured your unit tests. In order to work in parallel, the tests must be completely independent of one another. How easy or hard this is to accomplish depends very much on your environment. Experientially, the biggest area for collision with parallel tests comes when the unit tests use a shared resource, like a database. So if you plan on parallelizing your tests, keep this is mind. It will save you hours of debugging frustration.

Live Unit Testing

Visual Studio 2019 Enterprise includes a technology that allows your unit tests to be executed in real time. In other words, as you make changes to your code, the unit tests that cover the code you're changing get executed. This provides you immediate feedback into the code your writing, whether the changes that you're making are negatively impacting the code's previous functionality. This technology is named Live Unit Testing. And not only does Live Unit Testing show you which tests would pass or fail based on your changes, it also updated the code coverage information as well.

Live Unit Testing is not enabled by default. As you might imagine, there is a performance impact for continually running unit tests. And while Visual Studio is intelligent about the tests that need to be executed with every change, the tests are still run and that does take CPU cycles.

The starting point for Live Unit Testing is any test project. There is support for both .NET Framework and .NET Core testing projects. And for testing frameworks, Live Unit Testing supports MSTest, NUnit, and xUnit.net. For the examples that follow, we'll be using the test project created earlier in this chapter.

As mentioned earlier, Live Unit Testing is not enabled by default. You need to start it manually. This is done through the Test ➤ Live Unit Testing ➤ Start menu item in Visual Studio. When you start Live Unit Testing, the first step is to execute all of your current unit tests. This is the same as if you had run all the test manually. When the tests are complete, Test Explorer appears showing you the results. Again, this is the same as if you had run the test manually. Figure 3-26 illustrates Test Explorer when all of your tests have passed.

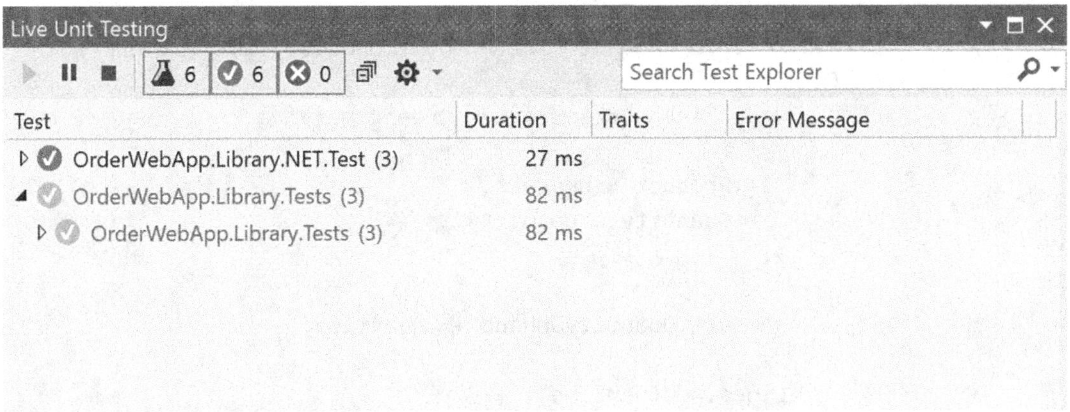

Figure 3-26. *Test Explorer with passing tests*

The difference with Live Unit Testing is visible when you look at your code. Figure 3-27 shows what a typical method would look like.

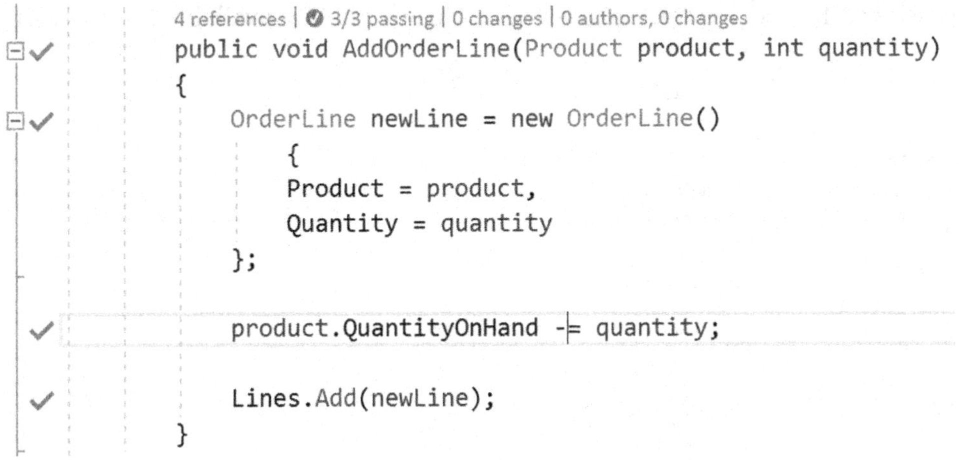

```
4 references | 3/3 passing | 0 changes | 0 authors, 0 changes
public void AddOrderLine(Product product, int quantity)
{
    OrderLine newLine = new OrderLine()
        {
        Product = product,
        Quantity = quantity
    };

    product.QuantityOnHand -= quantity;

    Lines.Add(newLine);
}
```

Figure 3-27. *A method with passing unit tests in Live Unit Testing*

The difference is the green check marks that appear next to each line and method that has every test that covers the line passing. The check marks (as if the green wasn't enough) indicate the success of the tests. But, as the section title suggested, this is **Live** unit testing. To see the live part in action, change the self-decrement operator in the line that updates the QuantityOnHand to a self-increment. Now the unit test fails, and the check marks change to red X's, as can be seen in Figure 3-28.

```
    4 references | ✔ 3/3 passing | 0 changes | 0 authors, 0 changes
⊟✗  public void AddOrderLine(Product product, int quantity)
    {
⊟✗      OrderLine newLine = new OrderLine()
            {
                Product = product,
                Quantity = quantity
            };

 ✗      product.QuantityOnHand += quantity;

 ✗      Lines.Add(newLine);
    }
```

Figure 3-28. *A method with failing unit tests in Live Unit Testing*

The X's aren't just an indicator of where the unit tests are failing. If you click one of the X's, you can see the specific tests that are covering the line of code, as well as which ones passed and failed. Figure 3-29 illustrates the information available upon clicking.

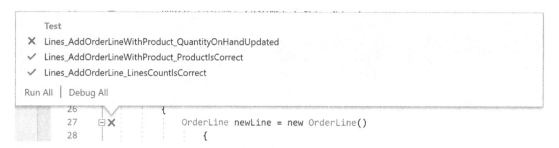

```
Test
✗  Lines_AddOrderLineWithProduct_QuantityOnHandUpdated
✔  Lines_AddOrderLineWithProduct_ProductIsCorrect
✔  Lines_AddOrderLine_LinesCountIsCorrect
Run All | Debug All
    26                {
    27  ⊟✗             OrderLine newLine = new OrderLine()
    28                    {
```

Figure 3-29. *Live Unit Testing details*

The information includes a list of the tests that cover the line associated with the X that you clicked. The X's and check marks beside each of the tests indicate whether the test passed or failed. If you double-click one of the tests, the file containing the test opens and your cursor is placed on the test method.

As well as the information about the test and their status, you can also run all of the tests or debug all of the tests. And if you select one of the test, you can also run or debug that individual test.

As was mentioned earlier, there can be a performance impact if you're using Live Unit Testing. There are a number of settings available to help mitigate any issues you might have. To get to the settings, click the Tools ➤ Options menu item and navigate to the Live Unit Testing node on the left side. Figure 3-30 should be seen.

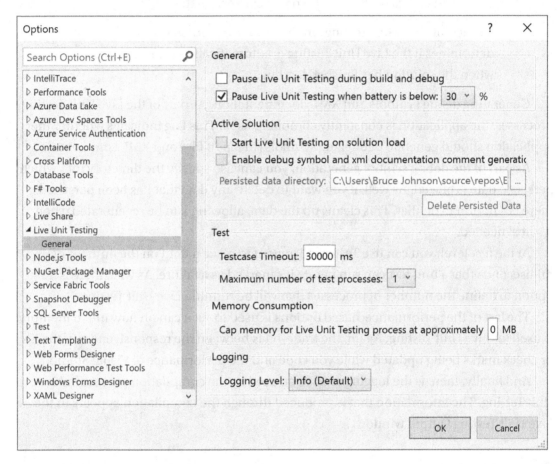

Figure 3-30. *Live Unit Testing settings*

The bulk of these settings are directly related to helping you ensure that performance levels are maintained. Using the options found in Figure 3-30, the following areas can be configured:

> Pausing Live Unit Testing when a solution is built and debugged –
> Stopping during a build makes sense, if you consider what Visual
> Studio is doing and the CPU effort involved. As for debugging,

unless you're planning on making changes to your application while debugging, there is no need to have Live Unit Testing running.

Pausing Live Unit Testing when the battery is below a certain percentage – Again, this is to help you conserve battery life.

Launching Live Unit Testing when a solution is opened – This determines if the Live Unit Testing is automatically turned on when the solution has finished loading.

Generating debug symbols and XML documentation. As part of the Live Unit Testing processes, the application is constantly compiling itself. This flag indicates whether the application should generate debugging symbols (the .pdb file) and XML comments.

As part of the debug symbol generation, you can also specify the directory into which persisted data is placed. As well, if you want to delete any data that has been persisted, there is a button to do that. This cleans up the data, allowing it to be regenerated when it's next needed.

At the test level, you can use Testcase Timeout to place a limit on the number of milliseconds that a unit test can run before it's marked as a failure. As well, there is an option to define the number of processes that will be running Live Unit Testing.

The last of the performance-based options is used to set a cap on how much memory is used for Live Unit Testing. Again, the trade-off is between the responsiveness of the X's or check marks being updated while you code and the performance of Visual Studio.

And finally, there is the logging level to be used by the compilation process in Live Unit Testing. The information that is produced through the compilation appears in the Live Unit Testing Output window.

Summary

Writing and executing tests, whether it's done manually or as part of Live Unit Testing, is a core function of the red/green/refactor process described at the top of the chapter. It's pretty much the heart of the red and green parts. This chapter has covered the support that Visual Studio provides in writing, running, and benefiting from unit tests within your application.

In the next chapter, you'll learn about the third leg of the development triad: refactoring. This is the process of taking code that works (according to the unit tests) and improving it by streamlining, reorganization, and restructuring.

CHAPTER 4

Refactoring Code

In Chapter 3, "Unit Testing," red/green/refactor was introduced as a development paradigm. Through unit testing, it was possible to achieve the red and green portion of that triumvirate. What was missing from the discussion was refactoring, which, fortunately for people who read books from front to back, is the topic of this chapter. After a brief description of the function and form of refactoring, you will learn about the many different tools that Visual Studio 2019 brings to bear to help with this step.

What Is Refactoring

To start, let's consider refactoring as a concept, away from the tooling used to make it happen. In plain terms, the purpose of refactoring is to make your code cleaner; easier to follow 6 months from now when you're reading through your application, wondering who wrote it; and less prone to errors caused by bugs being duplicated when you copied code from one place to another. All of these are the kinds of issues that creep into a code base over time. And they are what refactoring is intended to help address.

The idea behind refactoring is to make changes to the structure of your code without changing the functionality. Consider a simple example:

```
decimal CalculatePay(decimal hours, decimal? rate)
{
    return hours *
        rate.HasValue ? hourlyRate.Value : 15.0d;
}
```

This method calculates the pay by taking the number of hours and multiplying it by the hourly rate. However, the ternary operation used in the calculation includes the literal value of 15. It's not readily apparent from the code exactly what the 15 represents. As it turns out, that's the minimum wage. But are you really going to remember that

107

© Bruce Johnson 2020
B. Johnson, *Essential Visual Studio 2019*, https://doi.org/10.1007/978-1-4842-5719-7_4

6 months from now? Or 2 years? Or when the junior developer who takes over this code looks at it? Probably not. The solution is to refactor the code so that the 15 is defined as a constant, like the following:

```
const decimal minimumWage = 15.0d;
decimal CalculatePay(decimal hours, decimal? rate)
{
    return hours *
        rate.HasValue ? hourlyRate.Value : minimumWage;
}
```

At a minimum, it's now clearer what the code is intended to do. It also means that a person wanting to change the minimum wage only needs to do so in one place (where the constant variable is defined). And if, at some point, the calculation of the minimum wage becomes more complex (so that a function is a better implementation choice), the code is already set up to handle that with minimal modification.

You have just refactored the code. The structure of the code has changed, but the exposed functionality has not. That is the key idea behind refactoring. And it's why writing unit tests is so important. In the red/green/refactor workflow, it's critical that after performing a refactor, the unit tests stay green. That's how you know that the functionality has remained unchanged, even as the implementation is modified. If you refactored code that doesn't have unit tests, your ability to be certain that the functionality is the same is limited to running manual tests. Or just eyeballing it. It's much better (and less nerve-racking) to have unit test coverage.

You might ask yourself why special tooling is required to perform a refactoring like this. And, in this specific case, it might not be worthwhile. However, as you will see, the more complicated refactorings covered in this chapter benefit greatly from automation. It's not that you couldn't do it by hand. But it's easier and less prone to mistakes if you use a tool.

Available Refactorings

The quality of a refactoring tool is based on a couple of criteria. First is the number of different refactorings that are available – well, not just the quantity of refactorings but also their usefulness. A refactoring that you see only once a year isn't as useful as one that you see multiple times a day. The second criterion is the ability for a tool to recognize common refactoring patterns and surface the option to refactor in an easily discoverable manner.

Visual Studio 2019 satisfies both criteria. Before drilling down into the different refactorings that are available, let's look at how the refactorings that are available at any point in the development process are surfaced.

Surfacing Refactoring Options

Visual Studio 2019 uses its Quick Action menu (colloquially known as the light bulb icon) for a wide variety of notifications related to writing code. Figure 4-1 illustrates one of the locations for the light bulb icon.

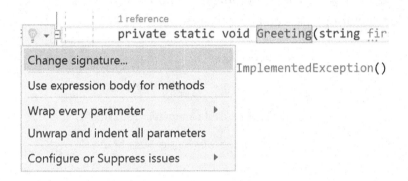

Figure 4-1. *The light bulb icon*

The light bulb icon that appears in the gutter of a line in the editor is your indicator that something about that line might be of interest. It appears when there are suggestions that could be made about your code. It could be syntax errors, or stylistic improvements, or if you have an undefined method or a data type unreferenced by using statements. There are many different situations that are covered by Quick Actions. And, pertinent to the topic at hand, it appears when there are possible refactorings available to be used.

The light bulb is part of a dropdown. When you click the triangle to the right of the bulb, a list of the items of interest for the line is displayed. The items that appear in the list are very context sensitive. In Figure 4-1, there are four different types of refactorings and one option to suppress the issues that were found on the line. But moving to other lines, indeed even where you place your cursor, can change the list completely.

You can gain access to the light bulb options using other techniques as well. As mentioned earlier, the actual name for the light bulb functionality is Quick Actions. If you right-click the line, there is a context menu option labeled Quick Actions and Refactorings. Selecting that option gets a similar list, as shown in Figure 4-2.

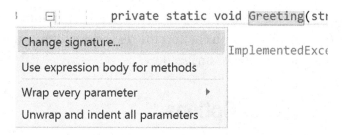

Figure 4-2. *Using the Quick Actions context menu option*

You will also occasionally see faint indicators under certain parts of your code. Hovering over the indicator displays another variation of the light bulb, complete with a set of possible refactorings, as seen in Figure 4-3.

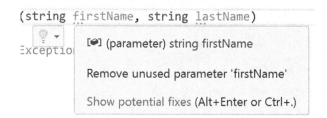

Figure 4-3. *Potential code fixes menu*

In Figure 4-3, the faint indicator is the three dots that appear under the beginning of the parameter names. The biggest difference between this interface and the others is that the options for addressing the issue are not readily available. Instead you click Show potential fixes to get the list of issues. The list for this specific situation is seen in Figure 4-4. Different situations will result in a different list, although the basic flow is roughly the same.

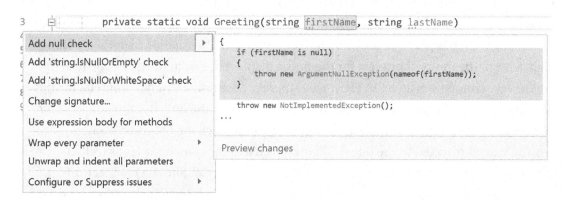

Figure 4-4. *Quick Actions with proposed code change*

110

One thing to notice in Figure 4-4, that hasn't been seen to this point, is the code block that appears to the right of the items list. As you hover over the items, when it's appropriate, a flyout appears to the right that contains a sample of the change that will be made, using the current context as the starting point. To be clear, the preview is appropriate when the change to be made by selecting the item doesn't require any further input from the developer. For instance, the Change signature option doesn't include the code preview because selecting that option displays a dialog that allows you to reorganize the parameters in the method.

If the sample change in the flyout isn't sufficient, click the Preview Changes link at the bottom left of the flyout. This causes a dialog similar to Figure 4-5 to appear.

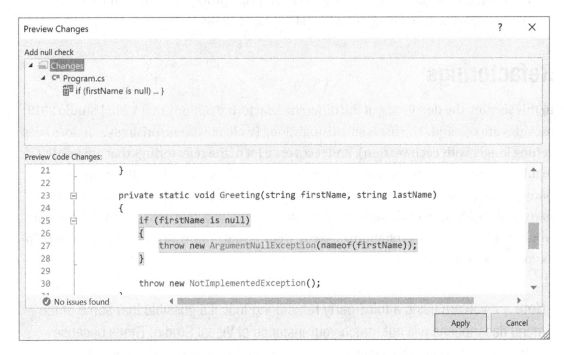

Figure 4-5. *Preview Changes dialog*

There are two parts to the Preview Changes dialog in Figure 4-5. At the top is a hierarchical view that contains all the places in your solution where the proposed change will take place. It is broken down by project, file, and line of code. At the bottom, the proposed change appears, with the changes highlighted. As you click different nodes in the top tree, the code window at the bottom changes to show the corresponding proposal. To make the changes, click the Apply button.

The light bulb icon is not the only way to start the refactoring process. There is a Refactor menu item available under the Edit menu, but the options there are not context sensitive. Nor are they nearly as granular as the light bulb choices. A second, and potentially more useful, way to start the refactoring process is to use a keyboard shortcut. When you are faced with the light bulb icon, you can trigger the list of options to appear by using the QuickActionsForPosition command, which has a default of Ctrl+.. By using this, you can trigger the refactor without taking your hands from the keyboard. A third way to start a refactoring is to right-click the line of code next to the light bulb. There is a Quick Actions option that acts the same as the keyboard shortcut. And in both cases, the options that are available are context sensitive.

Now that the mechanics of starting the refactoring process are out of the way, let's look at the different refactorings that Visual Studio 2019 offers.

Refactorings

In this section, the details about the different refactoring options that Visual Studio 2019 provides are covered. The list is surprisingly long (well, maybe surprisingly... it does keep getting longer with each version), and it covers a lot of the refactorings that are used regularly. That having been said, some people will end up comparing the list to third-party tools like ReSharper. The final choice ends up being a personal one. If the third-party tool has the exact refactoring you use ten times a day, then it's worth the price you would pay for it. But understanding exactly what Visual Studio 2019 has to offer can help as you make your decision.

Note   If you are using a third-party refactoring tool, it's possible that some of the menu descriptions will not match your instance of Visual Studio. That's because some tools override the various menus (both toolbar and context) related to refactoring.

The rest of this section looks at the many different refactorings that Visual Studio provides. While arranging them alphabetically might seem reasonable, your ability to find any particular one would depend on you knowing the name. And some of the names are not necessarily obvious. So instead, they are roughly grouped into three categories: class declarations, coding structures, and file organization. Hopefully this will help you more easily find the items that matter to you in the moment.

Class Declarations

In this section, we describe the refactorings that are related to the definition of classes and methods. Roughly, this translates into the changes that impact the methods and properties that are exposed by a class.

Change Method Name

The Change Method Name refactoring is well named. It is used to change the name of a method. More precisely, it allows you to rename a method at the point where it is declared and have the change propagate through to every place in the code where the method is used.

The starting point for this refactoring isn't a light bulb icon. Instead, you make a change to a method name by modifying the name in place. Then when you trigger the Quick Actions menu, you get an option that looks like Figure 4-6. Alternatively, you can get to the same place using the Rename option from the context menu that appears when you right-click the method name. Or use the Ctrl+R keyboard command while the cursor is in the method name to start the process.

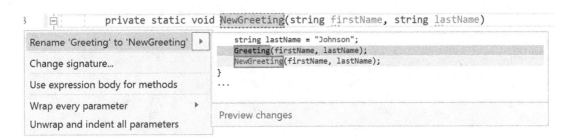

Figure 4-6. *Change Method Name*

The first option in the list is to rename "Greeting" (the old name of the method) to "NewGreeting" (the new name of the method). In the flyout, the code shows the old code in red and the new code in a pale green. If you select this option, then every place in your solution where the Greeting method is called, the name of the method will be changed from Greeting to NewGreeting.

To be completely clear, the changes only take place when the compiler can determine that Greeting is being called. The important distinction being the compiler has to be able to recognize the call. The refactoring process is not able to identify any runtime invocations of the Greeting method. Only compile-time calls are renamed.

As an example, consider a scenario where the name "Greeting" is embedded in a string in a configuration file. While your application is running, the configuration value is extracted, and the method is invoked using reflection. That usage is not detectable by the refactoring process, since there is no compile time checking on the method name stored in the configuration file.

Convert Anonymous Type to Class

Anonymous types have been available in .NET for quite a while. The following is an example:

```
var tempType = new {FirstName="Kyle", LastName = "Johnson"};
```

Anonymous types are incredibly useful, but they have the characteristic of only being usable in the local context. You can't return them from a method and you can't pass them as parameters to another method. If this becomes a limitation, there is a refactoring that allows you to convert the anonymous type into a class. Place the cursor on the new keyword and initiate the Quick Actions. You will see a display like Figure 4-7.

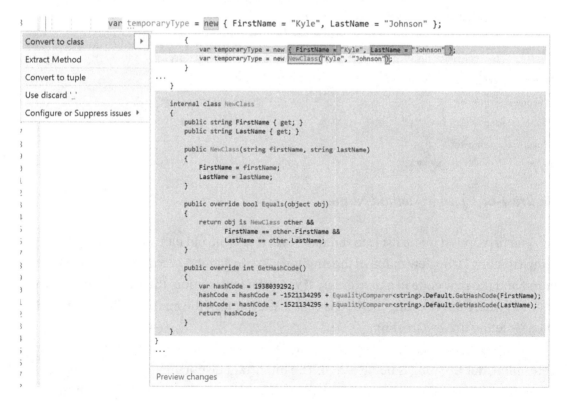

Figure 4-7. *Convert anonymous type to class*

Here you can see that a new class would be created. The class is marked with the access modifier of internal, and the constructor for the class takes the fields that are included in the anonymous type. As well, there is a custom implementation for the Equals and GetHashCode methods. These are required so that the comparison of two anonymous types remains consistent with the comparison of two instances of this class.

Convert Between Get Method and Property

It would be possible to get into a long discussion over the proper use of a Get method vs. a property when retrieving an attribute value for a class. But to start, consider the following code snippet:

```
public string Name { get; set; }

private string name;
public string GetName()
{
    return name;
}
```

First, you have a Name property, using the automatic property get and set functions. Second, you have a GetName method, returning the value of a private variable that is (presumably) set someplace else within the class. There might even be a SetName method to allow for setting the name's value.

The difference between these approaches (and the source for any disagreement between the "right" way) is semantic in nature. The idea is that a property should be idempotent. If you get a property's value, the state of the class shouldn't change in any way. If you set a property's value, the only thing that gets changed is that property. On the other hand, calling a method is not expected to be idempotent. It's not unreasonable for the mere invoking of a method to make changes to properties within the class that contains the method.

The purpose of this refactoring is to allow you to switch between the different modalities. Set the cursor into the Name property, and invoke the Quick Actions. Figure 4-8 is an example of what you might see.

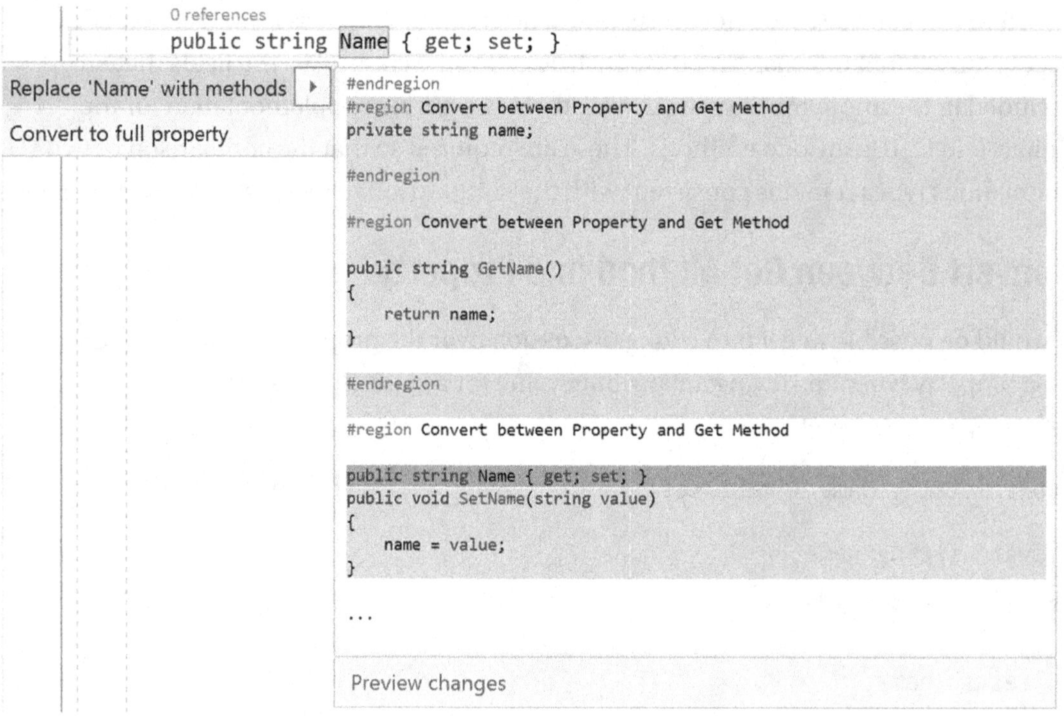

Figure 4-8. *Replacing a property with methods*

You can see that the Name property would be removed and replaced with both a GetName method and a SetName method that takes the new value as a parameter.

This refactoring also includes the opposite change, that is, moving from a GetName method to a Name property. The starting point is still having the cursor on the method name. But now initiating the Quick Actions reveals options like Figure 4-9.

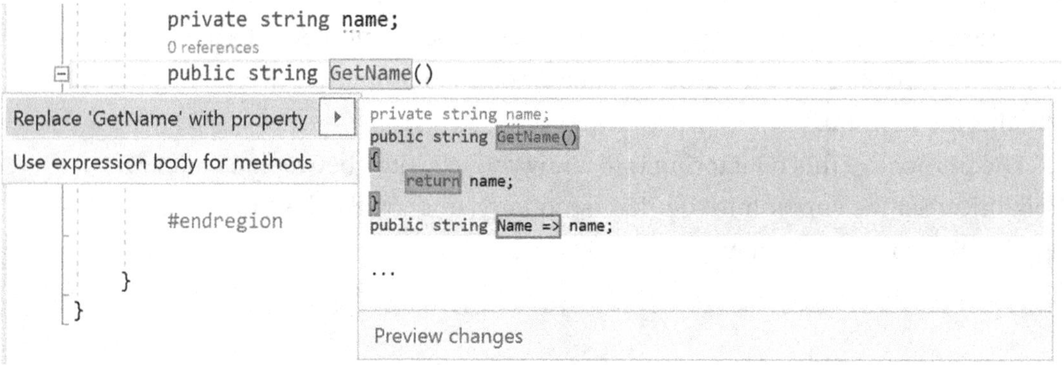

Figure 4-9. *Replacing a method with a property*

Here you can see that the GetName method is removed and replaced with the lambda form of a property declaration. If you also had a SetName method in your class, the refactoring preview is a little different (see Figure 4-10).

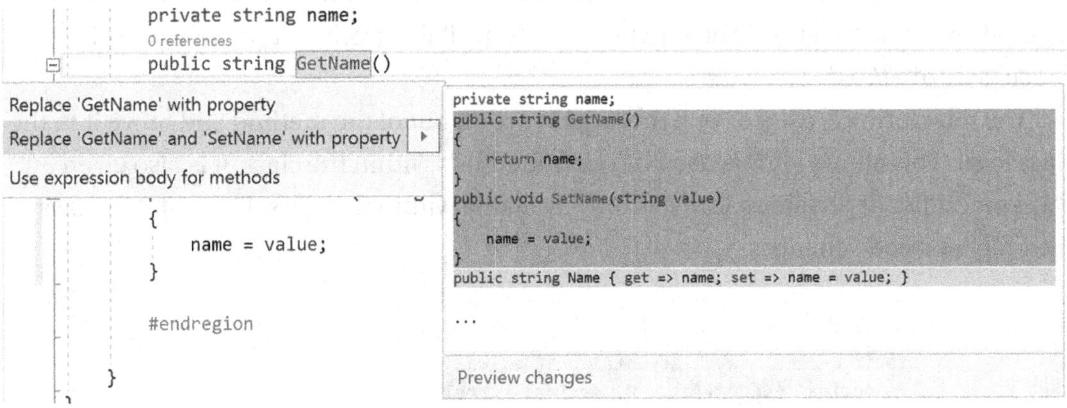

Figure 4-10. *Replacing two methods with a property*

Now both methods are being removed, to be replaced by a property that contains both a getter and a setter definition.

Convert Local Function to Method

This particular refactoring is a little esoteric, which is to say that it comes into play in a scenario that is rarely seen in most development environments. It takes a local function and converts it into a private method.

What makes this esoteric is the definition of a local function. It is a function that is scoped to a particular method. Consider the following code:

```
public  static decimal CalculateTotalCost(decimal price,
    decimal federalTax = 0,
    decimal stateTax = 0,
    decimal cityTax = 0)
{
    decimal TotalTax(decimal tax1, decimal tax2, decimal tax3)
    {
        return tax1 + tax2 + tax3;
    }
```

```
    return price * (1 + TotalTax(federalTax, stateTax,
        cityTax));
}
```

In this code snippet, the TotalTax function, defined within the CalculateTotalCost method, is a local function. The function is only available from within the scope of CalculateTotalCost.

The refactoring is used to pull the local function out of the method and move it to the class level. This allows it to be used by other methods within the class. It is also given an access modifier of private so that it is only available within the class. Figure 4-11 shows the proposed code changes.

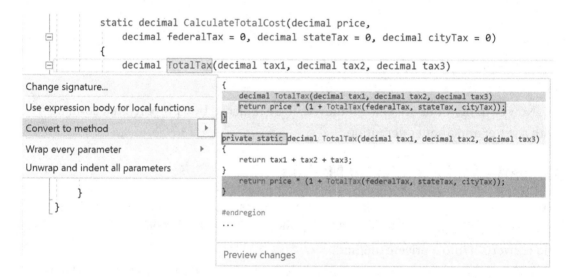

Figure 4-11. *Covert a local function to a method*

Encapsulate Field

Moving from the esoteric to the more common refactorings, the Encapsulate Field is used to modify a public field so that it becomes a public property. Consider the following code:

```
public double Age;
```

This is the declaration for a public field. If you invoke Quick Actions on the variable, Figure 4-12 is what you see.

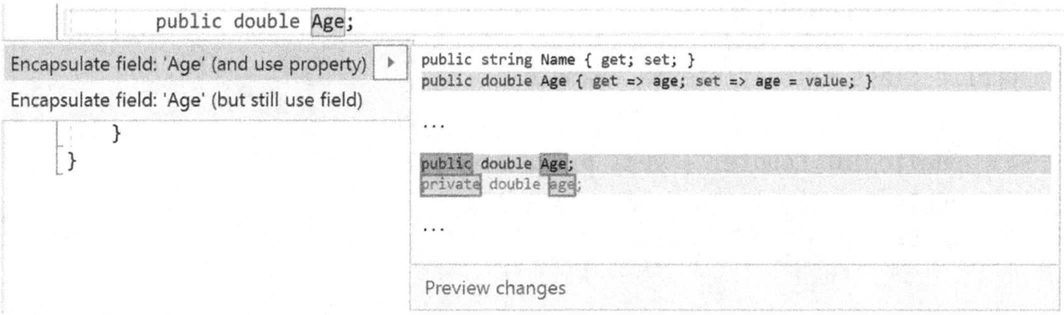

```
                 public double Age;
```

Encapsulate field: 'Age' (and use property)	▶
Encapsulate field: 'Age' (but still use field)	

```
        }
    }
```

```
public string Name { get; set; }
public double Age { get => age; set => age = value; }

...

public double Age;
private double age;

...
```

Preview changes

Figure 4-12. *Encapsulate Field*

You can see that two changes are being proposed. First, the public field is changed to a private one. Second, a property called Age is being added (using the lambda declaration). There are two things to note about these changes. First, the Age property is not necessarily placed where the public field is declared. Instead, Visual Studio places it where it first sees other properties declared. This fits within the standard of grouping declarations together, typically toward the top of a class definition. There is a refactoring (Move Declaration to Reference) that moves the declaration close to where the value is being used.

Second, there are two choices available in the Quick Actions menu for encapsulating the field. In terms of the visible proposed changes, they are the same. The difference is that if you select the first one (with "and use property"), then any reference to the field within the class will be changed to use the property instead. If you select the second one (with "but still use field"), then no changes will be made to any reference to the field.

Extract Interface

One of the more useful refactorings, especially if you are frequently working with writing testable code using interfaces, is Extract Interface. Its purpose is to look at the properties and methods that are declared in a class and create an interface using those elements. As it turns out, you can pick and choose which properties and methods get included on the interface. When it's finished, not only will the interface have been declared, but the class is configured so that it implements the interface.

Consider the following class:

```
public class ExtractInterfaceSample
{
    public int Counter { get; private set; }
    public string Title { get; set; }
    public void Increment()
    {
        Counter++;
    }
    public void Reset()
    {
        Counter = 0;
    }
}
```

The starting point is to place the cursor on the class declaration and invoke Quick Actions. Choose the Extract Interface option. This displays the dialog seen in Figure 4-13.

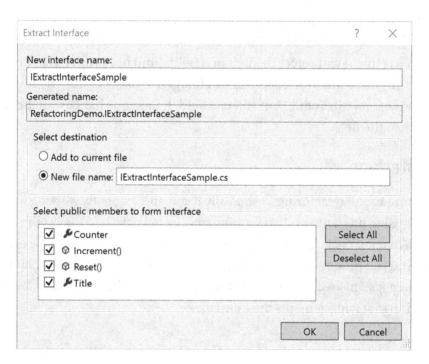

Figure 4-13. *Extract Interface dialog*

The dialog in Figure 4-13 is used to provide specific information about the interface being extracted. Starting from the top is the name of the interface (by default, it's the name of the class prefixed with an "I") and the fully qualified name (using the namespace of the class). Next you can specify the destination for the file that is created. While the default is to create a separate file, using the name of the interface, you can change the name or have the interface placed into the current file.

Finally, the public members (both methods and properties) are listed. By default, all these members will be included in the interface, but you can set the desired properties by unchecking those that you don't want to include. When you are ready, click OK and the interface is created, and the class is marked as implementing it.

Extract Method

Extracting a method is one of the more frequently used refactorings. It is used when you have a block of code that you would like to extract from its current location and place it into a new method. While you could copy and paste the code, where the refactoring shines is its ability to automatically set up the parameter list for you, complete with types and reference keywords (like out and ref).

The starting point is a block of code, typically embedded into a method. Consider the following code:

```
public bool Validate(Person person)
{
    bool result = true;

    if (String.IsNullOrEmpty(person.FirstName))
        result = false;
    else if (person.FirstName.Length > 50)
        result = false;

    if (String.IsNullOrEmpty(person.LastName))
        result = false;
    else if (person.LastName.Length > 50)
        result = false;

    return result;
}
```

Putting aside for a moment how contrived the code is, it's pretty obvious that there is a block of code that has been replicated and could easily be placed into its own method. To use this refactoring, select the code to be extracted (in this example, either of the two if blocks) and trigger the Quick Actions. Your editor will resemble Figure 4-14.

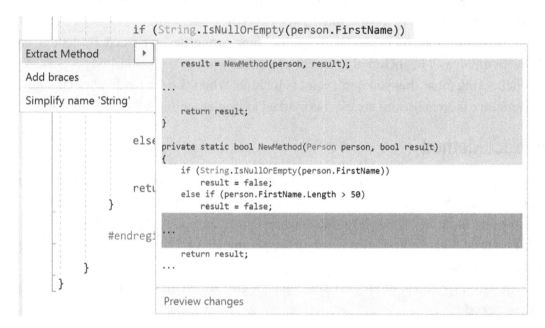

Figure 4-14. *Extract Method*

There are two main changes that are being proposed. First, at the site of the selected code block, the entire block has been replaced with a method call. The list of parameters is determined by considering the variables that were defined before the block and used within the block.

The return value is determined by looking at variables that are changed within the block. If more than one variable is changed, those will be labeled as ref or out in the parameter list. For instance, consider a method that looks like the following:

```
public bool Validate(Person person)
{
    bool result = true;
    bool result1 = false;
```

```
if (String.IsNullOrEmpty(person.FirstName))
{
    result = false;
    result1 = true;
}
else if (person.FirstName.Length > 50)
    result = false;

return result && result1;
}
```

Now if you perform the Extract Method refactoring on the if statement, the signature for the new method looks like the following:

```
NewMethod(person, ref result, ref result1)
```

One thing you might notice is that the method at both the calling and callee locations has been given the generic name of NewMethod. The cursor is placed at the method declaration. If you change the method name right now, it will also change the calling location. As well, in the top right of the editor, there is a small form associated with renaming the method. It can be seen in Figure 4-15.

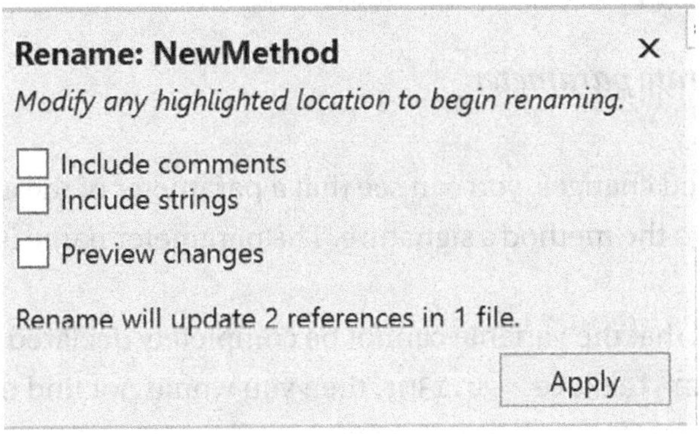

Figure 4-15. *Rename method settings*

The options in this form allow you to also make the changes within any comments or strings. Or you can use the check box to preview the changes when you click Apply instead of just updating the code immediately.

Generate Parameter

The goal of the generate parameter refactoring is to give you an easy way to add a
parameter to a method while keeping your focus on the code editor. To start, you need a
variable that is not declared within the method.

```
public void GenerateParameter()
{
    taxRate = 0.13m;
}
```

Then, with the cursor on the variable, trigger the Quick Actions command to see the
following (Figure 4-16).

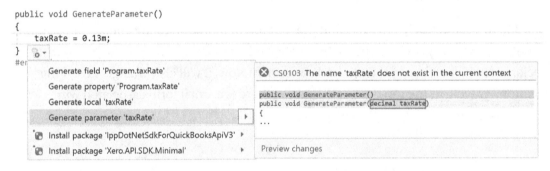

Figure 4-16.   *Generate parameter*

From the proposed changes, you can see that a parameter of the appropriate type
has been inserted into the method's signature. The parameter name is the same as the
variable name.

The one caveat is that the variable cannot be completely declared. In other words,
if the line had read `var taxRate = 0.13m;`, then you would not find the Generate
parameter option in the Quick Actions menu.

Pull Member Up

This refactoring works with classes that are implementing an interface or derived from a base class. The idea is that you have created the base class or the interface. Then you have created a class that derives from or implements that artifact. As you continue developing, you add a new method to the class and decide that the method really belongs in the base class or interface. So you pull the member up to the higher type or interface.

To invoke, start with your cursor on the method name and invoke the Quick Actions command. Figure 4-17 appears.

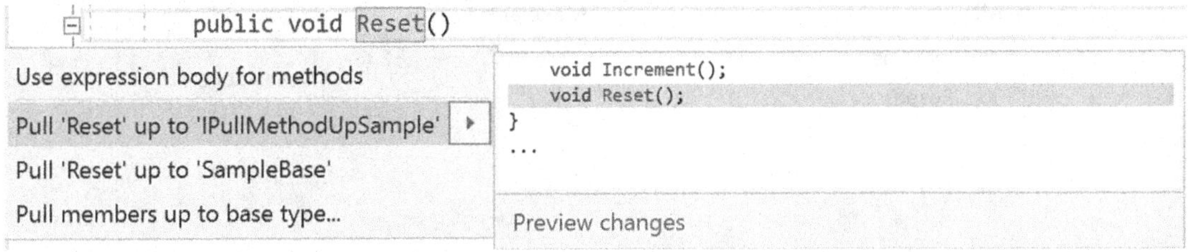

Figure 4-17. *Pulling a member up*

In the list of refactorings, there are two that are quite explicit in their functionality. There is one that pulls the selected method (Reset) up to the interface (IPullMethodUpSample) that the class implements. If the class implements multiple interfaces, you would have additional options in the list. Also, you have the option to pull the method up to the base class (SampleBase). In this case, both the method declaration and implementation are moved from the derived class to the base class.

The third option, Pull members up to base type, provides more control over the process. When you select this option, you will see a dialog similar to Figure 4-18.

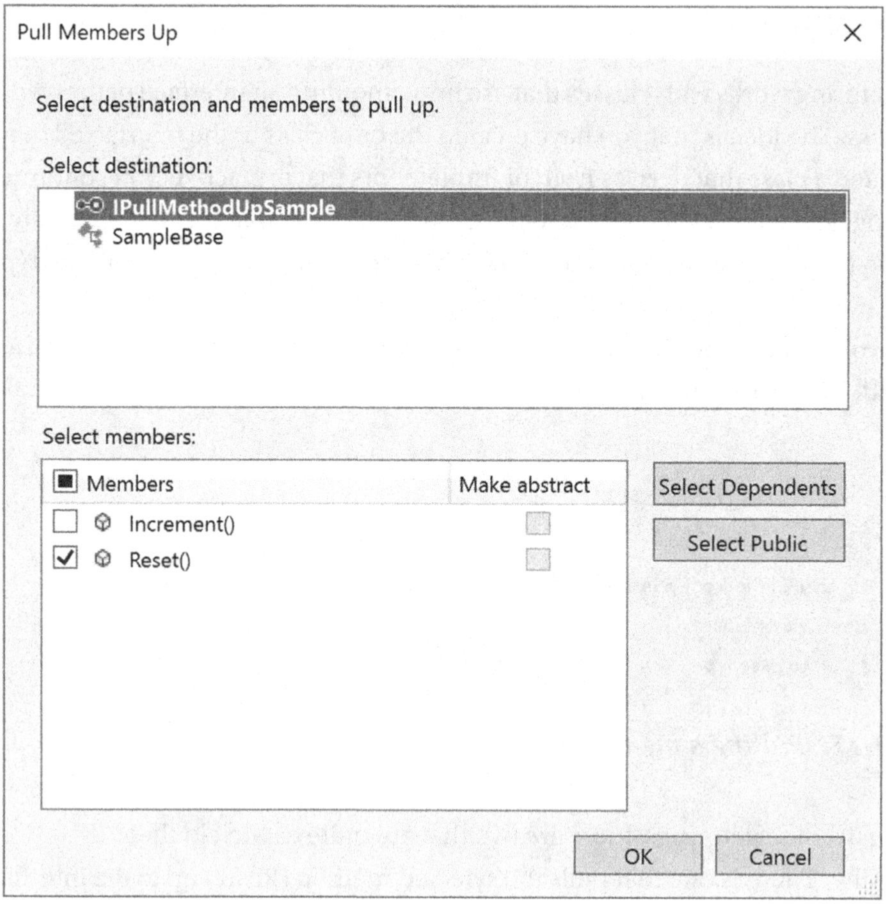

Figure 4-18. *Pulling members up dialog*

To start, you can select the destination, whether it be base class or one of the implemented interfaces. Next is a list of the members which are not already part of both the base class and the interface(s). For each member, you can decide if you want to pull the member up to the selected destination. When you have made all your choices, click OK to complete the refactoring.

Rename

The ability to rename things is one of the most basic refactorings. It applies to variables, properties, methods, classes, and interfaces. The user interface is pretty straightforward. Start by making a change to the item, and then trigger the Quick Actions command. Figure 4-19 shows an example.

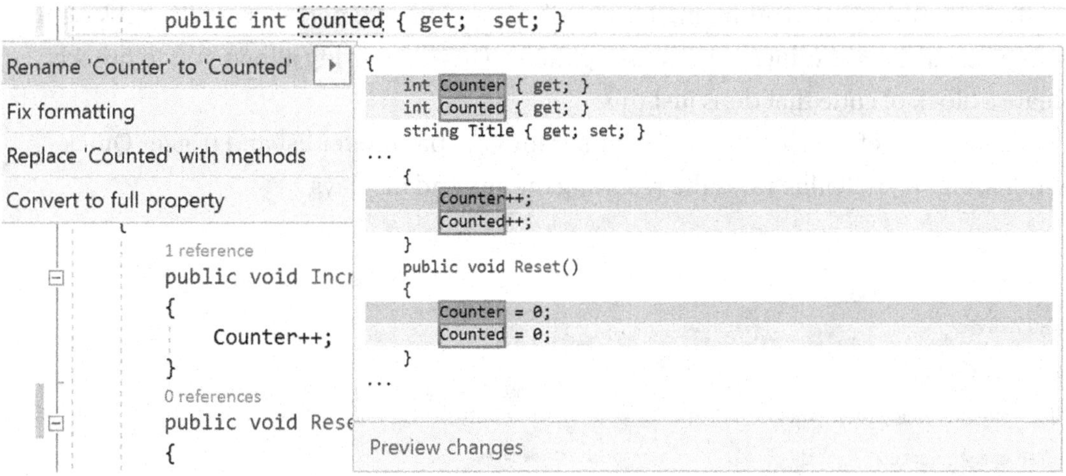

Figure 4-19. *Rename refactoring*

This flow is consistent across all the different types of things that can be renamed. And, as you become familiar with the steps, renaming all of these different items will become ingrained in your fingers. Change the name of a variable, do a Ctrl+., hit Enter, and keep going. Visual Studio makes the changes across all of the known references (standard disclaimers about not being able to rename values found inside strings apply).

Code Structure

Keeping code looking neat and tidy is, perhaps surprisingly, useful when it comes to understanding what code is doing. White space helps, as does converting code to a functionally equivalent version where the intent is more obvious. And to help with potential bugs, adding checks for commonly ignored scenarios. The refactorings that help with this process are covered in this section.

Add Null Checks for Parameters

As a developer, it is quite common to create methods that accept a reference to objects as a parameter – and then, without much thought, access properties or methods in that object. The problem occurs if a null value gets passed into the method. And null reference exception gets raised and it's up to the application (or, perhaps, a different developer) to figure out where the exception happened and what the cause is.

To help mitigate this problem, it is usually a good idea to perform a null check on the incoming parameter values prior to using them. This refactoring allows you to quickly create a block of code that does just this.

To start the refactoring, place the cursor into the parameter list and trigger Quick Actions. Figure 4-20 illustrates the resulting menus and displays.

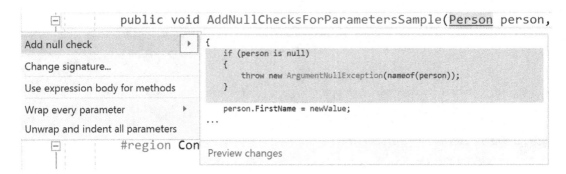

Figure 4-20. *Add null check refactoring*

You can see that, for the `person` parameter, a check for null would be added and an exception thrown if it was null. As an aside, the null check is only added for variables that are reference types. It doesn't include integer variables, for example.

Convert Anonymous Type to Tuple

Tuples are a lightweight way of incorporating a collection of related values as a single unit. Similar to classes, but without some of the syntactical overhead, they are great when needing to move the related values from method to method within a class. This refactoring is related to the Convert Anonymous Type to Class refactoring in the previous section, the difference being that the result is a tuple, not a class. More usefully, it's actually a named tuple, the difference being that a named tuple exposes field names as the values in tuple (as opposed to Item1, Item2, etc. found in regular tuples).

To trigger the refactoring, start with the declaration of an anonymous type. It can be done directly or as part of a LINQ query, for example. The following code is a sample:

```
var tempType = new {FirstName="Cam", LastName = "Johnson"};
```

Place the cursor on the `new` keyword or anyplace within the anonymous type and trigger Quick Actions. You'll see something like Figure 4-21.

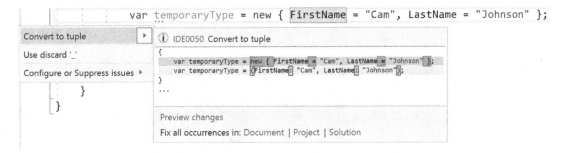

Figure 4-21. *Converting an anonymous type to a named tuple*

Once you have completed the refactoring, it becomes possible to pass the tuple into parameters, something not possible with an anonymous type. For example, the following method signature would accept the tuple created in Figure 4-21:

```
private void TakeParameter(
    (string FirstName, string LastName) temporaryType)
```

Convert Between For Loop and Foreach

C# provides a number of different ways to create loops. This refactoring is the first of a few that are used to move from one form to another. The starting point here is a for loop. More specifically, it's a for loop that contains all three of the standard parts: the initializer, the condition, and the iterator. The following code is an example:

```
List<string> data =
    new List<string>() { "a", "b", "c", "d", "e" };
for (int i = 0; i < data.Count; i++)
{
    Console.WriteLine(data[i]);
}
```

As you can see, the for statement includes all three required components. But there is one other element that needs to be present for the refactoring to be enabled. That is found within the loop itself. There needs to be an indexed reference to the collection that is the basis for the loop. For the example, that criterion is met with the reference to data[i]. When these conditions are met, place the cursor in the for keyword and trigger Quick Actions. The display seen in Figure 4-22 appears.

```
                    List<string> data = new List<string>() { "a", "b", "c", "d", "e" };

        for (int i = 0; i < data.Count; i++)
```

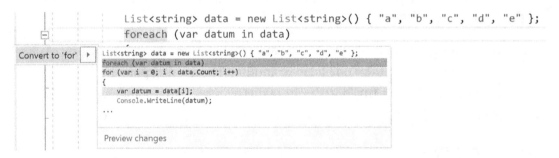

Figure 4-22. Converting for to foreach

The change from for to foreach is visible in the Preview Changes. As it turns out, there is also a refactoring to reverse the changes. Triggering the refactoring is pretty much the same, as it involves placing the cursor in the foreach keyword and executing the Quick Actions command. Figure 4-23 is the result.

```
                    List<string> data = new List<string>() { "a", "b", "c", "d", "e" };
            foreach (var datum in data)
```

Convert to 'for'

```
      List<string> data = new List<string>() { "a", "b", "c", "d", "e" };
      foreach (var datum in data)
      for (var i = 0; i < data.Count; i++)
      {
          var datum = data[i];
          Console.WriteLine(datum);
      ...
```

Preview changes

Figure 4-23. Converting foreach to for loop

While the reversal isn't quite character-for-character perfect, the result is more than reasonably close to the original code.

Convert Between Foreach and LINQ

Similar to the previous section, these two refactorings are used to move between a foreach structured loop and a LINQ query. The starting point is a little different, however. Consider the following code:

```
public IEnumerable<string> Sample()
{
    List<string> data =
        new List<string>() { "a", "b", "c", "d", "e" };
    foreach (var datum in data)
    {
        yield return datum;
    }
    yield break;
}
```

The big change between this code sample and the one from the previous section is the introduction of the yield keyword. This indicates that the method being called is an iterator. It is commonly used when working with enumerable collections, such as the generic class List. Here the implementation of the iterator is explicit, as opposed to the implicit implementation that the List hides from view. The result from LINQ query is also an iterator, which is why this form of code is required to enable the refactoring.

Place your cursor in the foreach keyword and trigger Quick Actions. The result appears in Figure 4-24.

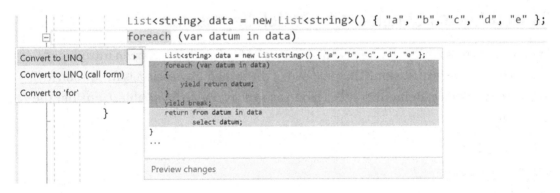

Figure 4-24. *Converting from foreach to LINQ*

In the section displaying the potential changes, you can see that the value returned from the method is now a LINQ query result. There is also a slightly different form of the refactoring available. If you chose Convert to LINQ (call form), instead of the inline syntax form of LINQ, the Select method is used. So the return statement would look like the following:

```
return data.Select(datum => datum);
```

There is also a refactoring that performs the reverse conversion. The starting point is the output from the previous refactoring (the inline syntax, not the call form), with your cursor in the `from` keyword. Then triggering the Quick Actions displays Figure 4-25.

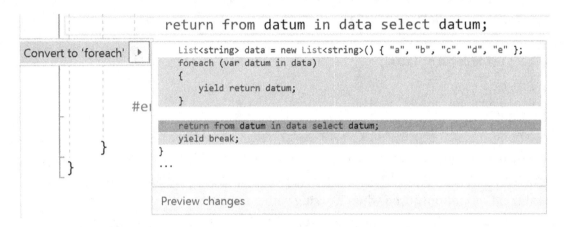

Figure 4-25. *Convert from LINQ to foreach*

The proposed changes are similar to the original code from the beginning of this section.

Convert Switch Statement to Switch Expression

This is a new refactoring that takes advantage of a feature that has been introduced in C# 8.0: a switch expression. The purpose of the switch expression is to condense the use of a switch statement that is used to assign a value to a variable. Consider the following code:

```
int place = 1;
string result;
switch (place)
{
    case 1: result = "First"; break;
    case 2: result = "Second"; break;
    case 3: result = "Third"; break;
    default: result = "Unknown"; break;
}
```

The purpose of the switch statement in the example is, ultimately, to set the value of result based on the value of place. A switch expression allows you to use a combination of a switch keyword and the lambda operator to more directly perform the assignment. The following is the equivalent switch expression:

```
int place = 1;
string result = place switch
{
    1 => "First",
    2 => "Second",
    3 => "Third",
    _ => "Unknown"
};
```

The refactoring is designed to make this transition for you automatically. Starting from the first code example, place your cursor on the switch keyword and start Quick Actions. Figure 4-26 should become visible.

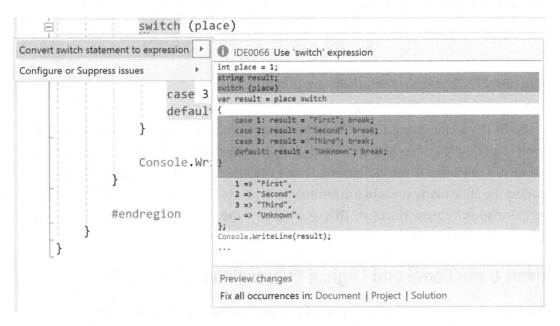

Figure 4-26. *Converting a switch statement to a switch expression*

Within the preview area, you can see the original code removed, to be replaced by the lambda syntax of the switch expression.

Inline Temporary Variable

The ability to refactor your code by inlining a temporary variable is nice, but not always critical. The premise is that you have some code where a temporary variable is being used. That variable is then being used in a different expression without modification. For example, consider the following lines of code:

```
double temp = diameter / 2;
double area = Math.PI * temp * temp;
```

It's not clear from the variable names what the purpose of temp is. As a result, you might want to inline the original calculation. Place your cursor in the declaration for temp and initiate Quick Actions. Figure 4-27 is the result.

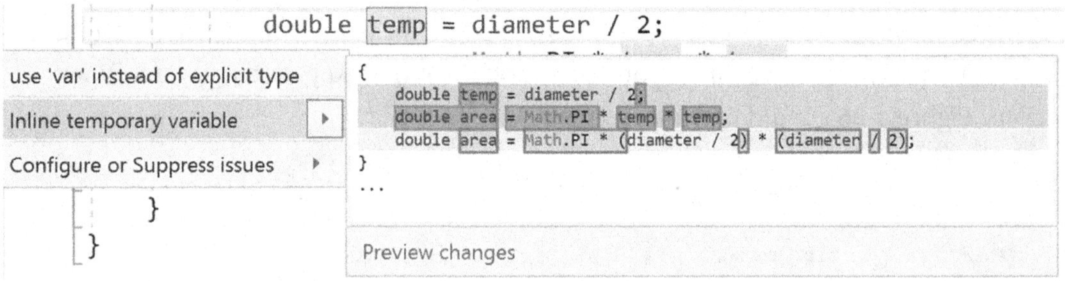

Figure 4-27. *Inlining a temporary variable*

While the refactoring is fine, in that the variable that was only being used to hold the result of a calculation has been removed, there is sometimes a benefit for keeping it. For instance, if the name of the variable had been radius instead of temp, then someone reading the code many years in the future would be able to more quickly pick up on the calculation being performed. This won't always the case, but it's worth considering before you use this refactoring.

Invert Conditional and Logical Expressions

Conditional values are a common part of any application. And how the conditional value gets set can be an important facet of future readability. As developers go back over code, if the logic associated with setting the value is convoluted, it can be difficult to unravel the original intent. What can make it worse is if the variable names used in the calculation are difficult to understand in the context of the condition.

Consider the following code:

```
bool continueProcessing =
    valueToTest > 100 ? false : canUpdate;
```

It might not be apparent from reading the code that continueProcessing is set to true so long as the valueToTest is less than or equal to 100 and canUpdate is true. While the statement works, in that the correct value is assigned to continueProcessing, it's not exceptionally readable. If you set your cursor anywhere within the expression and trigger Quick Actions, Figure 4-28 appears.

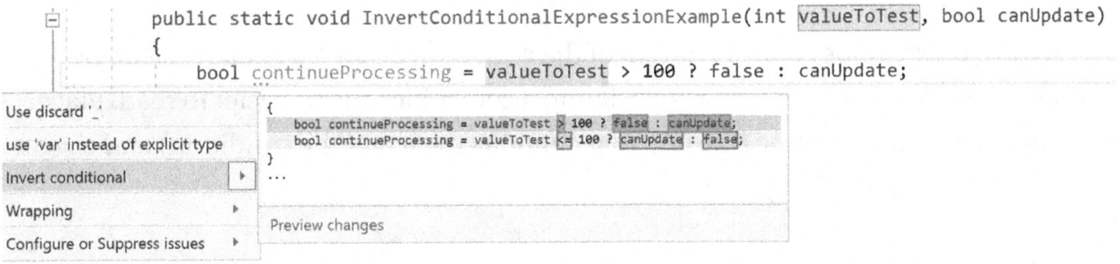

Figure 4-28. *Inverting conditional expressions*

Once the refactoring is finished, the result is the following:

```
bool continueProcessing =
    valueToTest <= 100 ? canUpdate : false;
```

While this is functionally equivalent to the previous statement, the ordering of the conditions makes it easier to read. And easier is almost always better when it comes to looking at existing code.

Invert If Statement

This refactoring is used for the same purpose as the previous one. It takes an if statement or an if-else statement and reverses the logic in the condition. At the same time, it swaps the blocks so that the code works the same. Consider the following:

```
public bool SampleMethod(int valueToTest, bool canUpdate)
{
    bool result;
```

```
    if (valueToTest > 100)
    {
        result = false;
    }
    else
    {
        result = canUpdate;
    }

    return result;
}
```

As with the previous code, the intent of the condition is not particularly clear. By inverting the if statement, you can make it into a code block that is easier to read. Place the cursor within the first line (the one that contains the if and the condition) and trigger Quick Actions. Figure 4-29 appears.

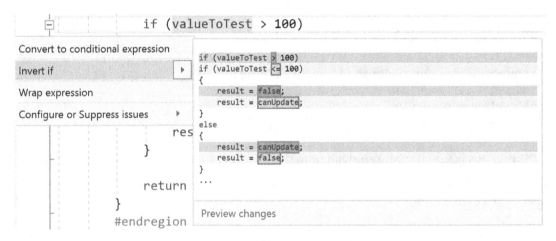

Figure 4-29. *Inverting an if statement*

The intent of the if statement is more apparent after the inversion. At least, it's plausible to argue that. Some people will always find a reason to disagree.

Move Declaration Near Reference

When it comes to where to place variable declarations, there are at least two main schools of thought. One is to collect all the declarations at the top of the method. The second is to declare variables near where they are first referenced within the method. Without weighing in on the pros and cons of each option, this refactoring allows you to easily move a declaration place. The following code is the starting point for the example:

```
int variableToMove;

ConvertAnonymousTypeToClassSample();
ConvertForEachLoopToFor();

variableToMove = 100;
```

Place the cursor in the variable declaration and initiate the Quick Actions command. Figure 4-30 shows the options available.

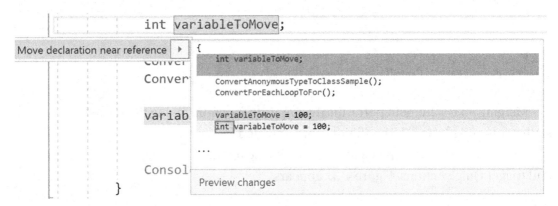

***Figure 4-30.** Move declaration near reference*

The change visible in the preview pane is to move the declaration from above the method calls down to just above where it is used.

Split or Merge If Statements

This refactoring also fits into the category of making code easier to read. Or you need to add functionality to different conditions within your if statement. The premise of splitting if statements is that you have a single if with multiple conditions. For example, consider the following:

```
if (valueToTest <= 100 && canUpdate)
{
    ...
}
```

This is a single if statement with two conditions. Splitting the if statement would result in the following code:

```
if (valueToTest <= 100))
{
    If (canUpdate)
    {
        ...
    }
}
```

Merging an if statement performs the opposite function, taking the nested if statements and placing the conditions into a single if.

To see the refactoring, place the cursor into the operator between the two conditions and trigger Quick Actions. Figure 4-31 appears.

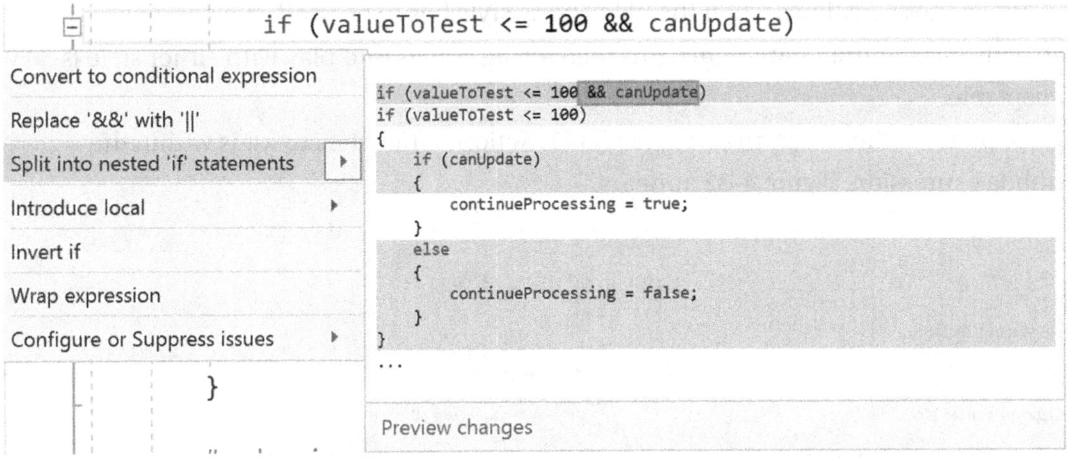

Figure 4-31. *Splitting an if statement*

You can see the split described earlier visible in the proposed changes pane. As well, if the original `if` statement contains an else block, that block is duplicated, so that regardless of which path is taking through the `if` statements, it will be executed when appropriate.

The merge refactoring is similar. The difference is that you need to place your cursor into the if command of the nested `if` statement. The option on the context menu indicates that it will merge the `if` statement with the outer `if` block.

Use Lambda Expression or Block Body

When using a lambda expression to define a function in C#, you have two syntactical choices. They are functionally equivalent, so the "correct" option depends on your preference. This refactoring allows you to easily move from one style to the other. As an example, the expression style of a lambda looks like the following:

```
delegate int del(int i); // Defines the delegate signature
del myFunction = x => x * x;
```

The same definition expressed in a block body style is as follows:

```
del myFunction = x => {
    return x * x;
}
```

While there are times when the block body style has to be used, such as when the body has multiple statements, this refactoring comes into play with either style is acceptable.

To perform the refactoring, trigger Quick Actions while the cursor is within the lambda expression. Figure 4-32 appears.

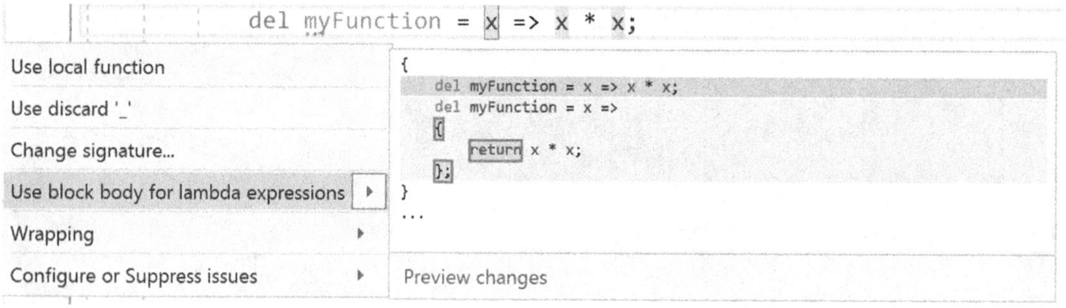

Figure 4-32. *Convert lambdas from expressions to block body*

As can be seen in the preview pane, the conversion from expression syntax to block body will be performed if you choose this refactoring. Going the opposite direction, from block body to expression, is also possible. Place the cursor inside the block and trigger Quick Actions. Figure 4-33 is the result.

Figure 4-33. *Convert lambdas from block body to expressions*

Unused Value Assignment, Variables, and Parameters

One of the subtle features of Visual Studio is that it fades out methods, parameters, and variables that are not used. A warning is also generated, so that it appears in any compiler output. There are a couple of benefits that accrue from this behavior. First, it's a quick way to find dead parts of code. And removing dead parts of code is good to do from a readability perspective. But sometimes seeing a variable unused can be an indication of an error. Perhaps the wrong method was called, because you're **sure** that you made a call to that faded out method?

Regardless, it's a nice feature for Visual Studio to indicate the lack of use. And there is also a refactoring to help you remove the offending variables, parameters, or assignments.

How you trigger the refactoring depends on what's being removed. For an unused variable or method, having the cursor on the variable declaration is sufficient. For an unused parameter, you need the cursor on the parameter. If the offending statement is an unneeded assignment, putting the cursor on the initial assignment enables the refactoring. Whichever situation you're in, the process is familiar by now. Trigger the Quick Actions command and you'll see the preview pane for your changes. Figure 4-34 is an example.

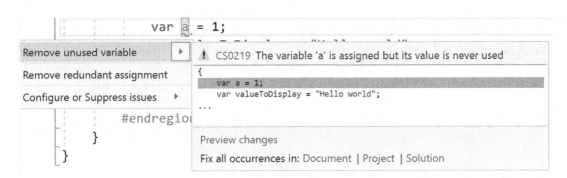

Figure 4-34. *Removing an unused variable*

The only change, in this example, is to remove the declaration for the variable. And that pattern holds for removing parameters or methods. The difference is if you're removing a value assignment. In that case, the issue is that a variable has been given a value when it is declared. Like the var a = 1 in the value, a is assigned the value of 1 immediately. However, if a is given another value before it is even used, the initial value assignment is redundant. This refactoring would remove the assignment found in the declaration.

Use Explicit Type

One of the features introduced into C# a few versions ago was the ability to declare variables with an implicit type. The simplistic example is as follows:

```
var a = 1;
```

The compiler has no problem figuring out from the statement that a is an integer. And so, it compiles your code having made that assumption.

All of that is fine and good, right until you have coding standards that required explicit type declarations for variables. For a case like the preceding one, that's not a big deal. But as the types get more complex, it's used to have a tool that helps convert from implicit type declarations to explicit typing and back again.

Start with your cursor on the variable name and trigger Quick Actions. Figure 4-35 appears.

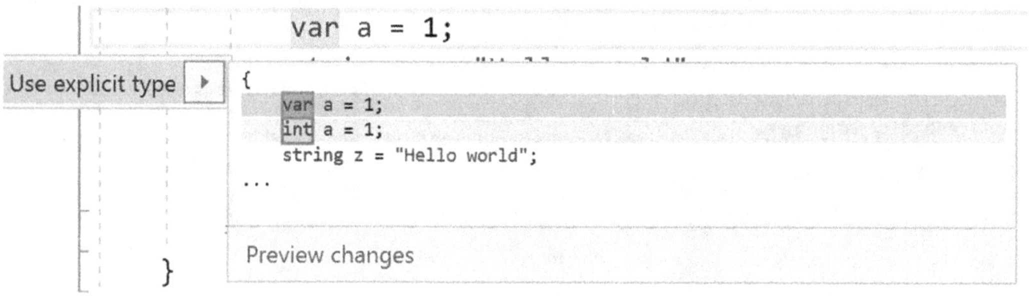

Figure 4-35. *Converting to an explicit type*

As you can see, the only change being made is in the variable declaration, which is exactly what you expect from the refactoring. And if the variable was originally declared using the var keyword, the refactoring option would read "Use var instead of explicit type." At that point, executing Quick Actions would display Figure 4-36.

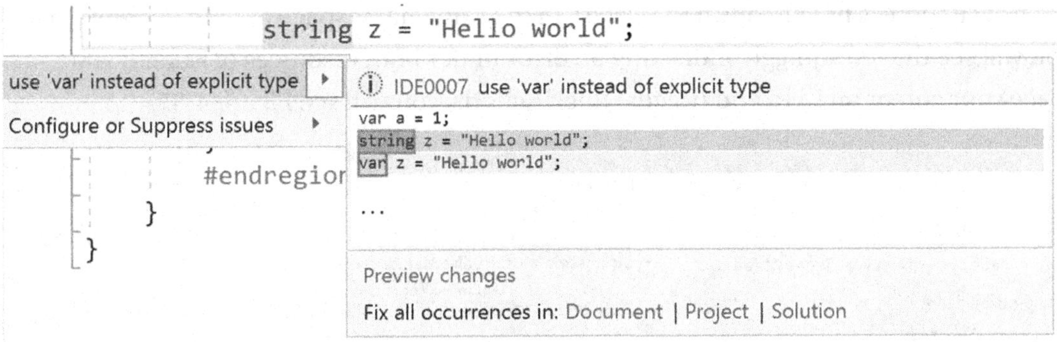

Figure 4-36. *Converting to an implicit type*

In this example, completing the action would convert the variable declaration to the implicit type declaration format.

Note   It's not always possible to convert from an implicit type declaration to an explicit type. This is particularly true if you are using anonymous types. In that situation, the refactoring will not be available to you. Instead, you can use the Convert Anonymous Type to Tuple refactoring described earlier in the chapter to create a concrete type.

File Organization

This section looks at the refactorings that are not about moving functionality around, but are instead about identifying where the code resides, adding required elements to a file, and in general, making your code and your projects more consistent.

IntelliSense Completion for Unimported Type

If you have been using IntelliSense for a while, you are likely familiar with a feature that allows you to automatically add a using statement to the top of your code while when you utilize a class that is not fully qualified. For instance, say you typed the following code:

```
File f = new File();
```

Now if there is not already a `File` class in the same namespace as your current class, you will see the red squiggly indicating an error under both instances of `File`. If you place your cursor on `File` and trigger Quick Actions, you will see Figure 4-37.

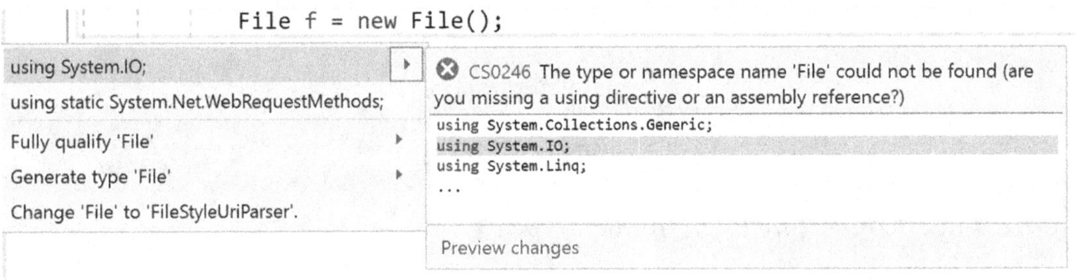

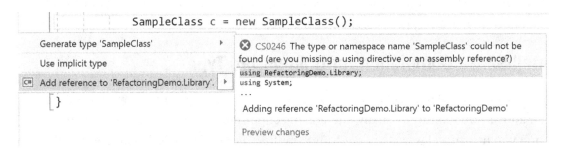

Figure 4-37. *Automatically adding a using statement*

In this case, you have a choice of using File as the class from either the System.IO namespace or the System.Net.WebRequestMethods namespace. The assemblies that contain the definition for each of these namespaces have already been imported into your project, either as part of the original project template or because you added a reference.

To this point, the limit on this refactoring is that the assembly needs to already be referenced within the project. What has been added to Visual Studio 2019 is the ability to not only add the appropriate using statement, but also to add the reference to a project or an assembly that isn't currently present.

The flow is the same as it was before. You place the cursor into the type and initiate Quick Action. Figure 4-38 is an example of the result.

Figure 4-38. *Adding a reference through Quick Actions*

Unlike Figure 4-37, where the options were to add a `using` statement to import the namespace, in this case, your choice includes adding a reference to the project in which the missing class is defined. RefactoringDemo.Library is a project within the current solution, so `SampleClass` is a class whose implementation is currently in your solution. However, while looking for possible references to add, IntelliSense doesn't just stop with the projects in your solution. It also considers the standard .NET Framework assemblies (at least the ones available to your project based on your target framework), as well as looking at NuGet for possible libraries to add. If you choose to perform the action, a reference to the project or assembly is added to your project, as well as adding the `using` statement at the top of the file. If you choose a NuGet package, a package reference is added along with the `using` statement.

Move Type to Matching File

When you are focused on the development of a feature, it's common to start placing implementation code, like enumerations or classes, in the file in which you are working. It might not seem like a big difference, but for some developers, it allows them to stay in the flow without moving from tab to tab or editor window to editor window.

Once development has finished (which is to say, all the tests pass… this is still red/green/refactor mode), it is good practice to move types and enumerations to individual files. It's easier for the next developer who works on the code base to find the implementation.

This refactoring does exactly what you need to bring your code into alignment with the goal of one type per file. To accomplish this, place the cursor in the name of the type and trigger Quick Actions. Figure 4-39 becomes visible.

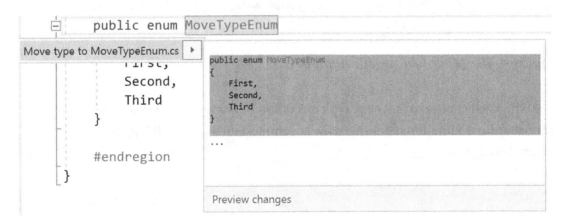

Figure 4-39. *Moving the type to a different file*

As you can see, the refactoring is offering to take the type definition and move it to a separate file. And the name of the file is the same as the name of the type.

Just for completeness, keep in mind that the namespace for the type will be the same as the namespace in which the type is currently declared. And the file is placed in the same folder as the file in which the declaration is currently found. While this will certainly keep the application compiling, it might not necessarily be the correct location, depending on your project's standards. Nor is it guaranteed to be in the correct namespace for your projects, again because it depends on your standards, which leads to the next refactoring.

Move Type to Namespace

The purpose of this refactoring is to modify the namespace for a particular class. To start, place your cursor in the name of the class and trigger Quick Actions. Figure 4-40 is the result.

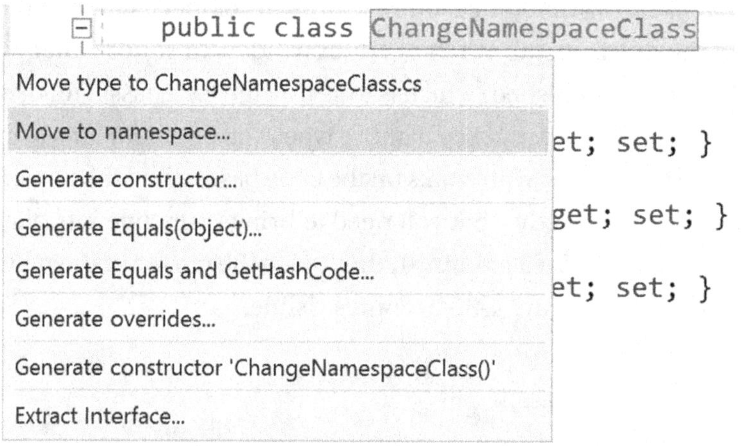

Figure 4-40. *Move to a specific namespace*

When you choose to move the type to a different namespace, the next step involves choosing the destination namespace. To accommodate this, the dialog shown in Figure 4-41 appears.

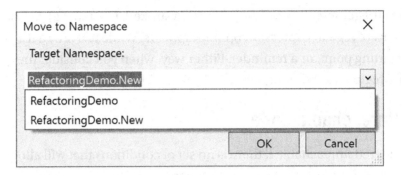

Figure 4-41. *Choosing the new namespace*

The dropdown list contains all of the namespaces currently defined within your project. When you select a different namespace and click OK, the namespace for the class is changed, and all of the references to the class within the solution are updated. Alternately, you can type a new namespace into the box and it will be created as part of the completed refactoring.

Regex Completion Through IntelliSense

While this IntelliSense functionality is not, strictly speaking, a refactoring, Visual Studio 2019 describes it in the "Refactorings" section of the documentation. And its usefulness is undisputed, regardless of how you categorize it.

The idea is that IntelliSense gives you hints about how to construct your regular expression string while you're in the middle of writing your expression. Consider the IntelliSense options visible in Figure 4-42.

```
Match m = new Regex(@"^([0-9]").Match(test);
```

\A	start of string only
\b	word boundary
\B	non-word boundary
\G	contiguous matches
\z	end of string only
\Z	end of string or before ending newline
\k< name-or-number >	named backreference
\1-9	numbered backreference

The \A a
the Rege

Figure 4-42. *Regex completion through IntelliSense*

When you trigger IntelliSense (the default keystroke is Ctrl+space), a dropdown containing a list of regular expression options appears. While it is only a list, at least it gives you a starting point, or a reminder. Either way, when you consider the challenge of creating good regular expressions, every little bit of help is appreciated.

Remove Unreachable Code

Code is considered unreachable if there is no set of conditions that will allow the code to be executed. As a simple example, examine the following lines:

```
throw new Exception();
Console.WriteLine("This will never be executed");
```

It's not possible for the second line (the Console.WriteLine method) to be executed. The previous line throws an exception, which immediately terminates execution in the current block of code. Console.WriteLine is considered unreadable.

In Visual Studio 2019, unreachable code is grayed out. As well, the beginning of the line contains a green squiggle indicating an issue. The tool tip on the issue explains that unreachable code has been detected.

The purpose of this refactoring is to easily remove the unreachable code. Place the cursor on the line of unreachable code and execute the Quick Actions comment. Figure 4-43 is displayed.

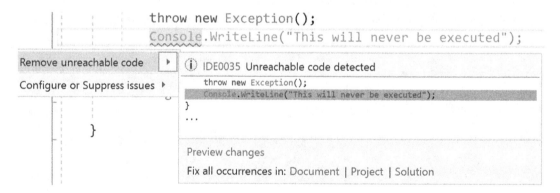

Figure 4-43. *Removing unreachable code*

When the refactoring is invoked, all of the unreachable code in the current section is removed.

Note   You might wonder why a refactoring like this is included in Visual Studio. After all, it's pretty trivial to just delete the line of code manually. One of the reasons has to do with the flow of developers. If you are familiar with the various keystroke commands, it is possible to trigger Quick Actions with a Ctrl+**.**. Then hitting Enter causes the refactoring to be performed. In other words, you can remove the unreachable code with two keystrokes. And, in the hands of an experienced developer, it would happen in a fraction of a second. And it's easier than selecting a row or two with a mouse. In other words, it's all about trimming seconds from the developer's workflow.

Sort Usings

This refactoring is the poster child for an aesthetic function. Its purpose is to sort the using statements found at the top of a code file into alphabetical order. Ostensibly, the reason is that it's much easier to find a particular namespace when the list is in alphabetical order. There are a few developers (the author included) who just feel compelled to sort the usings just because it looks prettier.

What is different about this refactoring is that it's not triggered through a Quick Actions command. Instead, the option is invoked by using the Edit ➤ IntelliSense ➤ Sort usings menu command. Or you can right-click the imports and choose the Remove and Sort Usings option from the context menu.

There is, however, a related refactoring that is available. If you have using statements that are no longer needed (which is to say that no classes from the namespace are referenced in the file), they are grayed out, similar to unreachable code. If you execute Quick Actions while the cursor is in the using section, there is a Remove unnecessary usings option that will delete the unneeded statements.

Sync Namespace and Folder

This refactoring also comes up when you're performing housecleaning on your project. A common action is to drag a file into a different folder, or decide that a number of files would be better off grouped into their own folder. Regardless of the rationale, you move files from folder to folder until you're happy with the result.

The problem is with how Visual Studio has defined the namespace in your files. When you first create a file, the namespace assigned by default is the name of the project followed by the hierarchy of folders in dot-separated notation. So if, in your RefactoringDemo project, you created a file in the Controllers ➤ Products folder, the namespace would look like the following:

```
namespace RefactoringDemo.Controllers.Products
```

Generally, this is exactly what you want the namespace to be. But you have just moved a number of files around to different folders. And their namespace has not been updated to file their new home. This is where the Sync namespace and folder refactoring comes in. Place your cursor on the namespace command and trigger Quick Actions. Something resembling Figure 4-44 appears.

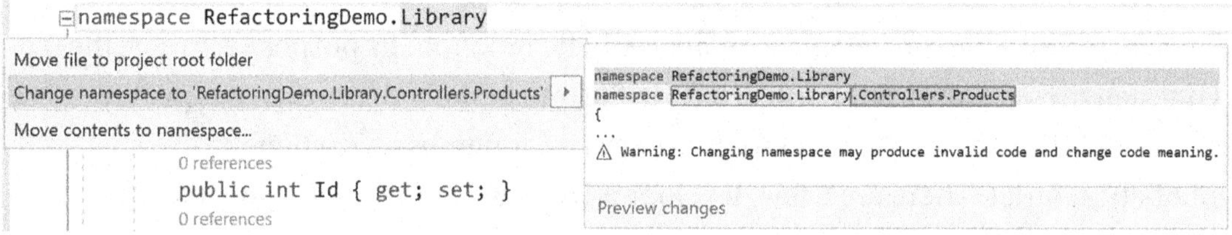

Figure 4-44. *Synchronizing the namespace and file location*

As you can see, the changes to the file are what you expect. And any references to the classes found within the file are updated as well.

Synchronize Type and File Name

This refactoring is similar to the previous one. In this case, it synchronizes the name of the type declared within the file with the name of the file name. It gets triggered a couple of different ways. First of all, if you change the name of a file using the Rename option in the context menu in Solution Explorer, you'll be prompted to see if you want to also change the name of the type within the file.

Alternatively, if the name of the type in the file is already different than the name of the file, you can place your cursor in the type name in the file and trigger Quick Actions. Figure 4-45 appears.

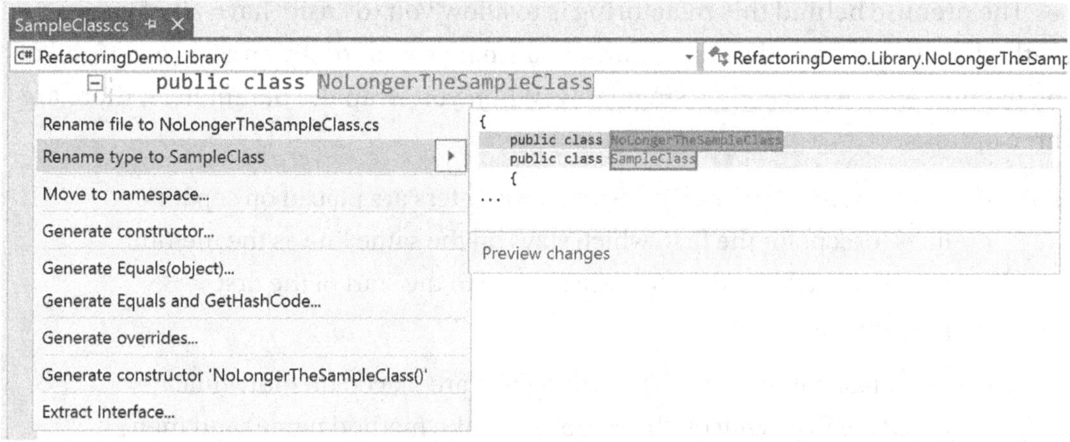

Figure 4-45. Changing the type to match the file name

The change made by this refactoring is pretty straightforward. And any reference to the original class name gets updated to match the new name, exactly if you had renamed the type manually.

Wrap, Indent, and Align Parameters

This refactoring most definitely fits into the category of aesthetics. Its purpose is to change the layout for the parameters found in method declarations or when methods are called. The starting point is either a method declaration or a method call. Place your cursor within the parameter list and execute the Quick Actions command. Figure 4-46, or something close to it, will be displayed.

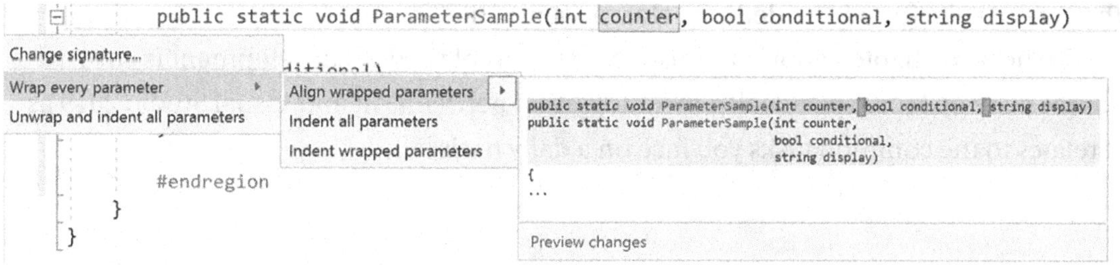

Figure 4-46. Wrapping parameters

The premise behind this refactoring is to allow you to easily have all of your method declarations and calls conform to a single standard. From Figure 4-46, all of the parameters are placed in a single row. When you wrap the parameters, there are three options:

- Align wrapped parameters – The parameters are placed on separate lines (except for the first, which stays on the same line as the method name). And the parameters are aligned to the start of the first parameter.

- Indent all parameters – The parameters are placed on individual lines (the first is *not* on the same line as the method name) and then are indented one tab-stop from the beginning of the line.

- Indent wrapped parameters – The parameters are placed on separate lines (the first parameter stays on the line with the method name) and are indented one tab-stop from the beginning of the line.

These options are also available when calling a method. And there is a refactoring to perform the opposite functionality. That is to take parameters that are on different lines and move them to the same line as the method name.

Summary

Over the last two chapters, you have taken a close look at the tools that Visual Studio 2019 includes to help you develop using the red/green/refactor paradigm. But even if that is not your preferred style of development, both unit testing and refactoring are at the core of solid (pun intended) development practices.

In the next chapter, another indispensable part of modern development is covered – source control. More specifically, the integration between Git and Visual Studio 2019 as it relates to the common tasks you face on a daily basis.

CHAPTER 5

Using Git in Visual Studio 2019

Modern development without using some form of source control is unthinkable. And while there are a number of options available, such as Subversion, Mercurial, and CVS (Concurrent Versions System), a cursory look at the popularity of the different products that are available, Git seems to have the advantage. Depending on how you count different things, GitHub (the most popular site for hosting Git repositories) would seem to be as much as seven times more popular than the next hosting site. And even accounting for variances in counting, it's pretty safe to conclude that Git is being used by millions of developers, to host everything from hobby sites to open source projects to commercial products, all of which lends support to the premise of this chapter, that is, to focus on the tooling that Visual Studio 2019 provides to developers using Git.

Integrating Git with Visual Studio

To go into a detailed description of Git would be far beyond the scope of this book. In fact, it would take its own book to do Git justice. Fortunately, there is such a book, found in Git's documentation section (`https://git-scm.com/book/en/v2`). The book, *Pro Git*, is also published by Apress and is available on Amazon.com.

This chapter is going to assume familiarity with basic Git concepts, such as repositories, commits, branches, tags, and pull requests. If something out of the ordinary is mentioned, there will be a description. But for the fundamental pieces, a base level of knowledge will be assumed.

Visual Studio 2019 provides a couple of components that enable you to easily interact with Git. However, those components are not installed with any of the current workloads. In order to work with Git, you need to add a couple of components.

© Bruce Johnson 2020
B. Johnson, *Essential Visual Studio 2019*, https://doi.org/10.1007/978-1-4842-5719-7_5

To start, launch the Visual Studio Installer. On the first screen (Figure 5-1), you should see the instances of Visual Studio that you have installed on your system.

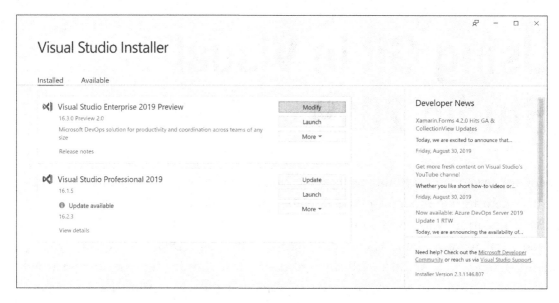

Figure 5-1. *Visual Studio Installer*

Next to the instance that you want to add Git support to, click the Modify button. This options up the form (Figure 5-2) that allows you to modify the workloads, components, and language packs for Visual Studio 2019.

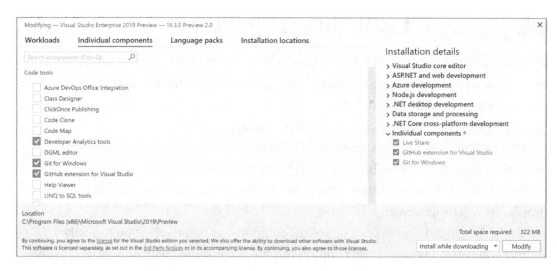

Figure 5-2. *Choosing Git components for installation*

In the Individual components section, scroll down until you get to the code tools section. There, you will see two components related to Git: Git for Windows and GitHub extension for Visual Studio. Of course, you could also enter Git into the search bar at the top of the left column to file the desired components.

Ensure that both of the components are checked and click the Modify button in the bottom right. This will start the installation process.

When the installation is finished, then it is possible that, after installing the components, the list of installed Visual Studio instances will reappear. It's possible that you might see a message indicating that updates are available. This message usually means that the Visual Studio Installer has detected that a new version of Visual Studio is available. It is not necessarily true that the update relates to the added components. Click the View details link and read the release notes to make sure.

Creating and Cloning Git Repositories

As a source control system, the fundamental purpose of Git is to track the changes that are made to a set of files over time. The files could be in a project, part of a solution, or just in a folder. This information is stored in a collection of files known as a repository. The details for a repository are stored in the .git folder.

Also, Git is a distributed source control system. Effectively, this means that there is no central storage for a project. Instead, the repository exists wherever the project is. On the server, there is a repository. On the client, there is a repository. When you push your changes, you are moving the changes in the repository on the client to the repository on the server. And when you clone a repository, you are taking the repository on the server and copying it to the client. Keep in mind that the repository includes all the files.

Visual Studio 2019 supports both the creation and cloning of Git repositories. And one or the other of those two operations is the key to getting started using Git with your development. We're going to start with creating a Git repository by creating a new project and adding it to source control. It is not the only way to create a Git repository. The Git command line includes an init command that can also create the files necessary for a Git repository. But we'll be demonstrating the Visual Studio way to do this.

Creating a Git Repository

As was mentioned earlier in the chapter, a Git repository is version information stored in a collection of files and folders. The key is to create the proper files in the proper places. Visual Studio 2019 provides an intuitive way to accomplish this.

To start, create a brand-new project. This can be done by using the File ➤ New ➤ Project menu item. In the Create a new project dialog (Figure 5-3), select a project template of ASP.NET Core Web Application and click Next.

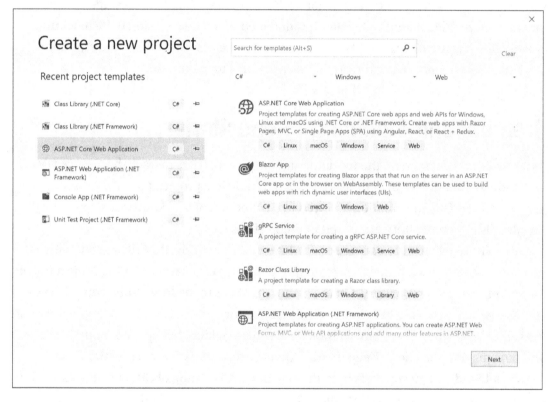

Figure 5-3. *Creating a new project*

In the next dialog (Figure 5-4), provide a Project name and a Location. You might also notice that there is a Place solution and project in the same directory option that has been checked. This is not the default setting but is being used here so that all of the files for the projects are in a single folder. This makes it easier to transfer the files to someone else, like as part of the download for a book.

Once the values have been provided, click Create to go to the next step in creating the application.

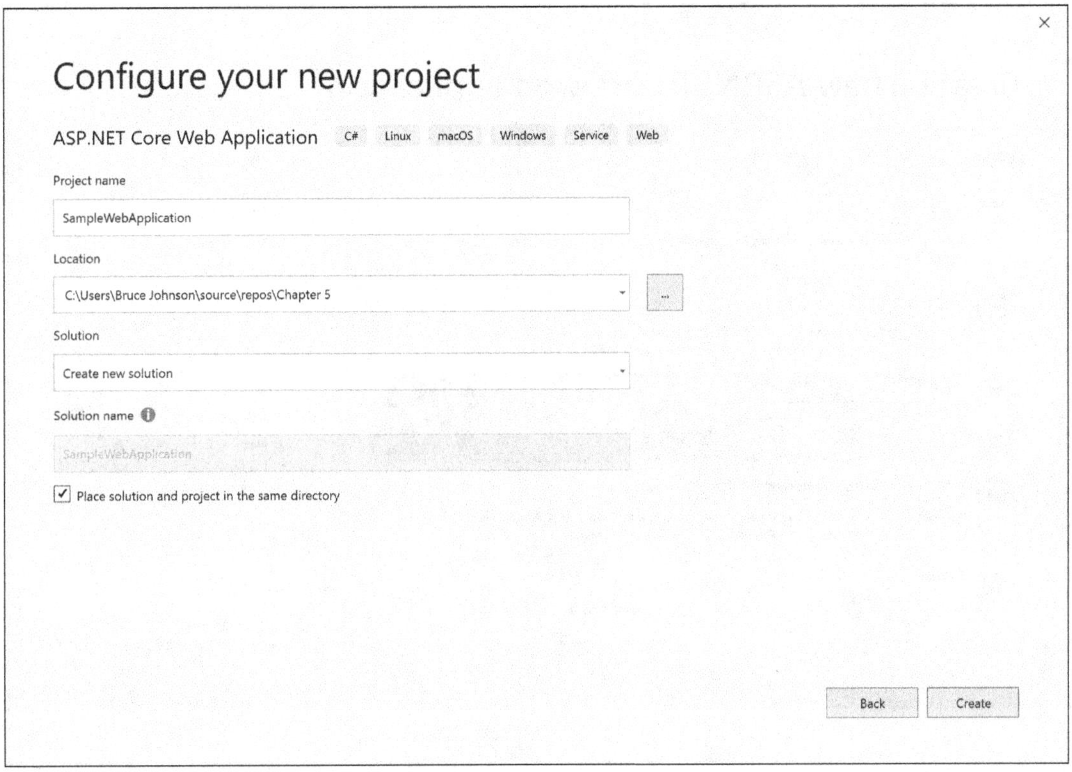

Figure 5-4. *Configure a new project*

The final step is to choose the template used to create the web application, seen in Figure 5-5.

Create a new ASP.NET Core web application   ×

.NET Core   ▾   ASP.NET Core 3.0   ▾

Empty
An empty project template for creating an ASP.NET Core application. This template does not have any content in it.

API
A project template for creating an ASP.NET Core application with an example Controller for a RESTful HTTP service. This template can also be used for ASP.NET Core MVC Views and Controllers.

Web Application
A project template for creating an ASP.NET Core application with example ASP.NET Core Razor Pages content.

Web Application (Model-View-Controller)
A project template for creating an ASP.NET Core application with example ASP.NET Core MVC Views and Controllers. This template can also be used for RESTful HTTP services.

Angular
A project template for creating an ASP.NET Core application with Angular.

Get additional project templates

Authentication
No Authentication
Change

Advanced
☑ Configure for HTTPS
☐ Enable Docker Support
   (Requires Docker Desktop)
Linux

Author: Microsoft
Source: .NET Core 3.0.0-preview8-013656

Back   Create

Figure 5-5. *Select ASP.NET Core Web Application template*

The example is going to use Web Application, to avoid sparking flame wars between proponents of the different technologies. But be aware that Git is completely neutral to the template type you use – just as it's neutral to the language you use to build your project, or the underlying technology used in deployment. Git is about storing the artifacts that are part of your project. It is agnostic about what you want to do with those artifacts.

Now that you have a project to work with, let's look at the steps associated with creating a Git repository for it.

You actually have a number of options available to you. The simplest can be found at the bottom right of Visual Studio (see Figure 5-6).

Figure 5-6. *Adding to source control*

158

When you click the Add to Source Control label, a list of the configured source control environments appears. Figure 5-6 shows Git as an option, which will be the case if you have installed the Git tools as described earlier in this chapter. If you have other source control tools configured in Visual Studio, they appear in this list as well.

Once you click Git, behind the scenes, Visual Studio is creating all of the requisite folders and contents. Once that has finished, which should only take a minute or so, the bottom right of Visual Studio will look like Figure 5-7.

Figure 5-7. *Status bar for a Git repository*

The label on the left is the name of the current repository. Clicking the label opens up the repository in Team Explorer. To the right of the name is the current branch. Clicking the branch provides a number of options to manage the branches, discussed later in the chapter.

Appreciate that the Git repository that you've just created only exists on your machine. It has not yet been saved to a central location. So, while you can perform a number of useful actions, like discarding changes to previously committed items, you are still open to the possibility of losing your work if something happens to your machine. In order to safeguard against this, it's necessary to push your code to a central repository. Once the repository has been created, along with changing the status bar, the Push pane in Team Explorer (Figure 5-8) is opened.

Figure 5-8. *Push pane in Team Explorer*

There are three possible destinations for pushing your code visible in the Push pane. The first is Azure DevOps. This is a hosted service associated with Microsoft Azure (perhaps that is obvious from the name). It uses the credentials you provided with Visual Studio to access the appropriate account and you can store an unlimited number of private repositories. If you wish to configure your repository so that others can used it, you may eventually need to pay to use the site.

The second option is GitHub. This is probably the most popular public Git repository site in the world, hosting hundreds of thousands of projects. As with Azure DevOps, there are limitations for the kinds of sites that can be hosted for free (public or private repos can have up to three collaborators in order to be free), but there are paid options for more extensive situations.

The final option is more generic. It allows you to specify the URL for a remote Git repository. The URL should represent an existing, empty repository on a remote server. This option allows you to, for example, use a corporate instance of a Git repository as the remote storage point.

While the option available at the bottom of the status bar for a project that does not already have a Git repository is great, if you are not starting with a project, there are a couple of other methods you can use.

The starting point is Team Explorer, which can be launched using the View ➤ Team Explorer menu option or using a keyboard shortcut (Ctrl+\, Ctrl+M is the default). Then click the green plug in the toolbar to display the Connect pane, seen in Figure 5-9.

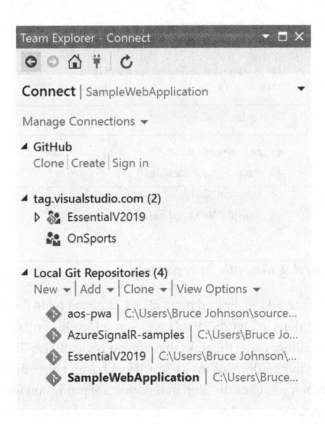

Figure 5-9. The Connect pane in Team Explorer

As with the Push pane, there are three places where you can create a Git repository. At the bottom, you can see a list of any local Git repositories. To create a new one, click the New label. This displays a text box, as seen in Figure 5-10, where the path to the Git repository can be specified.

Figure 5-10. *Specifying the path for repository*

When you have entered the desired path, click Create to create the repository.

The other two sections in Figure 5-9 relate to Azure DevOps and GitHub. For GitHub, you can create a repository using the links that appear beneath the GitHub label. First, you need to provide your credentials to GitHub, if you haven't already done so in a previous session. When you click the Sign in link, you are prompted for your GitHub user ID and password. Once you have signed in, you can create a repository by clicking Create. The dialog seen in Figure 5-11 appears.

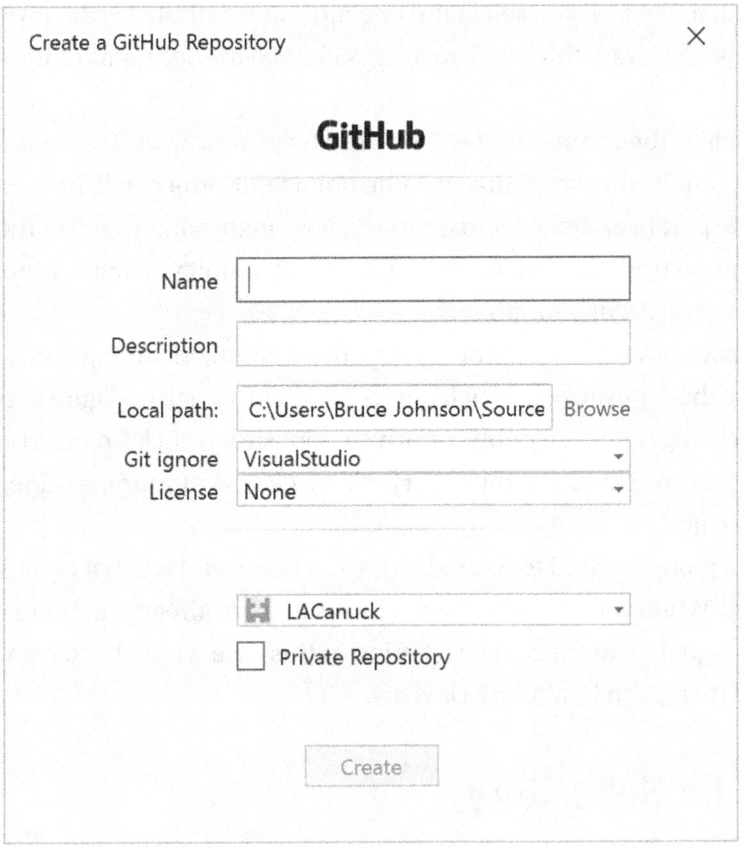

Figure 5-11. *Creating a GitHub repository*

The first three fields in this dialog are what you might expect. They are the name and description for the repository, and the local path where the repository will be cloned into after it has been created in GitHub. The next two fields are a little different and require some explanation.

The Git ignore option is a dropdown list that is used to select the `.gitignore` file that should be included in the repository. For the uninitiated, the `.gitignore` file is a collection of patterns that define files and folders that should not be included in the repository. In the Visual Studio world, a common file that shouldn't be committed is the `.suo` file. This is a file that contains settings for a Visual Studio solution that are specific to the current user. Since it is unique for each developer, it's a file that shouldn't be committed to the repository and should therefore be included in the `.gitignore` file. The dropdown list contains a list of different templates for the `.gitignore` file. And there are a lot of them. While the default is Visual Studio, because of how the repository is being created, make sure you select the one most appropriate for the project you are creating. But also be aware that you can always change the `.gitignore` file after it has been created.

The next field is the License that will be used by your project. The default is to not select a license, but if you expect that at some point your project will be commercially used or become part of an open source project, you might want to select the most appropriate license from the dropdown. Again, the decision you make is not irrevocable. It is just a starting point for your project.

Once you have provided all the necessary information, including the user who will be the owner of the repository (the field containing LACanuck in Figure 5-11) and the check box specifying if this is a public or private repository, click Create to create the repository. At the same time, the repository will be cloned to your machine, at the path that you've specified.

The second group, related to Azure DevOps, is not useful when it comes to creating a Git repository. While you can clone repositories that are already in Azure, you can't create one through this interface. The solution in this case would be to create a local Git repository and then push it to Azure DevOps.

Cloning a Git Repository

When it comes to cloning a Git repository, there are a number of paths that you can take to get there. One of the most straightforward ones comes right as you launch Visual Studio 2019. Figure 5-12 is an example of the startup screen.

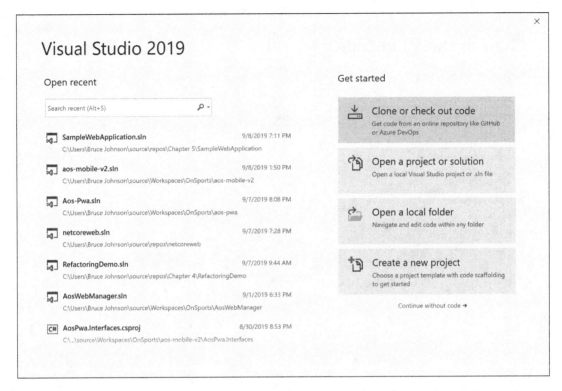

Figure 5-12. *Visual Studio 2019 launch screen*

On the right side is a collection of four buttons that are common starting points for developers. This includes both opening a project and creating a new one. And at the very top is the option to be able to clone or check out code. Clicking that button displays Figure 5-13, which is used to specify the location for the repository to be cloned.

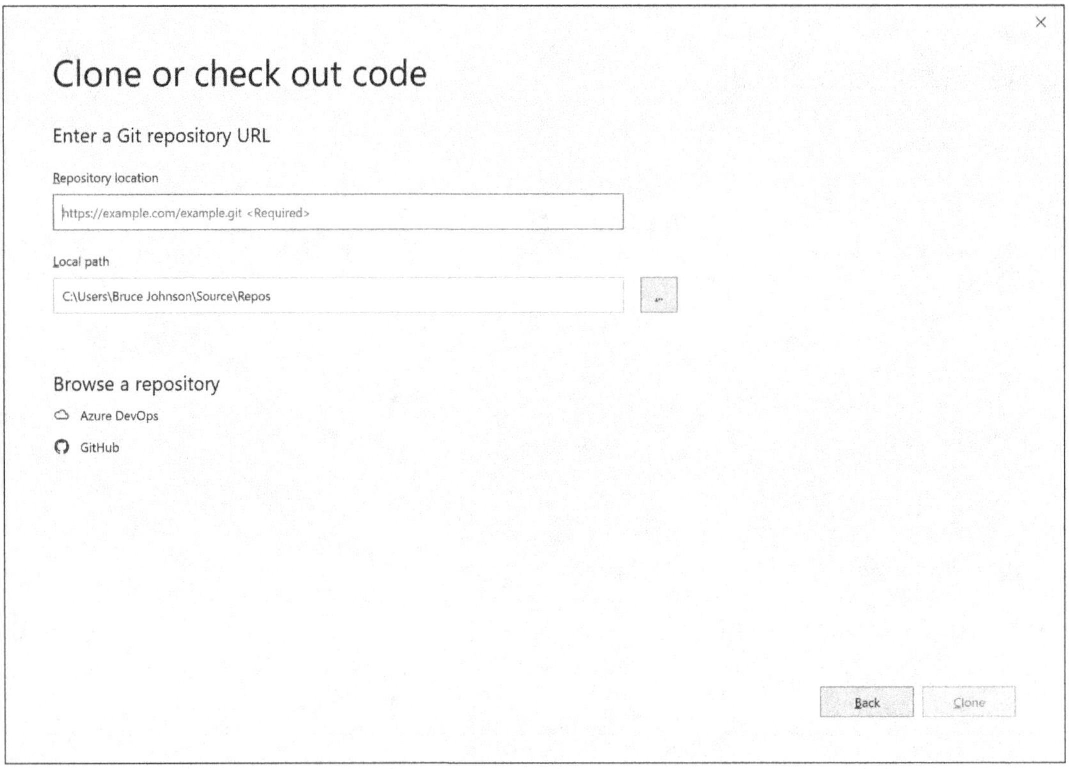

Figure 5-13. *Cloning or checking out a project*

For any arbitrary repository, there will be a URL that identifies the location. That URL needs to be entered in the first text box, while the second contains a path on your local machine. When you click the Clone button, the repository found at the specific location will be cloned into the specified path. Along with all of the project artifacts, an upstream link between the local and remote repositories will be established. This link makes it easier to push commits from the local to the remote repository.

Aside from the two text boxes, there are two other links, under the Browse a repository label, aimed at allowing you to find a repository if you don't know the appropriate URL.

If you click the Azure DevOps link, you are taken to a dialog similar to Figure 5-14.

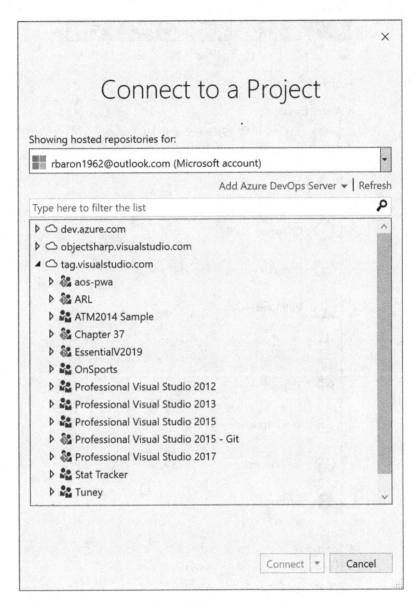

Figure 5-14. *Browsing an Azure DevOps account*

At the top is a dropdown containing the different Microsoft accounts that you have added to your computer. When an account is selected, the different Azure accounts that are accessible appear in the tree that takes up the majority of the dialog. Here you can navigate to the repository that you're looking for. When you select the repository and click Connect at the bottom of the dialog, the Visual Studio IDE appears and the Team Explorer pane is displayed (Figure 5-15).

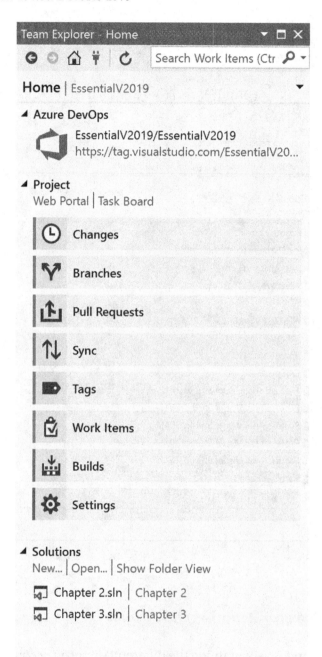

Figure 5-15. *Home pane for Team Explorer*

As mentioned earlier, there is more than one way to clone a Git repository. The workflow just described is available when you first open Visual Studio. However, that flow is also accessible from within the Visual Studio 2019 IDE itself. If you use the File ➤ Clone or Check Out Code menu option, the dialog seen in Figure 5-13 appears and the described flow continues from there.

A completely different flow is available through Team Explorer. To start, navigate to the Connect pane (Figure 5-16) by clicking the plug icon in the toolbar.

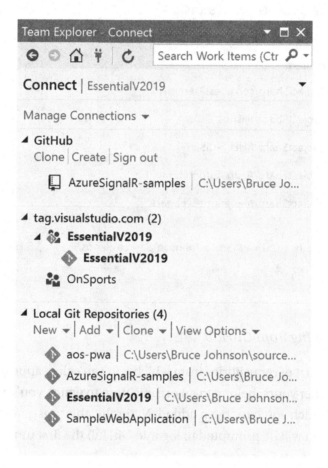

Figure 5-16. *Connect pane in Team Explorer*

On this pane, you have two different ways to clone a repository. At the top, under the GitHub section, there is a Clone option. The result of clicking the option is a screen (Figure 5-17) that lets you find a repository on GitHub and then clone it to your local machine.

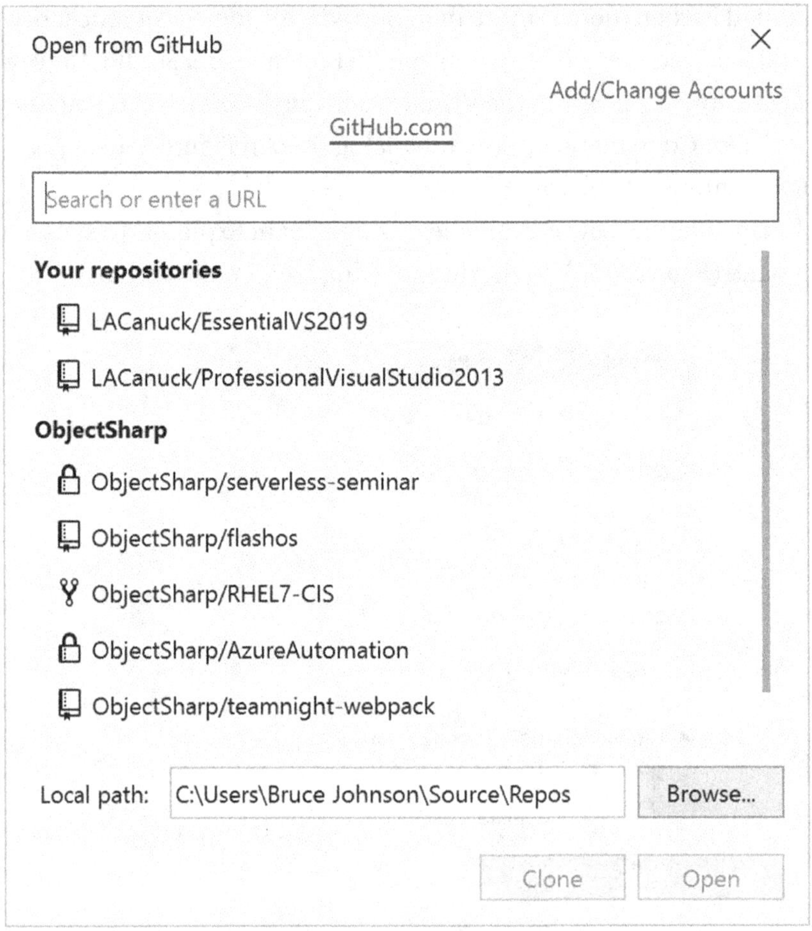

Figure 5-17. *Cloning from GitHub*

In this dialog, a list of repositories from which you can select appears. There, repositories are either yours, belong to an organization to which you've been added, or are projects to which you have been added. Naturally, this presumes that you have a GitHub account. You will be prompted to log into GitHub the first time you access this dialog.

If the repository you want to clone isn't already in the list, you can provide the URL for it at the top of the dialog. As well, you can enter a search term in that top text box. However, the search is performed only within the repositories that appear in the list. If you want to search the repositories within GitHub, you'll need to visit GitHub and search there directly.

The text box at the bottom of the dialog is the local path into which the repository will be cloned. Once all the necessary information has been provided, the Clone button becomes enabled. Clicking it starts the cloning process.

In the lower section of the Connect pane, there is a second method for cloning a repository. Underneath the Local Git Repositories heading, there is a Clone option. When clicked, it reveals an area that looks like Figure 5-18.

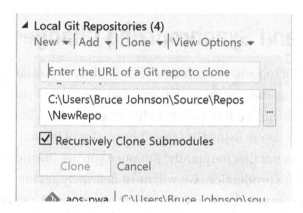

Figure 5-18. *Cloning a non-GitHub Git repository*

The required information is similar to what you needed for a GitHub repository with which you were not already associated. In the top text box (it has a pale-yellow background), you specify the URL to the Git repository. In the second text box, you specify the local path into which the repository will be cloned. The button on the right (with the ellipsis) is used to open the Open File dialog. When those pieces of information are provided, the Clone button is enabled. Clicking it starts the cloning process. The Recursively Clone Submodules check box is used to allow for submodules to be cloned, if they are part of the base repository.

Git Submodules   The idea behind a submodule in Git is to attach an existing repository into the folder structure of another repository. While there are a number of benefits to this mechanism, the main ones involve being able to reference a single repository from within multiple repositories and having the changes to that single repository be available to the other repositories when they're willing to take them in.

When you have cloned a repository using any of these steps, you end up with a local version of the code that you can modify. This is referred to as a local repository or just a local repo. This repository is also associated with the repository that was the source of the clone. That repository is known as the remote repository or the upstream repository. This relationship becomes useful when you are finished with development, as described in the next section.

Committing and Synchronizing Changes

Once you have your Git repository on your local machine, the usual next step involves making changes, testing, making more changes, and so on, until you are satisfied with your work. While Visual Studio has tools to help (as was covered in earlier and later chapters), the fact that you're using Git doesn't have a lot of impact on your development workflow. Well, at least not that frequently. But once you are finished with your code and are ready to move it into production, Git will most definitely get involved.

The first step is to get your code into your local repository. This is done by performing a "commit."

The commit process consists of two separate steps. The first is to identify the files which are to be included in the commit. This is known as *staging* the files. The second is to record the identified changes (i.e., the staged files) in the local repository.

In Visual Studio 2019, the starting point for the commit process is the Commit pane within Team Explorer (Figure 5-19). It can be accessed by clicking the Changes option in Team Explorer's Home pane.

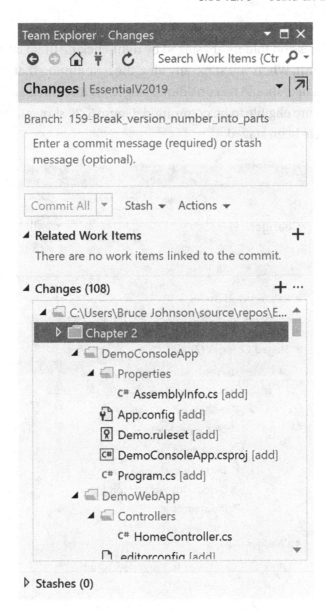

Figure 5-19. *Changes pane in Team Explorer*

The large section in the middle, labeled Changes, is the collection of files that have been added, deleted, or modified since the last time a commit was performed. These files (or a subset of them) will be part of your commit.

In Visual Studio, by default all the changed files are initially considered staged. This is an effort to make it easier for developers to perform a commit. A high percentage of the commits performed by developers includes all changed files, so this optimization frequently saves a step. However, you can always be judicious about the files that get staged. Individual files and folders are staged by right-clicking them and choosing Stage from the context menu. When you stage any files, the assumption that Visual Studio started with (that all files should be considered staged) is discarded and only those that are explicitly staged are eligible to be committed. Figure 5-20 shows the Changes pane where some files have been staged.

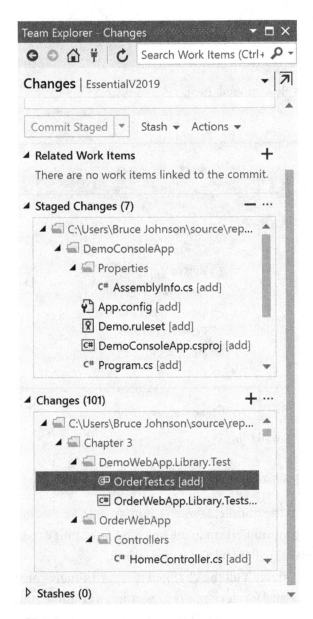

Figure 5-20. Changes pane with some staged files

Along with adding files and folders, you can also stage the entire set of changes by clicking the plus sign to the right of the Changes label. It's also possible to unstage files that have been staged by clicking the individual files and selecting Unstage from the context menu. Or all the staged files can be unstaged using the minus sign to the right of the Staged Changes label.

Along with staging and unstaging files, there is one additional way to keep a file from being included in the commit. That would be to undo all the changes that had been made. This is useful if you had modified a file temporarily (by, say, modifying a connection string) or if you're doing some experimental development. Maybe you're not entirely sure how to solve a problem, and after following a particular path, you decide the result is not to your liking. Regardless of the reason, the changes made to a file since the last commit can be undone through the context menu. Select the file or files that you want to revert in either the Changes or Staged Changes section. Then right-click and choose Undo changes from the context menu. After a few moments, the version of the file (or files) that was last committed will replace the current file(s).

At this point, a collection of files has been staged. The next step is to commit them. Functionally, this involves updating the local repository with the changes found in the staged files. In terms of the steps you take, they are all still on the Changes pane in Team Explorer.

There is one mandatory field for committing files. In Figure 5-21, at the top, there is a text box. If it is left empty, the background color is a pale yellow.

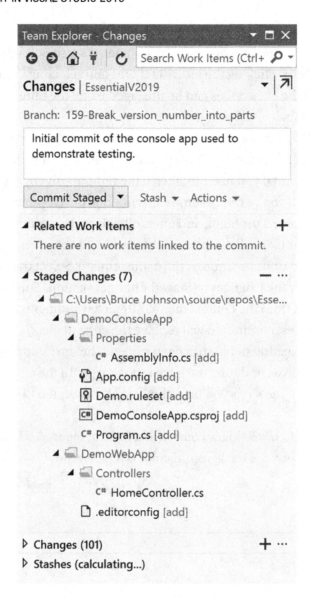

Figure 5-21. *Commit comment field in Changes pane*

This field is used to provide a comment for your commit. The comment is associated with the set of changes and is used to identify, at least at a high level, the reason for the changes, which means that while it's tempting to put something short and potentially meaningless into the comment, it will be more useful in the long run if you're diligent about keeping your comments meaningful.

Once the comment has been entered, the Commit Staged button immediately below the comment text box is enabled. Click this button to commit your staged changes to the local repository.

There is a dropdown button immediate to the right of that button. That's because Team Explorer offers you a couple of other choices while committing.

> Commit Staged – Takes the staged files and updates the local repository with the changes.

> Commit Staged and Push – Performs the same functionality as Commit Staged. But once the commit is finished, the changes are pushed to the upstream repository. This is the equivalent of performing a `git commit` followed by a `git push`.

> Commit Staged and Sync – Starts by performing the same functionality as Commit Staged. This is followed by integrating any outstanding commits from the upstream repository into your local repository. Finally, any changes are pushed back to the upstream repository. The equivalent commands are `git commit` followed by a `git pull` then a `git push`.

Getting more into the details of which command is appropriate for your environment is beyond the scope of this book. In fact, there are sources available to help you understand how to utilize Git in your workflow.

But while we're on the topic of pull and push, you can always perform these actions independently of committing your code. At the bottom right of Visual Studio, shown in Figure 5-22, there is an area that indicates your current branch.

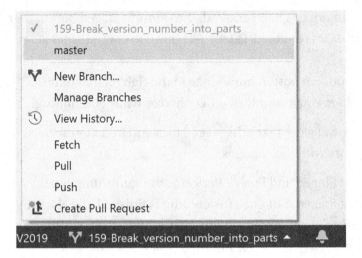

Figure 5-22. *Git commands available on the status bar*

When you click the branch name, a menu with a number of options appears. The Branch and Pull Request options are covered later in this chapter. But the Pull, Push, and Fetch commands relate to the commit functionality just described.

> Pull – Retrieves any commits from the upstream repository and merges them into your local repository.

> Push – Takes any commits in your local repository and pushes them to the upstream repository.

> Fetch – Retrieves any commits from the upstream repository and lets you decide whether you want to merge them into your local repository. This is similar to a pull, but without the automatic merging to your local repository.

Stashing

As you work with Git, it's inevitable that you will eventually be faced with the following situation: you have been working happily on your own branch, making changes, getting tests to pass, and so on; you get asked to review code that exists on another branch (or someone needs help with a problem or whatever other reason you can come up with to need to change branches); you can't switch branches without committing your code, but your work is not yet ready to commit. How do you change to the desired branch without losing your work?

The answer comes in the form of the Stash functionality. By stashing your changes, you can remove them from your current branch while saving them so that they can be restored in the future. And once the changes are not in your current branch, you can switch branches with impunity. After you've finished with the work on that new branch, you can come back to your original branch (or any other branch, actually) and update that branch with the changes you've stashed.

The starting point for the stashing feature is the Changes pane in Team Explorer. As you can see in Figure 5-23, there is a Stash option immediately to the right of the Commit Staged button.

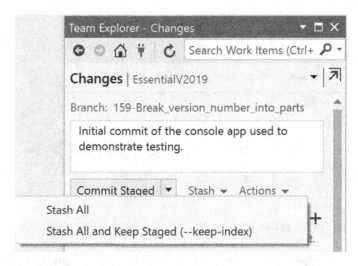

Figure 5-23. *Stash menu options in the Changes pane*

The first option, Stash All, records all the changes (not just the staged changes... all the changes) into a stash. It then removes all the changes, reverting the code back to the state prior to the changes. You might see this referred to as discarding the changes, undoing the changes, or reverting, if you are familiar with a different Git client. The second option, Stash All and Keep Staged, records all the changes and keeps any changes that have been staged. Unstaged changes are reversed.

Once the stash is created, it appears at the bottom of the Changes pane in Team Explorer (Figure 5-24).

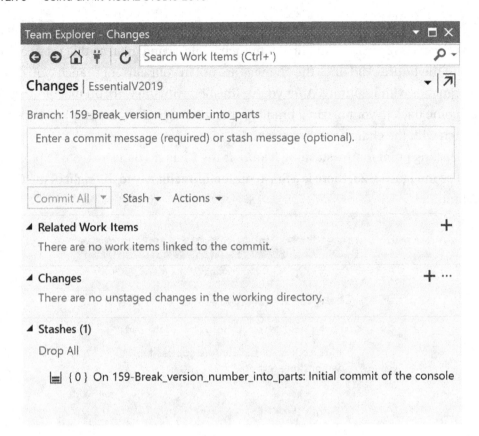

Figure 5-24. *Stashes in Team Explorer*

Each stash is identified with the branch on which it was originally created, along with the commit message.

You have four actions that can be performed on an individual stash. The options are available by right-clicking the stash. From the context menu that appears, you can take the following actions:

View Changes – Displays the changes that are part of the stash. They appear in a format that is similar to the Staged Changes/Changes sections in the Changes pane. Figure 5-25 provides an illustration.

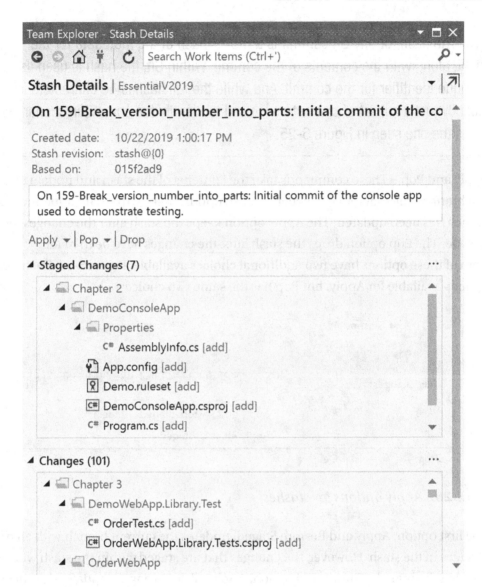

Figure 5-25. Stash Details

Here, you can see that files that had been staged are still separated from the files that had just been modified. As well, the description of the stash is available, along with the date on which it was created, the revision of the stash, as well as an indicator of which specific commit the stash was based on. The collection of characters that indicate the base for the stash (in Figure 5-25, it's 015f2ad9) is part of the hash for the commit that is done most recently in the branch.

> **Note** The hash for any Git commit is a SHA-1 hash of the metadata for the commit, along with the contents of the commit. Within Git, the hash is used as the unique identifier for the commit. And while the full hash is 40 characters long, frequently just a subset of characters is used to identify the commit in scenarios, such as the one seen in Figure 5-25.

Apply and Pop – These commands take the contents of the stash and update the current branch. The difference between the two options relates to what happens after the branch has been updated. The Apply option keeps the stash after the changes have been made. The Pop option drops the stash after the changes have been made.

Both of these options have two additional choices available. Figure 5-26 illustrates the options available for Apply, but Pop has the same two choices.

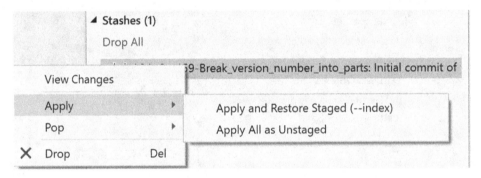

Figure 5-26. *Apply options for stashes*

The first option, Apply and Restore Staged, updates the current branch with all of the changes in the stash. However, the changes that are staged within the stash will also be staged in the branch. The second option, Apply All as Unstaged, updates the current branch with all the changes, but even if the changes were staged in the stash, they will be unstaged in the branch.

Drop – The fourth command available to you actually deletes the stash from your repository. Nothing is updated in the current branch and this choice is permanent. There isn't a mechanism that undoes the deletion of a stash.

Drop All – If you have more than one stash in your repository, you will also see a Drop All option. This option will delete not only the currently selected stash, but every other stash as well.

Working with Branches and Tags

The previous section mentioned branches, especially as part of the discussion on stashing, but didn't really go into any detail about what they are and certainly didn't touch on how they can be manipulated within Visual Studio 2019. This section rectifies that situation.

If you're familiar with Git (or any of the most commonly used source control systems), you're not a stranger to the concept of a branch. If you're new to Git, the best way to think of a branch is a separate stream of development. Figure 5-27 illustrates a simple sample of branching.

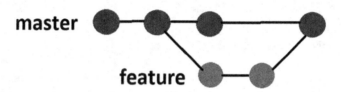

Figure 5-27. *Simple branching*

There are two branches in Figure 5-27: *master* and *feature*. *Master* is the name of the default branch in Git. Consider each of the circles on the top row to indicate different commits made to the *master* branch. After the second commit, a new branch is created, based on the current state of master. That branch is called *feature*. Now development can take place on both *master* and *feature* independently of one another. If things go horribly awry in *feature*, that branch can just be discarded with no impact on *master*. Or the more likely scenario is that the work in *feature* is successful. In that case, the changes in *feature* can be merged back into *master* so that everyone can share in your success.

One of the strengths of Git is the ability to quickly create new branches, as well as move from branch to branch. That gives a lot of freedom to developers to experiment with different solutions, safely discarding what doesn't work. Or you can move from working on a feature to fixing a bug in a different branch and easily come back when finished. Naturally, the Git support in Visual Studio allows you to take advantage of all of these abilities.

Creating a Branch

The first step in using a branch is to create it. Visual Studio provides a number of different mechanisms for you to achieve this, depending on where you are working. The most fully featured option is from Team Explorer. Figure 5-28 shows the Branches pane in Team Explorer.

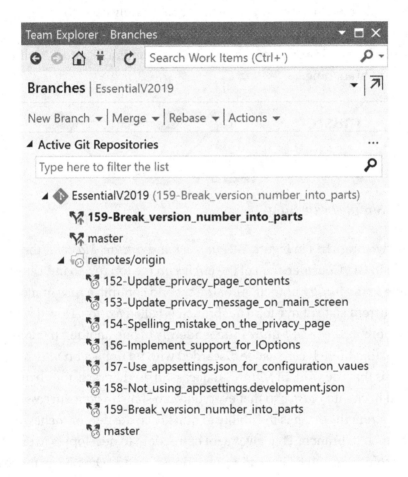

Figure 5-28. *Branches pane in Team Explorer*

The Branches page shows all of the branches that have been defined in both your local repository and the remote repository. The list is further segregated by the active repositories. In Figure 5-28, there is a single active repository, called EssentialV2019. In the local version of that repository, there are two branches, master and 159-Break_version_number_into_parts. The branch that is currently checked out (i.e., the one that is currently being worked on) has the name bolded. The remote repository is indicated by the *remotes/origin* node and there are a number of branches found in that repository.

To create a new branch, click the New Branch link just below the Branches title. The top portion of the pane expands to provide the necessary options, as seen in Figure 5-29.

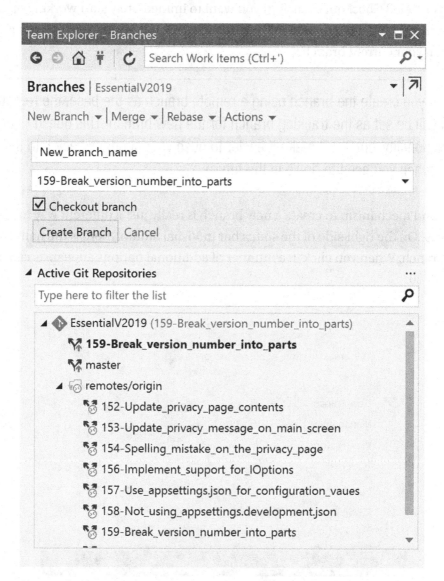

Figure 5-29. *New Branch information in Branches pane*

In order to create a branch, two pieces of information need to be provided. First, the name for the new branch is entered into the top text box. Then, the base for the branch is identified. Immediately below the branch name is a dropdown that contains all the branches available to you, both locally and in the remote repository. Choose the desired existing branch and click Create Branch to create the branch. You might notice a check box labeled Checkout branch. If you want to immediately start working on the new branch after it's created, then make sure the check box is checked. Otherwise, you will stay on your current branch.

Note   If you create the branch using a remote branch as the base, the remote branch will be set as the tracking branch for the new branch. This doesn't affect any functionality, but it will make it easier to push your changes back into the base branch, when you need to do so in the future.

A second mechanism to create a new branch is really just a different way to get to Figure 5-29. On the right side of the status bar in Visual Studio, there is the name of the current branch. When you click it, a number of additional options appear, as can be seen in Figure 5-30.

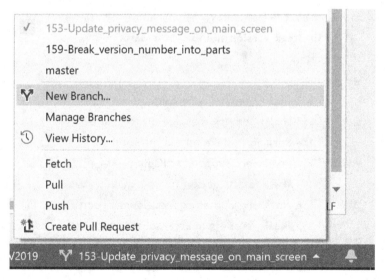

Figure 5-30. *Branching options from the Visual Studio status bar*

To create a new branch, click the New Branch... menu option. This launches Team Explorer (if it's not already open) and displays the Branches pane, with the controls needed to create the new branch visible. In other words, it looks exactly the same as Figure 5-29.

There is one additional way to create a new branch. In the Branches pane, you can right-click any of the branches, either remote or local. The context menu includes a New Local Branch from... menu option. When you click the option, then the fields needed to create the new branch are revealed (again, just like Figure 5-29), with the difference that the branch on which you right-clicked is used as the selected value for the dropdown list of branches.

You might have noticed that the only branches we've created have been local ones. While it's possible to create remote branches using the Git Hub web portal, there isn't a mechanism for doing so in Visual Studio. At least, not directly.

By default, creating a local branch from a remote branch sets the tracking branch. Now when you issue a pull, push, or fetch, Visual Studio automatically executes that command against the tracking branch. And each of those operations is performed without giving you a chance to change the tracking branch. The trick is to start by unsetting the tracking branch. To accomplish this, from the Branches pane, right-click the local branch and select the Unset the Upstream Branch menu option. At this point, there is no longer a relationship between the local branch and any remote branch.

The next step is to reconnect the branch to a remote branch. There is no way to do this through Visual Studio directory. If you had not associated the current repository with a remote repository, you'd have the ability to do so through the Sync pane. Instead, open the Visual Studio 2019 Developer Command Prompt and navigate to the directory where your local repository is found. Then execute the command `git branch <branchName> -u origin/<remoteBranchName>`, where `<branchName>` is the name of the local branch and `<remoteBranchName>` is the name of the upstream branch.

Switching Branches

In order to make use of branches, you need to be able to quickly switch between different branches. This allows you to take advantage of the lightweight nature of Git branches to switch development contexts as your job demands.

In Visual Studio, you have two areas where the current branch can be changed. For one, in Team Explorer, go to the Branches pane (Figure 5-31).

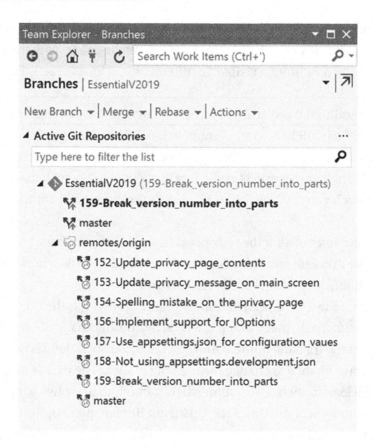

Figure 5-31. *Branches pane in Team Explorer*

Underneath the repository is a list of both local and remote branches. If you right-click a branch, there is a Checkout option in the context menu. Choosing that option causes the current branch to be switched to the selected branch. And if you had checked out a remote branch, a local branch with the same name is created and then the new branch is set to be the current branch. And the remote branch (the original source for the branch) is set as the upstream branch. You can accomplish the same functionality by double-clicking the branch instead of using the context menu.

The second place to change branches is from the status bar at the bottom on Visual Studio. If you click the current branch at the right of the status bar, a menu appears (Figure 5-32).

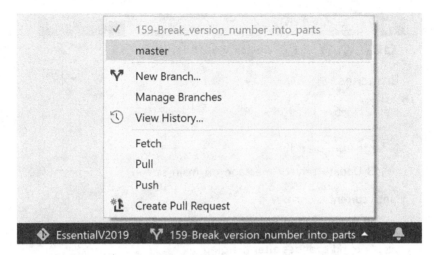

Figure 5-32. *Switching branches from the status bar*

At the top of the menu is a list of the local branches. The currently checked out branch is grayed out and has a check mark on the left. To check out another branch, click it.

Merging Branches

The typical development flow in Git involves creating a local branch, developing until finished, committing your changes into the local branch, and then pushing your updated branch back into a remote branch.

If you're working on a system with multiple developers, then there is a possibility that other people might have updated the remote branch while you were doing your development. If that happens, the actual steps in the process involve pulling any changes from the remote branch, which merges the remote changes with your changes, then pushing the result back to the remote branch. A key part of this process is merging.

While the details of how a merge is successfully performed are beyond the scope of this book, the premise is straightforward. If the same file has been changed in both branches, the individual lines of code are compared. If this comparison finds changes at the same place within the file in both branches, then a conflict is identified. Otherwise, both changes are included into the merged file.

While this merging and conflict detection happens automatically as part of a Git pull, you can also perform this merge manually at a time of your choosing. To do so, go into the Branches pane in Team Explorer. If you right-click a branch, one of the options is Merge from.... Selecting this option opens an area at the top of the Branches pane, as seen in Figure 5-33.

189

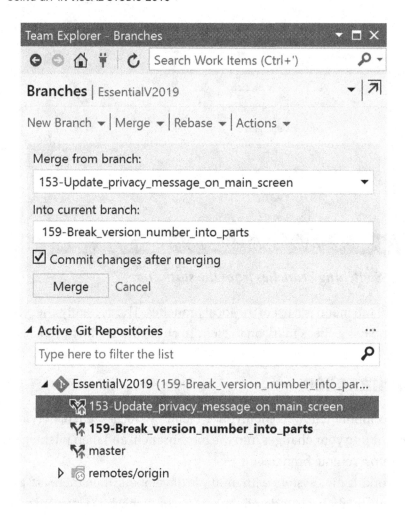

Figure 5-33. *Merging branches in Team Explorer*

The first field, a dropdown, contains a list of the local and remote branches. Here you select the branch from which you are merging. The second field is the name of your current branch. This is here just for information purposes. You can't make changes to it and can only merge into your current branch. As well, there is a check box indicating if you would like to perform a commit immediately after a successful merge. When these values have been set as you desire, click the Merge button to start the process.

If there are no conflicts, the two branches will be merged and you can continue on with your development. However, if the merge detects a conflict, you must either resolve the conflicts or revert the merge before continuing.

You are notified that there is a conflict by a message that appears in the Branches pane (Figure 5-34).

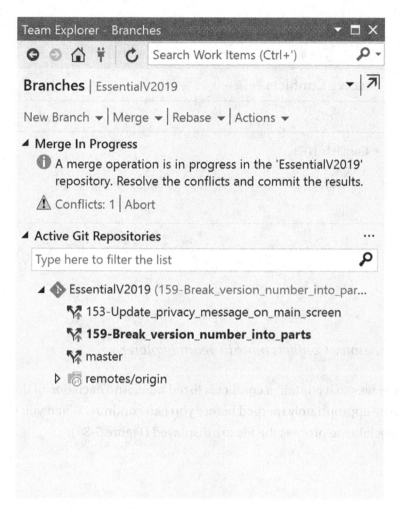

Figure 5-34. *Merge conflict in Branches pane*

There are two options found immediately below the conflict message. If you don't want to continue with the merge, click the Abort link. In order to resolve any conflicts (and you can see from the number that there is only one conflict in this instant), click the Conflicts link. This displays the Resolve Conflicts pane seen in Figure 5-35.

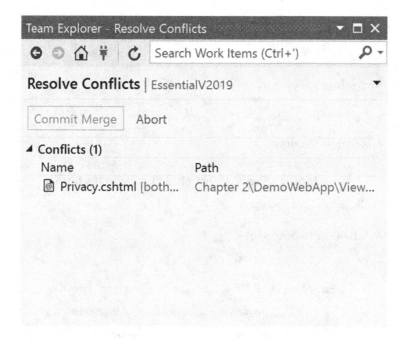

Figure 5-35. *Resolve Conflicts pane in Team Explorer*

Each of the files that contain a conflict is listed here. And each one of the conflicted files needs to be appropriately merged before you can continue. When you click a file, the options available to process the file are displayed (Figure 5-36).

Figure 5-36. *Conflict resolution options*

Once a file has been selected, you have a number of options to help you decide how to complete the merge. There are three different links on the page: Compare Files underneath the conflict message and two Diff links next to the Edited on messages. Each of these links launches the Visual Studio Diff tool. The difference (pun intended) between the links is the files that are being compared.

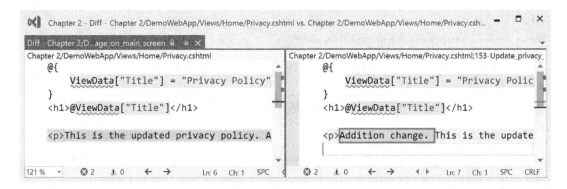

Figure 5-37. *Diff tool from Visual Studio*

Figure 5-37 shows a sample view of the results from the Diff tool. The idea is basically to highlight the differences that exist between two different files. There is a target and a source for the Diff process. When a line has changed, it will appear in pale red in the source and pale green in the target. If a line has been deleted between the source and target, the line appears in pale red in the source. And if a line has been added to the target, it is highlighted in pale green.

The three links mentioned earlier all result in the same view. But they use different sources and targets. The Compare Files link compares the files that have been committed to the two branches being merged. The Diff links compare the current local file (not necessarily committed) with the instance of the file in the specific branch.

To help complete the merge by resolving the conflict, Visual Studio includes a built-in three-way Diff/Merge tool. Unless you have modified the settings for Git (discussed later in this chapter) to use a different tool, Figure 5-38 contains an example of what you will see.

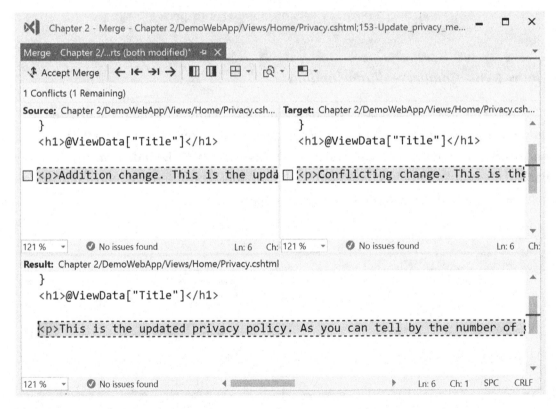

Figure 5-38. *Diff/Merge tool in Visual Studio*

The idea with the Diff/Merge tool is to allow you to easily define the correct result for the merge. There are a number of icons and messages at the top of the pane to help you navigate through the file.

First, lines that are in conflict appear in a pale orange/brown color. Next to each line is a check box. To indicate that a particular line should be included in the merged file, simply ensure that the check box is checked. You can include either one or both of the lines at the same time. The result appears in the pane at the bottom. That bottom pane can also be directly edited, so that you can add any additional code that you need to create the correct result.

There may be other differences between the two files that do not result in conflicts. They are denoted by the same color scheme described earlier in the Diff tool.

A message at the top of the page indicates how many conflicts were identified and how many have not been resolved. You can navigate through the file looking for conflicts manually (they appear as orange-brown dots in the scroll bar). Or you can use the first four icons on the toolbar to navigate to the first, previous, next, and last conflicts (in order).

The next two icons (they are three rectangles with either the leftmost or rightmost shape filled in) are used to just take all of the changes from either the left or the right file.

The next icons (that look like the basic layout of the panes seen in Figure 5-38) are used to change the organization of the panes. Besides the two over one layout that is in the example, you can arrange the panes either vertically or horizontally.

Next up is an icon that is used to launch the Diff tool directly from the merge. The same three choices are available as were described in the Resolve Conflicts pane. You can perform a diff between the source and target, the source and base (the local version), or the target and base.

Finally, the last icon is used to set focus on one of the three panes. While it's not likely that you'll use these menu items directly (it would be easier to just click the pane), there are shortcut keys associated with these options that allow you to shift focus between panes without having to move your fingers from the keys.

Using as many of these tools as you require, get the file to a state that is correct for merging the two conflicted files. When you have the file ready, click Accept Merge to complete the conflict resolution process. This takes the merged file and makes it the local file. If you have more conflicted files, fix each one in turn. When you are finished, the merge is automatically identified as complete. If you have indicated when initiating the merge that you wanted to commit the merged files when the merge is complete, then the commit will be done. And, more importantly, you are able to continue developing normally.

You don't even need to use a merge tool in order to resolve merge conflicts. Git indicates the information necessary to see both the source and target in the file itself. For example, the following would be the lines of code that generated the conflict in Figure 5-38:

```
<<<<<<< HEAD
<p>Conflicting change. This is the updated privacy policy. As you can tell
by the number of characters in this page, privacy is something that we take
very seriously.</p>
=======
<p>Addition change. This is the updated privacy policy. As you can tell by
the number of characters in this page, privacy is something that we take
very seriously.</p>
>>>>>>> 153-Update_privacy_message_on_main_screen
```

The collection of left and right pointing chevrons are the telltale signs of a conflict. The section that starts with `<<<<<<< HEAD` and ends with `=======` is the code currently in your local file. The section that starts with `=======` and ends with `>>>>>>>` `<branchName>` is the code that is coming from the merge file. The `<branchName>` is the name of the branch from which you are merging. You can go into your favorite text editor, make the changes directly, and then remove the lines that are used to delimit the conflicting sections. Once those changes are made and the file saved, it is no longer considered in conflict.

Rebasing Branches

The idea behind merging files in Git is to combine the contents of two files to create a version of the file that contains both changes (or a modification of the changes, based on manual intervention). For most situations, this is the easiest way to take the contents of one branch and add it to another.

However, Git has a second technique for combining two branches: rebasing. With rebasing, rather than combining files, you are taking the commits from one branch and reapplying them to the current branch. The actual steps are as follows:

Locate the most recent common ancestor between the two branches (current and incoming).

Collect the file diffs generated by the changes in each commit in the incoming branch.

Reset the current branch to the most recent commit.

Apply each of the file diffs from the incoming branch commits, in the order they occurred.

Perform a fast-forward merge.

When you're finished rebasing, you should have a set of files that are the same as you would get with a merge. In other words, from a results perspective, rebasing and merging get to the same source. The difference is the history found in the repository. During the merge, the history of the two branches is combined. Most Git history visualizers will show the merge as being two separate paths of history that separated when source branch was created and then joined again with the merge. The history of a rebased file is linear. You see all the changes up to the most recent commit. Then you see the commits from the file diffs. The result is that the history is linear, rather than branched.

Within Visual Studio, the process of rebasing is pretty similar to merging. It starts in Team Explorer. In the Branches pane, there is a link at the top labeled Rebase. Clicking the clink opens an area at the top of the pane, as seen in Figure 5-39.

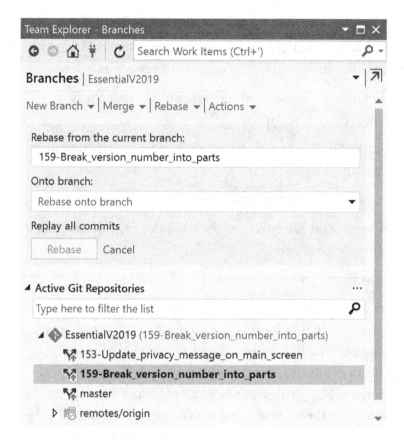

Figure 5-39. *Rebasing in Team Explorer*

The rebase is performed by taking the current branch and pushing the changes to another branch. When you click the Rebase link, the top text box contains the current branch name (and you can't change it). Below that field is a dropdown containing the local and remote branches. If you select a local branch, clicking the Rebase button causes the current branch to be rebased onto the selected branch. If you select a remote branch, then that branch is pulled into a local branch with the same name as before the rebase is performed.

It's also possible to get to the rebase options by right-clicking a branch in the full Branches pane. In that case, the branch that you right-clicked becomes the target for the rebase (unless you right-click the current branch, in which case the dropdown is left blank).

Deleting Branches

Deleting branch is a simple process in Visual Studio. Start in the Branches pane in Team Explorer. Right-click a branch and select Delete from the context menu. If the branch has commits that had not yet been pushed to its upstream repository, you'll get a message saying so. You can choose to continue (the equivalent of the --delete option) or cancel the deletion.

If you right-click a remote branch, the deletion option is labeled Delete Branch from Remote. You'll get a message asking to confirm the deletion, and if you accept, then the branch will be deleted from the origin.

Pull Requests

To this point, when we're talking about pushing code to another branch, you are responsible for the entire process – making sure that the incoming code is good, performing the merge, and making sure that the merged code is tested. If you're responsible for the project, that's good. But as more and more people are involved, there are typically one or more people who take on the role of gatekeeper for the incoming code. In this scenario, the gatekeepers become responsible for ensuring that quality and functionality are maintained as code is added to the project. You would typically see this structure in open source or large projects that have a team or teams of developers.

When you have that situation, allowing everyone to push code can be dangerous. While most developers wouldn't cause a problem, all it takes is one bad commit to seriously impact the quality and reputation of a project. To combat this problem, Git supports the idea of a pull request. With a pull request, rather than merging your changes directly into a branch, the changes are packaged up so that they can be reviewed. This package, which is the pull request, includes other information, like a title, description, and related work items. The pull request is then reviewed by people who have the authority to approve the pull request. When the pull request is approved, the code is merged into the target branch.

Visual Studio 2019 provides support for creating pull requests only in that it launches the New Pull Request web page in Team Foundation Service or GitHub, with the appropriate information filled in. To launch the page, from the Branches pane in Team Explorer, right-click a branch and select the Create Pull Request option from the context menu. The same option is available from the menu that appears when you click the branch at the right side of the status bar. When the option is clicked (and you're connected to a repository hosted in TFS), the following page (Figure 5-40) is opened in your default browser.

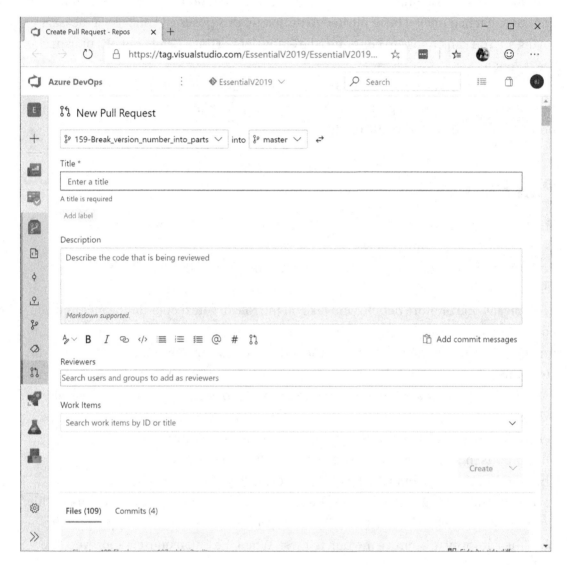

Figure 5-40. *Creating a new pull request*

One of the criteria for being able to create a pull request is that both branches (the source and the target) need to be available on the server. In other words, you can't pull request from a local branch to a remote branch. So in order to even create a pull request, you'll have to commit to the local branch and then push the commit to the upstream branch. When you get to the New Pull Request screen, the selected branch (or its upstream companion) appears in the dropdown at the top left. To the right of the dropdown is the target for the pull request. Both of these can be modified on this screen.

Below the target and source branches are the metadata for the pull request. The title is required, and the description is strongly suggested. There is a link at the bottom right of the description to add the commit message to the description. Still, that might not be sufficient. When writing the description, consider that someone in the future will be going over the description to get an idea of what's in the pull request. In other words, do your future self (because, inevitably, you'll be the person reading the description) a favor and be as clear and complete as you can be about what is in the pull request.

Under the description is a list of people who are the reviewers for the pull request. The policy for the repository can automatically add reviewers (either individuals or groups), but you can also specify specific people. Those people will be emailed to let them know that the pull request has been created.

There is also a place to associate work items with the pull request. If you do this, the pull request becomes part of the associations for the work item. It allows others to see which pull requests might have been accepted to complete the development or fix the issue described in the work item.

Below the metadata (and not visible in Figure 5-40, except for the headings) are the changes made in each file, along with the commits that are part of the pull request. It's a good idea to review these to ensure that only the changes you expect are part of the pull request.

When the information is ready, click Create to create the pull request. There is also an option to create the pull request as a draft. This allows you to come back later to fill in missing information or add files. One thing to keep in mind is that while the pull request is open, subsequent commits to the same remote branch become automatically included in the pull request.

Once created, the page containing the pull request information looks like Figure 5-41.

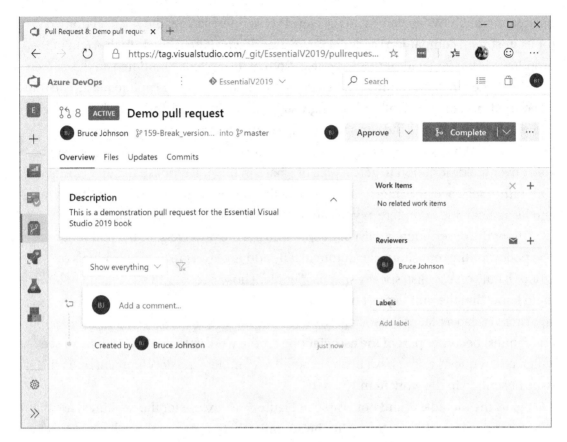

Figure 5-41. *An existing pull request in Visual Studio Online*

This view is seen by both reviewers and the person who created the pull request. At some point, the reviewers will approve the pull request (or reject it). This could be after making comments that need to be resolved. But at the point where the pull requests are reviewed, it can be completed by clicking the Complete button. At that point, the changes that are part of the pull request will be merged into the target branch.

Viewing the History of Your Code

The ability to track the changes made to a file over time is a great way to identify the source for newly arising bugs. After all, if the code used to work and now it doesn't, it stands to reason that any change made in the intervening time would be a good place to start your bug hunt.

The starting point to viewing the history for any file is the Solution Explorer. Right-click the desired file and choose View History from the context menu. That will display the History form, an example of which can be seen in Figure 5-42.

Figure 5-42. *Simple history view in Visual Studio 2019*

Each change made to the file appears in this list, including the commit hash, the commit message, the date and time of the commit, the developer who made the commit, and, if available, a picture of the developer. This is the simple view of history. Click the second icon from the left in the toolbar to see the details history view (Figure 5-43).

ID	Author	Date	Message
▲ Local History			
820c3853	Bruce Johnson	10/27/2019 3:53:38 PM	Adding a conflicting change to this branch
47266d74	Bruce Johnson	6/28/2019 6:04:39 AM	Corrected the spelling of 'privacy'
be29a761	Bruce Johnson	6/28/2019 5:41:51 AM	Update the text for the privacy page
aa09c8e1	Bruce Johnson	6/27/2019 2:57:05 PM	Initial commit for Chapter 2

Figure 5-43. *Detailed history view in Visual Studio 2019*

The information available in the detailed view is pretty much the same as the simple view, with the exception that the developer's picture is not visible. It's left to the reader to determine how much of a loss that is.

There is an even more complete history that can be displayed. First, the last icon on the right is used to show any tags that were applied to the commits. And the second to last icon on the right includes the remote branches from which any commits came from. Also, the fourth button from the right (the one with the clock) shows a complete history. By default, the merge commits are excluded from the display. The complete history brings those commits to the list. Figure 5-44 illustrates the different remote branch labels and with the merge commits.

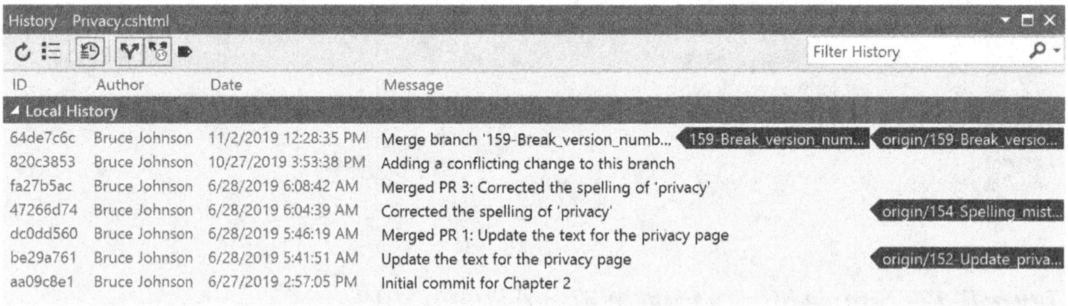

Figure 5-44. *History view with all commits and remote branch labels*

There are operations that can be performed on the individual commits so that you might more closely see the changes that have been made. To start each of these, select two different commits by clicking the first and Ctrl+Click the second. Then the context menu will include the following options:

Compare – This launches the Visual Studio Diff tool described in the "Merging Branches" section.

Compare Commits – This option opens the Compare Commits pane in Team Explorer (Figure 5-45).

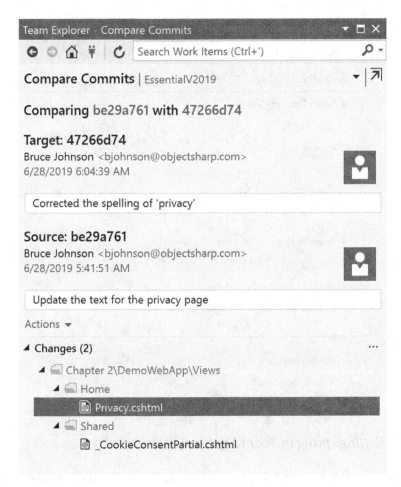

Figure 5-45. Compare Commits pane in Team Explorer

The goal of this pane is to give you a view of the two commits that you are comparing at the file view. The details of the two commits take up the bulk of the pane. Below that are the files that were modified between the two commits. If you double-click any of the files, the Diff tool is opened comparing the selected file in the two different commits.

Git Settings

Git has a wide variety of settings available to be manipulated. In general, the settings are configured using the Git command line. However, Visual Studio does allow some basic information and defaults to be set, both across all Git functions and for each repository. The settings can be accessed by clicking the Settings button on the Home page in Team Explorer. This displays the Settings pane, shown in Figure 5-46.

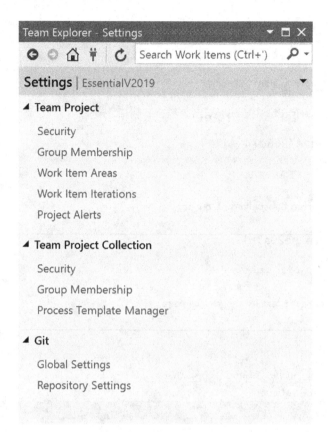

Figure 5-46. Settings pane in Team Explorer

At the bottom of this list of settings are two links that take you to separate panes related specifically to Git. The Global Settings pane (Figure 5-47) controls settings across every Git repository.

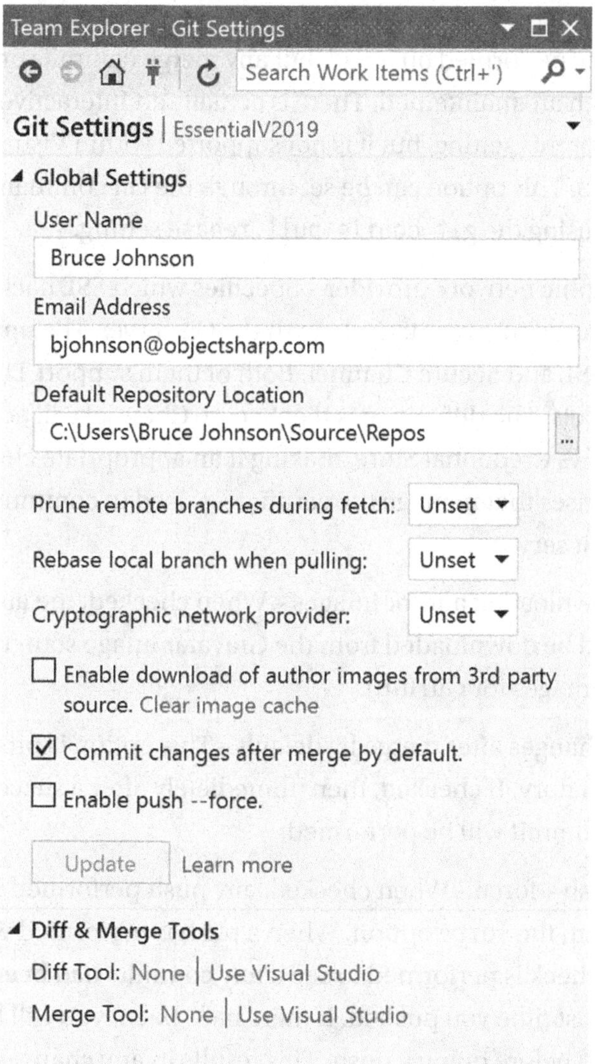

Figure 5-47. *Global Git Settings pane in Team Explorer*

At the top of the pane, you can set the username, email address, and the default location for any new repositories. The next few settings are less straightforward.

Prune remote branches during fetch – If set to True, then when a fetch is performed, if there is a local branch that has an upstream branch that no longer exists, the local branch is deleted.

Rebase local branch when pulling – This setting controls whether a rebase is automatically performed on a pull. If set to True, every pull results in a rebase. Setting this to False means that a pull

207

performs a merge and not a rebase. A Preserve option causes the rebase to be performed on a pull, but any merge commits on the local branch are maintained. There is actually an Interactive option available for this setting, but it is not supported within Visual Studio 2019. This option can be set through the Git command line, if desired, using the `git config pull.rebase` setting.

Cryptographic network provider – Specifies which SSL back end should be used to communicate with the Git server. The options are OpenSSL and Secure Channel. Both of them support TLS and SSL protocols. The difference is that Secure Channel will access the Windows Credential Store, making it an appropriate choice for enterprises that manage the certificates used to communicate with the Git server.

Enable download of author images – When checked, the author images will be downloaded from the Gravatar image source (the source of images for GitHub).

Commit changes after merge by default – This option is pretty self-explanatory. If checked, then immediately after a successful merge, a commit will be performed.

Enable push --force – When checked, any push performed will execute with the `force` option. When a push is performed without a force, a check is performed to see if any commits had been made since the last time you pushed. If there have been, you will be told to do a pull before doing a push. This results in any changes being merged into your branch, complete with any necessary conflict resolution, before you can push. Using the `force` option can be dangerous, because there is the possibility of overwriting changes in the upstream branch.

At the bottom of the Global Settings pane are the Diff and Merge tools being used. Typically, these tools are set using the `git config` command-line command. However, if you want to set the Visual Studio tools as the default, you can click the Use Visual Studio link.

The Repository Settings are similar to the Global Settings. Figure 5-48 illustrates a typical repository.

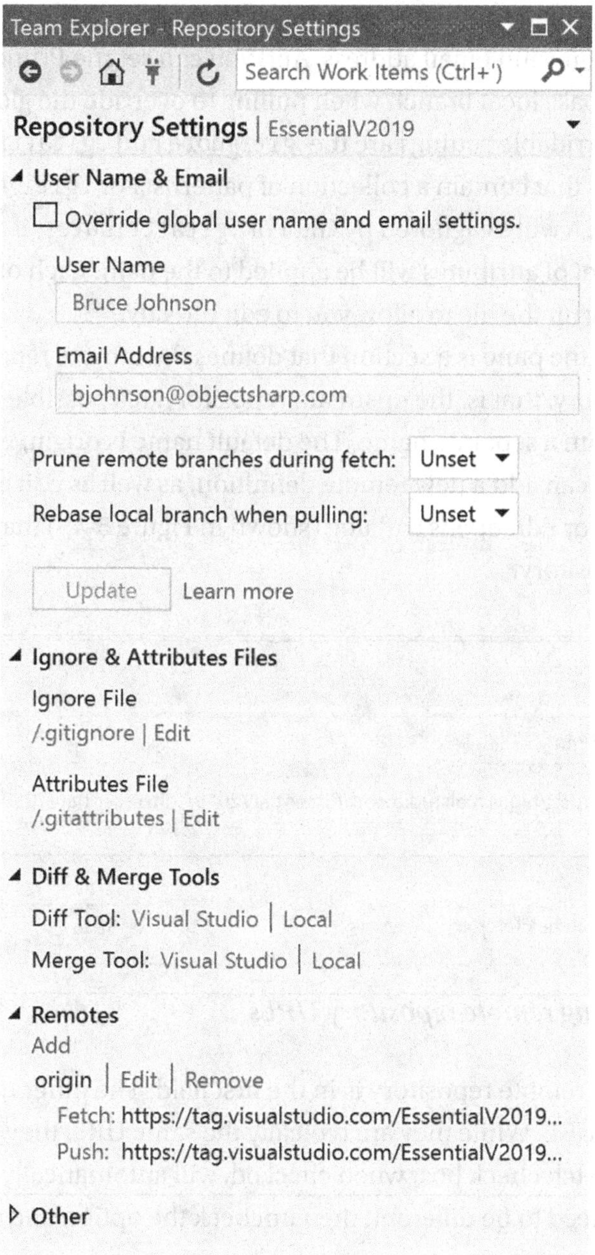

***Figure 5-48.** Repository Settings in Team Explorer*

The top half of the pane contains some of the settings from the global pane. You can overwrite the username and email address. And you can set the Prune remote branches during fetch and Rebase local branch when pulling to override the global values.

Below those overridable settings are the .gitignore and .gitattributes files. These are standard Git files that contain a collection of patterns. For .gitignore, if a file path matches the pattern, it will be ignored by Git. For .gitattributes, if a file path matches the pattern, then a set of attributes will be applied to the path. Each of the files contains an Edit link, opening up the file to allow you to edit directly.

At the bottom of the pane is a section that defines the remote repository for the current local repository, that is, the upstream repository. It's possible to have different repositories, each with a separate name. The default name is origin, which is visible in Figure 5-48. But you can add a new remote definition, as well as edit an existing remote server. Clicking Add or Edit opens a dialog (shown in Figure 5-49) that lets you specify the paths to the repository.

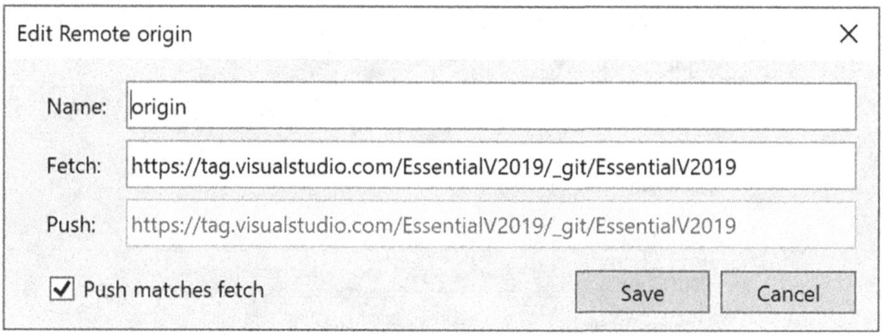

Figure 5-49. *Editing remote repository URLs*

The name of the remote repository is in the first field. The other two text boxes are for the Fetch and Push URL. While they are typically the same URL, they don't need to be. The Push matches fetch check box, when checked, will automatically sync the Fetch and Push URLs. If they need to be different, then uncheck the option and set each URL to the appropriate value.

Summary

Git has been tightly integrated into Visual Studio 2019. Part of that is because of the widespread usage of Git across many different development environments and platforms. It's also at least partly informed by the fact that Microsoft recently purchased GitHub, a leading Git repository for projects, both open source and personal. It's likely that, over time, there will be even more Git functions available.

While Git is a collaborative tool, in that many developers can be working on the same code base simultaneously, it's not the full extent of collaboration that is available in Visual Studio. In the next chapter, we look at some of the interactive, collaborative experiences that Visual Studio 2019 enables.

CHAPTER 6

Collaboration

At the heart of the Git functionality described in the last chapter is the concept of collaboration. You make changes to code. Other developers make changes to code. The changes are merged together into a single functional unit. And pull requests go a step further, along potential commits to be reviewed and commented on prior to being accepted into a branch.

But that is not the limit of collaboration that is available in Visual Studio 2019. There are a couple of new features that take the idea of code reviews, pair development, and assisted debugging to new levels. In this chapter, the focal points of collaborative development, Live Share, and integrated code review are covered in detail.

Visual Studio Live Share

The premise behind Visual Studio Live Share is very impressive. Using either Visual Studio or Visual Studio Code, you can edit and debug your application in collaboration with another developer in real time – with the participants able to see the application code and debugging information, execute terminal commands, forward localhost requests, and communicate over voice calls. Picture a combination of Skype, Visual Studio, and remote debugging, and you have the idea, at least of the combination of features. The implementation is even more impressive.

System Requirements

For Visual Studio 2019, the main requirement is to install a workload that supports Live Share. This includes ASP.NET, .NET Core, C++ (the desktop development with C++ workload), Python, and Node.js. For Visual Studio 2017, you need to be running at least version 15.6. As well, you need to install an extension called Visual Studio Live Share. It's available in the Visual Studio Marketplace. For Visual Studio Code, the same extension (Visual Studio Live Share from the Marketplace) is required.

© Bruce Johnson 2020
B. Johnson, *Essential Visual Studio 2019*, https://doi.org/10.1007/978-1-4842-5719-7_6

For completeness, not every language is supported to the same level. You can break Live Share functionality into three high-level groups:

- Shared Language Services – The participants see edits done by one person appear immediately in their editor. You can also see their cursor position and selections. As well, you can follow other participants (automatically navigate to where they are navigating) or send and receive focus notifications (asking participants to focus their attention on your editing).

- Shared Debugging – Participants are able to work within the same debugging session. This includes the ability to view state and step through the execution in sync with one another.

- App Sharing – Participants share in the execution of an app. For a web application, for instance, they can make requests to the website, even if it's running on the localhost of another participant. For non-web applications, they can interact with the application as if it were running locally.

For a given language and platform (Visual Studio vs. Visual Studio Code), there are different levels of support provided. Mostly because the range of languages available in Visual Studio Code is so vast. For Visual Studio, the most commonly used languages (this includes C#, Python, C++, VB.NET, and F#) are supported for Shared Language Services. The most notable exception, at the time of writing, was R, although it is supported in Visual Studio Code. And most of these languages are also available for Shared Debugging (interestingly, R **is** available for co-debugging). The exceptions are languages where execution is not really happening (CSS, HTML, XAML, Markdown, SQL).

If a participant is using Visual Studio Code, the list of supported languages for both Shared Language Services and Shared Debugging is longer and much more exotic.

When it comes to App Sharing, the supported development platforms are also extensive. Most of the expected environments are supported (web front- and back-end, console applications). As well, there are a number of environments that might be surprising, including Kubernetes, Azure functions, Ethereum, and mobile development using Cordova or React Native. All in all, the list is complete enough to cover a majority of collaborative situations.

Connectivity

There are three connection modes that are supported by Live Share:

- Direct – The host machine and guest machine can communicate directly over a local network.

- Relay – The communication between the host and guest machines is done through the Azure Service Bus.

- Auto – Allows connections either directly, through the local network, or through the Azure Service Bus.

When establishing a Live Share connection, there are a number of steps that are gone through. First, the host machine establishes the session. While doing so, it can specify that all connections must be made through one of the two connection modes. In other words, it's possible for a host to ensure that only participants on the local network can join by specifying a connection type of Direct.

Once the host session is established, guests are allowed to connect. As with the host, they can choose either Direct, Relay, or Auto connection modes. For a guest, the Auto mode will start by checking to see if a direct connection can be made to the host. If available, that connection is used. If not, then the session falls back to Relay mode.

All connections are SSH or SSL encrypted, so none of the communications are visible to anyone but the participants. However, there are ports that need to be open in order to be able to host or participate. For Direct connections, ports between 5990 and 5999 are used. For Relay connections, then you must have access to `*.servicebus.windows.net:443`.

Security

In order to either host or connect to a Live Share session, you must be authenticated through an Azure Active Directory account, a Microsoft Live account, or a GitHub account. It is not possible to connect to Live Share using an on-premise Active Directory account, or a GitHub Enterprise account, although they are being considered by Microsoft as a future enhancement.

Hosting a Live Share Session

To start a Live Share session, there are two steps you need to take. First, you need to be signed into Visual Studio. This is a question you get asked when you first install Visual Studio. If you're already signed in, the top-right corner will look similar to Figure 6-1.

Figure 6-1. *Signed-in account information in Visual Studio*

You stay signed in, so if you haven't had to authenticate yourself since installation, don't be surprised. If you haven't signed in, then there is a Sign In label where the circle in Figure 6-1 is found. Clicking that label launches the authentication process. Once that is complete, you are halfway to Live Sharing.

The second, and less onerous, step actually has two parts. Start by opening a solution, or creating one. The idea is to get the solution that you want to share open in Visual Studio. Once the solution is ready, click the Live Share label, as seen in Figure 6-2.

Figure 6-2. *Live Share link*

If you don't see this Live Share link, it's probably because you haven't installed any of the workloads that include it. You can do so (the list is found at the beginning of the chapter), or install it directly from Visual Studio Marketplace.

Clicking Live Share starts the process of sharing your environment. The first time you do this, you are likely to get a number of dialogs asking you to configure your Windows environment. Figure 6-3 appears if you are using Live Share in Auto mode and the appropriate port range has not been enabled in Windows Firewall.

Figure 6-3. *Live Share Firewall Access dialog*

If you click Ok, then you will almost immediately see the dialog shown in Figure 6-4.

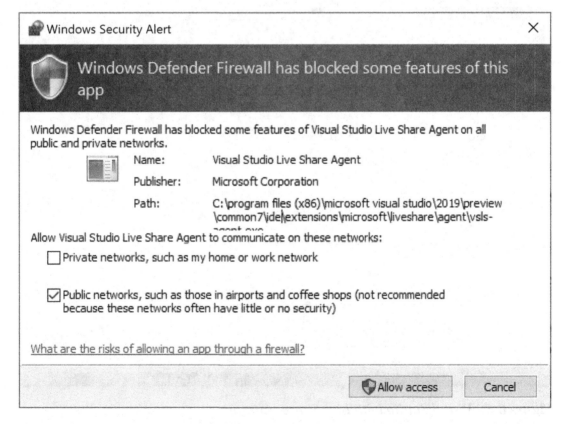

Figure 6-4. *Windows Firewall alert for Live Sharing*

217

This dialog is surfaced by Windows Firewall, and it indicates that an application, the one described by the Name, Publisher, and Path details, is requesting access. In this instance, it is the agent that is used to host Live Share. Clicking Allow access opens up the necessary ports.

If you're using a different firewall or security package, the dialog that you see after Figure 6-3 might be different. Or you might require that your administrator open up the ports through global settings. Keep in mind that these dialogs appear because the Live Share mode is Auto. It's possible to change that default through the Live Share Settings screen, covered later in this section.

Once port access has been configured, the Live Share session will begin. It might take a couple of minutes to get set up, depending on the speed of your machine and network connection. But once it's going, your Visual Studio will look something similar to Figure 6-5.

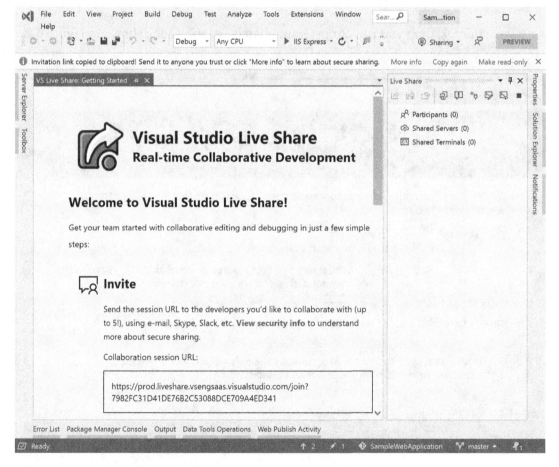

Figure 6-5. *Visual Studio with Live Share running*

The second and subsequent times you share, you won't see the Getting Started window open. Instead, just the Live Share pane (on the right) and the Invitation link message (in yellow, immediately below the toolbar) appear. However, you can get it back by clicking the More info label in the Invitation link message.

Along with showing the Getting Started page, the Invitation link message is also a quick way to get to information you are likely to be interested in at the beginning of a List Share session. By default, a URL that can be used to join the session is pasted to your clipboard. That way, you can send the link to anyone who might be interested with a minimum of effort. From the link message, you can re-add the link to your clipboard by using the Copy again link. You can also convert the session to be read-only using the Make read-only link.

But the Invitation link message is just a convenience. The real source of functionality is found in the Live Share pane. Figure 6-6 shows a Live Share pane for an active session with one participant (i.e., one participant other than the host).

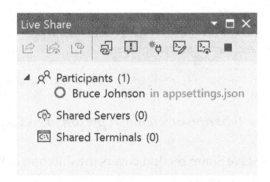

Figure 6-6. *Live Share pane for an active hosting session*

The body of the pane is a list of the active participants, servers, and terminals that are part of the session. Listed under each heading are the instances of each type of component. However, when it comes to actions you can take, most of the capabilities are found in the toolbar. And, with two exceptions, they will be covered in the upcoming sections.

The two exceptions are the icon at the extreme right (the red square) and the icon to the right of the divider (looking like a combination of the copy icon and the link icon). The square icon is used to terminate the Live Share session. The copy link icon is used to place a copy of the URL used to connect to the Live Share session onto your clipboard. The URL can then be sent to anyone who might be interested in joining the session through whatever means (email, Skype, Teams, Slack, etc.) you prefer.

The Live Share pane is visible to everyone who is part of the session, although not every function is available.

As the host of a Live Share session, you receive a notification whenever an invitee joins your session. You see the notification in the bottom right of Visual Studio (Figure 6-7).

Figure 6-7. *You've got notification*

The notification itself (Figure 6-8) indicates the name and email address of the person who joined.

Figure 6-8. *Notification that appears when a person joins Live Share session*

The remainder of the Live Share section covers the different collaboration tools that are available while a session is active.

Live Editing

One could easily describe live editing (or coediting) as the fundamental functionality in Live Share. The premise is straightforward. You can see the changes, selections, and cursor positioning of everyone else in the session in near real-time. When someone opens a file, that file will open in your Visual Studio instance. When someone makes a change, that change appears in your editor. As well, the name of the participant is available to you. Figure 6-9 provides an example of what each of two instances of Visual Studio will see.

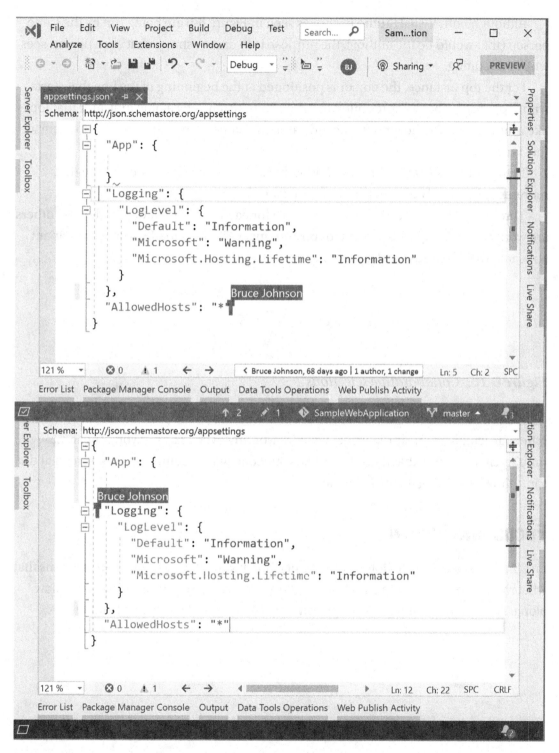

Figure 6-9. *Live Editing in multiple Visual Studio instances*

Although both Visual Studio instances seen in Figure 6-9 are being run by the same person (that would be the author), the purpose is to demonstrate what each person sees while live editing.

For the top instance, the cursor is positioned at the beginning of the line that starts with "Logging". That is represented in the bottom instance by a blue indicator that looks like a fat T. When you hover over the indicator, the name of the participant whose cursor that is appears as a tool tip.

In the bottom instance, the cursor is at the end of the last line. You can see that represented as the T indicator in the top instance.

Through this simple interface, it's possible for each participant to see what the others are working on. Along with just cursor positioning, selections made by one participant appear to the others, as illustrated in Figure 6-10.

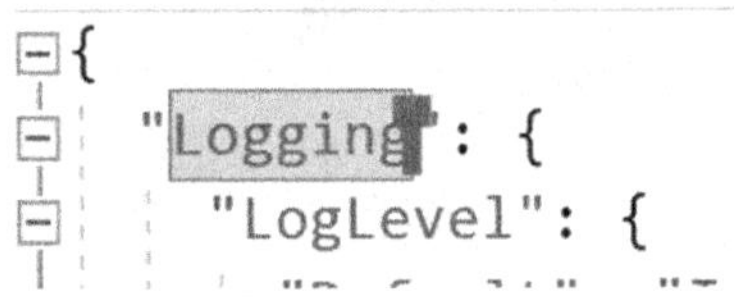

Figure 6-10. *Collaborative selections*

As well as selections, any editing that is done by one participant is visible to all the other participants in near real-time. If you're working over a fast network, "near real-time" is close enough that it just looks like your colleague is editing on your screen at the same time he's typing on his machine.

Focus and Follow

Live Share has a concept of following a participant. If you follow a participant, it means that whatever that person is doing in Visual Studio, your instance of Visual Studio will follow along. This includes editing, cursor placement, selecting, and navigating to other files.

Figure 6-11. *Following participants in Live Share*

Figure 6-11 illustrates the two different ways to see who you are currently following. In the toolbar at the top right of Visual Studio, there is a collection of circles, one for each participant. They contain the initials for the participant, but if you hover over them, the full name is visible.

The double circle surrounding the BJ participant indicates that you are currently following that person. You can stop following at any time by clicking the circle, or by clicking the circle of another participant.

As well as on the toolbar, the Live Share pane also indicates who you are currently following. Each of the other users is visible in a list under the Participant's node. Next to each name is a circle. If the circle is hollow, then you are not following that person. If the circle has a center dot (as seen in Figure 6-11), then you are following that person. You can change who you follow by clicking another participant. Or you can stop following someone by clicking their name. There are also context menu options to follow and unfollow individuals.

If you are in a Live Share session, there might be times when you want the other participants to pay attention to what you're doing. This is accomplished using a feature called Focus. You send a notification to each of the participants, requesting that they follow you.

You can send the Focus notification through two different techniques. First, in the toolbar at the top right of Visual Studio, there is a dropdown that is labeled either Sharing (if you're the host) or Joined (if you're a participant). This dropdown contains a number of execution points for Live Share commands. In this instance, from that dropdown, select Focus Participants. This generates a notification that is sent to each participant (seen in Figure 6-12).

Figure 6-12. *Focus notification*

As well as the notification, the participants are automatically set to follow you. Naturally, they can always choose to unfollow, using the techniques mentioned in the previous paragraphs.

Co-debugging

One of the more useful features offered by Live Share is the ability to collaboratively participate in a debugging session. Starting a co-debugging session is as simple as launching a debugging session in Visual Studio. Once the host's debugger has attached to the process, each of the participants' Visual Studio instances is connected to the debugging session. From the participants' perspective, it looks and feels like they are debugging locally.

When breakpoints are hit, the instances for each participant stop as well. Again, the look is like a typical debugging session. And, in fact, the participant can explore the values associated with the debugging session in the same manner as if they were running it locally. Consider the two Visual Studio instances displayed in Figure 6-13.

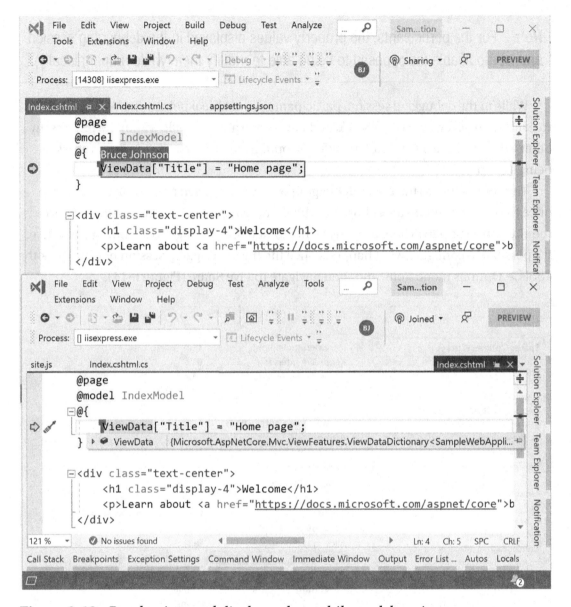

Figure 6-13. *Breakpoints and display values while co-debugging*

The hosting session is the instance that appears at the top of Figure 6-13. However, in the bottom instance, hovering over the ViewData variables displays the tool tip that contains the current property values.

Note   For the participants, the property values displayed in the debugging session are not modifiable (as opposed to being able to modify them while running locally).

While in the debugging session, participants can set breakpoints, view values of the variables in use, review the call stack, and navigate to any other file within the process. In other words, you are free to explore different options to help identify cause for the issue being examined.

The connection to the host's debugging session happened automatically. That is, once the host was set up for debugging, the participants were attached with no effort required on their part. There are times when that behavior might be counterproductive. It's possible to configure what happens once the host debugging session begins. Click the Tools ➤ Options menu item, and then navigate to Live Share (Figure 6-14).

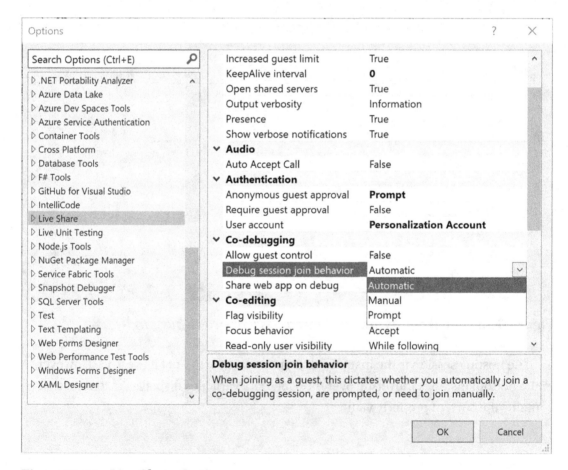

Figure 6-14. Live Share Options

The Debug session join behavior options are Automatic (the default), Manual (so that you have to join the session using the technique described in the next paragraph), and Prompt.

You might not be connected to the host's debugging session, because you have chosen the Manual option, responded No when prompted, or just stopped the debugging session (which stops you from following it, but the session continues for everyone else). If you wish to join a running debug session, you can do so in the same manner that you start a local debugging session. In the toolbar, the Run option includes a dropdown providing you with a number of startup options. Figure 6-15 illustrates an example while you are in a Live Share session.

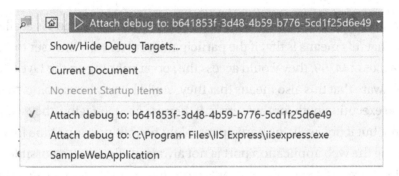

Figure 6-15. *Run options while in Live Share*

Choosing the item that indicates that you're attaching to a GUID will join you to the Live Share debugging session. The GUID is the same GUID that appears in the link that is used to connect to a Live Share session.

Shared Servers

Modern applications can be a complex network of different servers. Authentication servers, microservice endpoints, and REST-based endpoints all can be part of a running application. When engaging others in the process of debugging, it can be helpful to allow Live Share participants to have access to the different endpoints. That way they can interact with the application in a manner similar to what happens when debugging locally.

When you launch a web application for a co-debugging session, the web server is automatically shared with other participants. You can see the shared server in the Live Share pane (Figure 6-16).

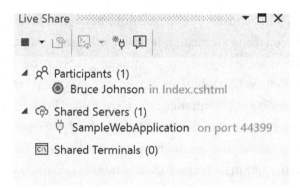

Figure 6-16. *Live Share pane with a shared server*

In this example, the web application called SampleWebApplication is available on port 44399. What this means is that if the participant were to use a browser to navigate to `http://localhost:44399`, they would access the server running on the Live Share host's machine. Be aware that this also means that they would hit any breakpoints that have been defined in the execution path for that server. If they are co-debugging, they would see the breakpoint hit, but if not, well, the participant might be waiting a long time for a response.

But sharing the web application port is not always sufficient. It's possible for the host to specifically share additional servers for the participants to interact with. This is done by using the Manage Shared Servers command. You can click the icon in the Live Share pane toolbar (second from the right in Figure 6-16) or use the Sharing dropdown in the Visual Studio toolbar. The Shared Local Servers can be seen in Figure 6-17.

Server Name	Port	
SampleWebApplication	44399	Add
		Remove
		Open in Browser
		Copy to Clipboard

Shared Local Servers

Ok   Cancel

Figure 6-17. *Shared Local Servers dialog*

This dialog is used to manage the servers running on the host's machine that are accessible by the Live Share participants. At the moment that the image for Figure 6-17 was captured, the SampleWebApplication server is running. A different server can be added by clicking the Add button. You will need to provide a port number and a name for the server. Once the server is added, it will become visible in the Live Share pane for the participants. And they will be able to access it through browser or code or whatever method they prefer.

On this dialog, you can also remove shared servers (by selecting and then clicking Remove), open the particular server in a browser window, or copy the URL for the server to the clipboard.

Shared Terminal

There might be times when command-line functionality needs to be used by or demonstrated to Live Share participants. To support this, Live Share includes the ability to share a terminal session with participants. This means that they can see commands that the host enters into a terminal window, as well as the results. It also means that they can execute commands themselves.

In both cases, sharing a terminal session is started from one of two places within the host's environment. From the Live Share pane, click the Share Terminal icon (third from the right, seen in Figure 6-18) and choose from one of the two options.

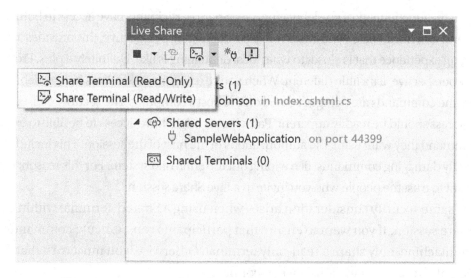

Figure 6-18. *Sharing a terminal in the Live Share pane*

Alternatively, the Sharing icon in the Visual Studio toolbar includes the same two options visible in Figure 6-18.

And there are two choices available to you. In the first, the Read-Only terminal, you are sharing the terminal window, along with all the contents to each participant. But you are not sharing the ability for the participants to execute commands. With the second option, the Read-Write terminal, you are allowing participants to execute their own commands, complete with all the potential security implications of that ability.

With either option, sharing a terminal will launch a separate terminal window. At least, that's the default behavior for Visual Studio. As Visual Studio doesn't include an integrated terminal window out-of-the-box, a separate window is a requirement. However, you will see a notification below the toolbar (shown in Figure 6-19).

Figure 6-19. *Terminal sharing notification*

One of the links in the notification message, Install integrated terminal, will direct you to the Visual Studio Marketplace where you can install the Whack Whack Extension, an integrated terminal window for Visual Studio.

Security in Live Share

As part of the functionality of co-debugging, Live Share participants have access to both the Command and Immediate windows. From a co-debugging perspective, this provides a rich debugging experience that is closer to what local debugging is like. Definitely a plus. From a security perspective, it's a little different. When you're using these windows in a co-debugging session, the commands are being executed on the host's computer. The security consequences of this access should be readily apparent. Participants might have access to be able to execute any command they want using the authorizations of the host of the session. This includes potentially damaging commands, like wiping out the entire file system. For this reason, it's important to trust the people who you invite to a Live Share session.

The same security consideration arises when using a Shared Terminal within a Live Share session. If you want to ensure that participants can't execute commands on your machine, only share a read-only terminal. Otherwise, you must trust that the participants won't act maliciously while connected.

Along the same lines, while editing within a Live Share session, it's possible for participants to see the entire file tree of the shared project. And the participants don't need to be following you, allowing them to navigate through the tree at will. If there are secrets embedded into the files (like server or database passwords), they could be discovered by the participants.

When it comes to file access, it is possible to mitigate some of the risks. The .vsls. json file contains settings that are used to control the access that participants have to the files. The following is an example of a .vsls.json file:

```
{
    "$schema": "http://json.schemastore.org/vsls",
    "gitignore":"none",
    "excludeFiles":[
        "*.cer",
        "*.config",
        ".gitignore"
    ],
    "hideFiles": [
        "bin",
        "obj"
    ]
}
```

There are three attributes in the file that are used to control access:

- excludeFiles – Defines a list of files and folders that participants are not allowed to open. This restriction includes instances where you might expect to have access to these files, such as when you're stepping into a file during a debugging session. The intent is to include files that should never be visible to participants.

- hideFiles – Defines a list of files and folders that are not visible in the tree. However, the participants will be able to navigate to the files if it comes up through navigation (like going to a definition) or during debugging.

- gitignore – By default, files that are in the .gitignore file are treated as if they were hidden. However, you can change that behavior using this attribute. The possible values are as follows:

  - none – The .gitignore contents have no impact on what's visible in the project tree.

  - hide – The .gitignore contents are treated as if they are part of the hideFiles attribute.

  - exclude – The .gitignore contents are treated as if they were part of the excludeFiles attribute.

There is one potential issue when using the exclude option for the gitignore attribute. Frequently, the node_modules directory is included in the .gitignore file. But it can be useful to debug into the files in node_modules while trying to isolate behavior. To alleviate this problem, Live Share supports the ability to negate visibility defined in .gitignore. For example, the following .vsls.json file would still allow you to debug into the node_module files, even though they had been excluded in the .gitignore file:

```
{
    "$schema": "http://json.schemastore.org/vsls",
    "gitignore":"exclude",
    "excludeFiles":[
        "!node_modules"
    ],
    "hideFiles": [
        "node_modules"
    ]
}
```

Note also the use of node_modules in the hideFiles attribute. The exclusion and hiding logic are processed independently of one another. So this setting would allow the node_modules files to be hidden from the solution tree (to reduce clutter), but would still allow the files to be viewed or stepped into.

Summary

Collaboration has definitely been a focus for the features added to Visual Studio 2019. Live Sharing in particular has the potential to help greatly when it comes to solving particularly pernicious bugs. Having multiple eyes on the issue is good. Having people look over your shoulder while your debugging is better. Allowing the participants to poke and prod at your code while also debugging gives a high degree of flexibility, which is just what is needed when working through challenging issues.

However, the co-debugging option is not the only debugging feature that has been added to Visual Studio 2019. In the next chapter, we look at some of the other debugging functionality that has been added, all in service of trying to make it easier to track down issues.

CHAPTER 7

Debugging and Profiling

As a developer, you are going to spend a large part of your time debugging code. Not your code, naturally. Your code is completely covered by unit tests and has no bugs whatsoever. But other people's code. People who don't have the benefit of your many years of experience, or your skills in crafting bulletproof solutions. Or maybe third-party or open source code. Sometimes there are bugs in those too.

Hopefully the tongue-in-cheek nature of that opening paragraph was obvious. But the point is still valid. You are going to spend a significant portion of your time debugging your application. And Visual Studio has a large number of tools available to help with the process. Because it's a process that, at least on occasion, requires all the help you can get.

This chapter is not going to talk about the basics of debugging applications in Visual Studio. The presumption is that the techniques of setting breakpoints, viewing the current value of variables, and using the Locals, Watch, and Quick Watch features are already well understood. None of those are new to Visual Studio 2019, having been in the developer's arsenal for years. Instead, the focus will be on features that have been introduced or enhanced in Visual Studio 2019, or are just useful but underappreciated.

Breakpoints

It might seem odd, after that introduction, to start by talking about breakpoints. After all, breakpoints are the grand old man of debugging techniques. They designate a place within your application where execution should halt and give you the chance to examine the current state of the runtime. It's one of the first things that would be taught to any developer. But there are parts of using breakpoints that are underutilized. And one of the more exciting additions to Visual Studio 2019 happens to target this venerable piece of functionality.

As was just mentioned, breakpoints are used to pause your application at a specific line of code. However, the default behavior is to pause whenever that line of code is hit. For certain situations, that's great. For others, it's not. You might want more control over when execution is paused for a given breakpoint.

© Bruce Johnson 2020
B. Johnson, *Essential Visual Studio 2019*, https://doi.org/10.1007/978-1-4842-5719-7_7

Conditional Breakpoints

You can add conditions to the breakpoint through the Breakpoint Settings pane. This pane is accessed through the Settings option on the context menu that appears when you right-click a breakpoint indicator (in the left gutter of the editor). The context menu, seen in Figure 7-1, includes a number of options useful for more advance breakpoint functionality.

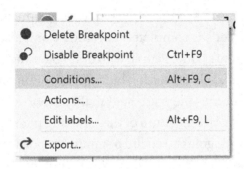

Figure 7-1. *Context menu for a breakpoint*

Click the Conditions option to display the pane, shown in Figure 7-2.

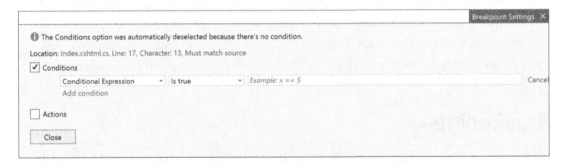

Figure 7-2. *Breakpoint Settings pane for defining conditions*

There are a number of options available for determining the type of condition applied to the breakpoint. First, there is a dropdown containing the type of the condition being used. There are three options available.

Conditional Expression

The premise is that the large text box on the right of the line where the condition is defined will contain an expression. The middle field contains a dropdown that controls how the expression is used. There are two choices in the dropdown. For the Is true option, if the expression evaluates to True, then execution stops at the breakpoint. For the When changed option, execution halts the first time the line on which the breakpoint has been set is encountered. The expression is evaluated, and the value is remembered. Then each subsequent time the breakpoint is hit, the expression is again evaluated using the current variables. If the result is different than the previous value, execution stops at the breakpoint.

Note   If you're debugging native code, the behavior is slightly different for the When changed option. In that instance, the debugger doesn't consider the first evaluation to be a change in value. The result being that the first time the breakpoint is hit, execution does not stop.

The language used for the expression depends on the language of the file in which the breakpoint is set. A C# file will use a C# expression. A JavaScript file will use a JavaScript expression. Determining the relationship between file type and expression language for other situations is left as an exercise for the reader.

While the expression does have IntelliSense, it does not do immediate syntax checking. And it certainly can't tell if your expression will generate a runtime exception. In both of those cases, execution is halted at the breakpoint the first time it happens. That is, in the case of a syntax error, the first time the breakpoint is encountered, and for a runtime exception, the first time the exception is thrown.

When you have collection of objects, using the conditional expression can get frustrating. There is no obvious way to distinguish between the different objects in the collection short of creating additional conditions tied to a unique property in the object. Visual Studio 2019 provides a mechanism that allows you to generate an object ID that can then be used in the breakpoint expression. In the Locals window, right-click the desired object and select Make Object ID from the context menu (Figure 7-3).

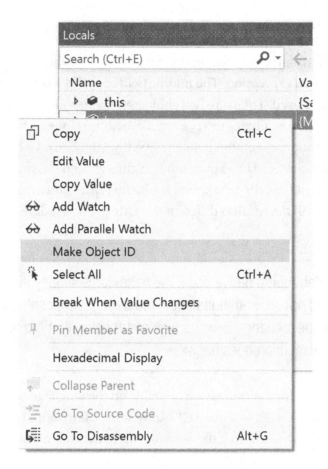

Figure 7-3. *Context menu for a Locals variable*

A new variable is now added to the Locals window (Figure 7-4).

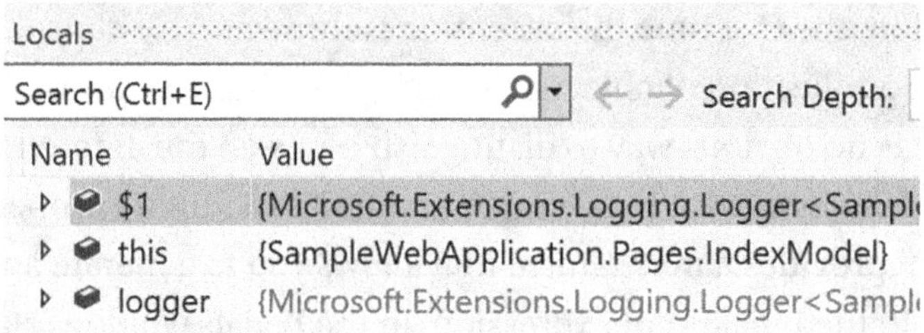

Figure 7-4. *Object ID tracking variable*

The format for the variable name is $n where n is a sequential number. To use this object identifier in the conditional breakpoint, you would add the expression `item ==` $n, where $n is the object identifier.

As useful as this option might be, there are a couple of drawbacks. First, object identifier does not live past the current debugging session. You would need to make an object identifier for each debugging session. There's a possibility that the numeric part of the identifier would be the same (the sequential number is reset to 1 with each debugging session), but that something you should make sure of.

Also, the relationship between the original object and the tracking object is a weak reference. What this means is that existence of the tracking object will not prevent the original object from being garbage collected. Depending on the specific situation you are debugging, this could be a significant issue.

Hit Count

There are times when conditions just don't cut it. Instead, you want the execution to break after a line has been executed a certain number of times. This would be common if you have code that is being executed in a loop or is accessed many times by other parts of your application.

Defining a hit count condition is done through the same Breakpoint Settings pane. The difference is that the first dropdown is set to Hit Count (Figure 7-5).

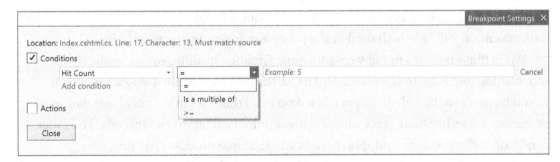

Figure 7-5. *Hit Count settings for a breakpoint*

The expression for a hit count is numeric. In fact, no nonnumeric input is allowed. How this number is processed depends on the value in the middle dropdown. The choices available are as follows:

> Equals (=) – Execution is halted when the breakpoint has been hit the number of times found in the expression.

> Is a multiple of – Execution is halted when the number of times a breakpoint has been hit is an even multiple of the number in the expression.

> Greater than or equal (>=) – Execution is halted when the breakpoint has been hit the number of times found in the expression. And then execution is halted every time after that.

Filter

Applications have long since reached a point where multiple applications need to be running in order to function. One of the strengths of Visual Studio is the ability to start more than one application as part of a debugging session. However, this can cause a bit of a problem with debugging such a solution. When execution is halted at a breakpoint, all of the processes are halted, not just the one in which the breakpoint is located.

There is a setting that can change this behavior. In the Tools ➤ Options dialog, navigate to the Debugging ➤ General node. There, near the top of the list, you'll find an option named Break All Processes When One Process Breaks. If you uncheck that option, then execution will only be halted in the process containing the breakpoint.

While that's nice, it's not always sufficient. Creating multithreaded applications is becoming much more common. And those threads run within a single process. It would be useful to be able to target a breakpoint so that execution only halts within a single thread, rather than every time the breakpoint is hit across all threads. The Filter condition is designed for multiple threads and multiple process targeting.

Figure 7-6 illustrates the Breakpoint Settings pane for a Filter condition.

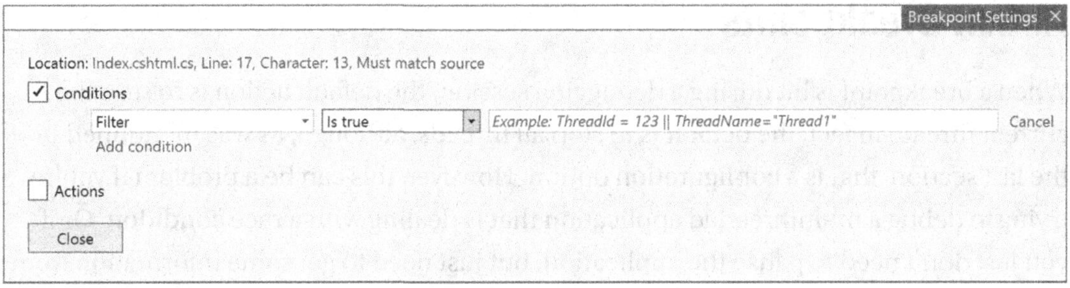

Figure 7-6. *Filter settings for a breakpoint*

The first two fields have no options. The third field is the expression. And it too is limited. While the expression can have ANDs (&), ORs (||), NOTs (!), and parentheses, the values that can be tested are restricted to thread, process, and machine values. Specifically, the ThreadId, ThreadName, ProcessId, ProcessName, and MachineName can be used.

Additional Settings

You might have noticed that there is an Add condition link that appears below the condition type dropdown. Once you have any condition filled in, you have the ability to add additional conditions, with the caveat that you can only add one condition of each type. In other words, you can have a breakpoint where execution halts when the Hit Count is 5 and the ProcessName is "demo.exe". But you can't have a breakpoint where the condition is "Hit Count is 5 and Hit Count is 7".

As well as multiple conditions, you can also be precise about where the breakpoint gets placed. This is useful if you have more than one statement on a single line of code. At the top of the pane, there is a location where the breakpoint is set. Clicking the value allows you to edit the values directly, as can be seen in Figure 7-7.

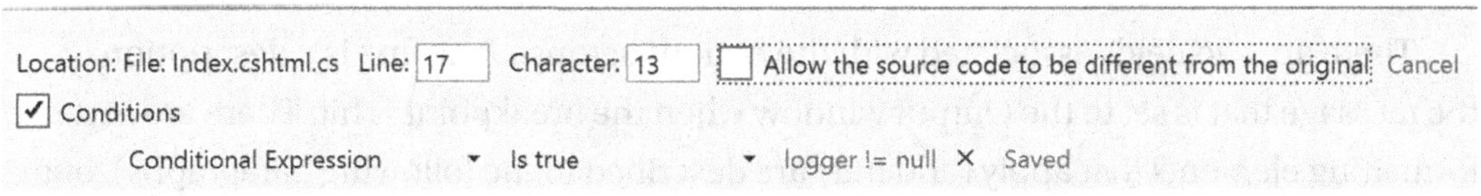

Figure 7-7. *Setting the location for a breakpoint*

Here you can specify the line number within the source code file and the character position within that line. And there is a check box to indicate whether you're willing to allow the breakpoint to be active if the current source code is different than one used to compile the executable that's running.

241

Action Breakpoints

When a breakpoint is hit during a debugging session, the default action is to stop the current thread. In fact, the default is to stop all threads, although, as was mentioned in the last section, that is a configuration option. However, this can be a problem if you're trying to debug a multithreaded application that is dealing with a race condition. Or if you just don't need to pause the application, but just need to get some information from the debugger at the time the breakpoint is hit.

These scenarios can be addressed with an action breakpoint, also known as a tracepoint. Creating an action breakpoint is the same as creating a regular breakpoint. In fact, it's what you do with the settings for a breakpoint that makes it an action breakpoint. As with the conditional breakpoint, right-click the breakpoint indicator (in the left gutter of the editor) and choose Actions from the context menu. The Breakpoint Settings pane appears, this time with the Actions visible, as seen in Figure 7-8.

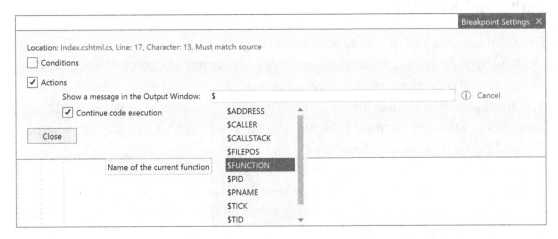

Figure 7-8. *Actions settings in the Breakpoint pane*

There are two fields associated with the Actions settings. The first is a description of the message that is set to the Output window when the breakpoint is hit. There are several formatting elements that apply (and they are described in the following paragraphs), but that is the basic purpose of the action breakpoint. In this way, it is similar to a Debug or a Trace statement in your code. The difference is that the Action breakpoint is dynamically set and therefore doesn't require a recompilation of your application.

The second field is a check box indicating whether the execution of the program should continue when the breakpoint is hit. By default, the application does not pause execution. In this way, it's the exact opposite of a regular breakpoint, and this behavior works well in the multithreaded scenario described at the beginning of the section. However, if you still want execution to pause, then clear this check box.

The message to be displayed is not an expression. That is to say, the expectation is not that a string value will be defined, complete with concatenation symbols. Instead, the format is closer to the templating you use in a `String.Format` string, with special variables used for intrinsic values and a curly brace notation for variable values. For example, consider the following:

`$FUNCTION: The value of x.y is {x.y}`

When this action breakpoint is encountered, we will start with the name of the current function (i.e., the `$FUNCTION` value), followed by the string `The value of x.y is` and then the value of the `y` property on the `x` object. So the message consists of a combination of built-in variables, text, and curly brace notation for local variable values.

The list of built-in variables is available through IntelliSense (and visible in Figure 7-8). The meaning of each is found in the following:

$ADDRESS – The current instructions

$CALLER – The name of the function that called the current method

$CALLSTACK – The current call stack

$FILEPOS – The current position within the code file

$FUNCTION – The name of the current function

$PID – The current process ID

$PNAME – The name of the current process

$TICK – The current tick count

$TID – The current thread ID

$TNAME – The name of the current thread

The presence of an action breakpoint (as opposed to a regular breakpoint) is indicated by a different breakpoint indicator. Instead of the red circle, a red diamond appears in the left gutter of the editor, although that is only true if the `Continue code execution` check box is checked. If it is unchecked, then the red circle appears as usual.

Function Breakpoints

One of the underlying premises of setting breakpoints manually, whether you add conditions or not, is that you have access to the source code where you want to apply the breakpoint. You can open up the file, find the line in question, and apply a breakpoint. But it's not always the case where that is going to work. Visual Studio 2019 provides a couple of different functions which are designed to help in these situations.

Function breakpoints are intended to be used when you know the name of the function where you would like to pause execution, but you don't know where in the source code the file is found. Or if you have a number of overloads of a function, using a function breakpoint is easier than putting a breakpoint into each of the overload methods.

A function breakpoint is created using the Debug menu, specifically selecting Debug ➤ New Breakpoint ➤ Function Breakpoint. The dialog seen in Figure 7-9 appears.

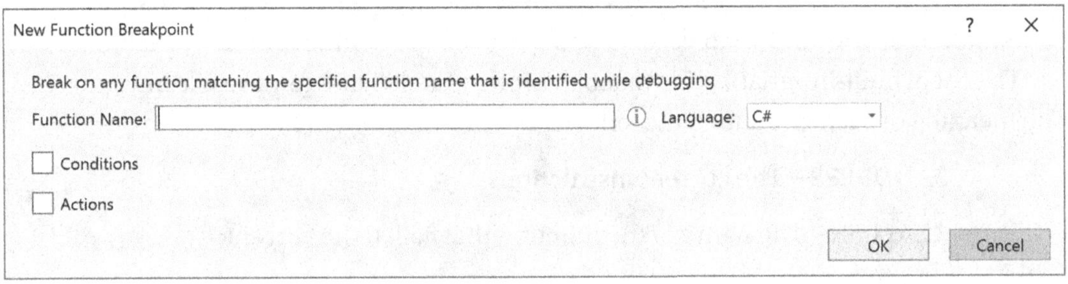

Figure 7-9. *Function Breakpoint dialog*

In the lower half of the dialog, there are two check boxes, labeled Conditions and Actions. These are used to set any conditions you want to apply to the breakpoint, or any actions that should occur when the breakpoint is reached. These work the same as the Conditions and Actions found in the regular breakpoint dialog. The options initiated with these check boxes are described in the "Conditional Breakpoints" and "Action Breakpoints" sections earlier in this chapter.

What sets function breakpoints apart from other breakpoints is how you define when execution is paused. That is accomplished in the Function Name text box. At its simplest, you enter the name of the function. The name must be fully qualified, so, for example, it would look something like the following:

```
SampleApplication.Models.Order.Add()
```

In this example, the namespace for the method is `SampleApplication.Models`. The name of the class containing the method is `Order`, and the name of the method is `Add`. Also notice the parentheses with no parameters. This notation would match every call to `Add` regardless of the parameters used. In other words, it will break on every overloaded instance of the `Add` method.

The goal of the Function Name is to provide as much specificity or variability as you need to break at the appropriate time. For instance, while the preceding example will break on all `Add` methods, regardless of the signature, you can be more accurate with the breakpoint by providing parameters and data types.

```
SampleApplication.Models.Order.Add(Customer c)
```

Now execution is paused only if a single parameter of type `Customer` is passed into the `Add` method.

Instead of using a namespace for the method, you can specify the module in which the method is found. For example, the following would pause execution when the Add method is called from the Order.dll module.

```
Order.dll!Add
```

Finally, if you are debugging in native C++, you can include the offset in the information used to identify the breakpoint location.

```
{Add, , Order.dll}+2
```

This notation sets a breakpoint at the second line from the start of the Add method in the Order.dll module.

The other field related to the function name is the Language dropdown. This is used to impact the syntax that you use to declare the function name. The example shown previously, passing a parameter into the method, was using C# syntax, which means that the Language property would need to be set to C#. The dropdown contains a number of different choices, including JavaScript, TypeScript, F#, and Basic. The syntax used to define the function name needs to match the language that has been selected.

Data Breakpoints

A new feature for Visual Studio 2019 is the concept of a data breakpoint. The idea is that instead of breaking at a line of code, execution is paused when the value of a variable changes. This is an incredibly powerful idea, as quite regularly the key to solving a bug is identifying where in the application the value of a variable is modified. And while this functionality is already available for C++ developers, it has been a regular request for managed code developers for a long time.

First, the bad news. At the moment, creating a data breakpoint is only available in .NET Core 3.0 or higher. On the plus side, .NET Core 3.0 supports Windows desktop applications using WPF or Windows Forms, so the limitations you have on the types of applications you can use have been significantly reduced. But if you're not running on .NET Core 3.0, then this functionality is not available to you.

To set a data breakpoint in managed code, you need to be running your application. Then in either the Locals, Autos, or Watch window, right-click the property you want to watch and select Break When Value Changes from the context menu. Figure 7-10 shows this sequence in action.

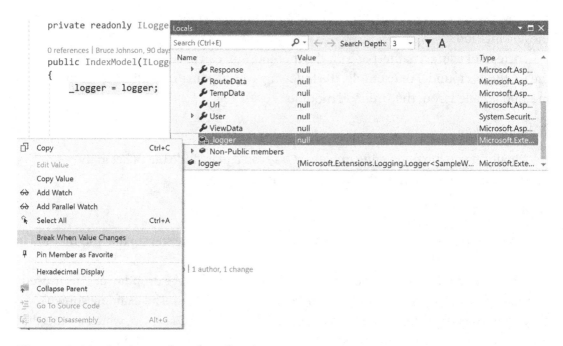

Figure 7-10. *Setting a data breakpoint*

Once the breakpoint is set, there will be a red circle next to the variable in the window.

During execution, if the value of a variable is changed, then execution pauses and a message appears indicating the reason for the breakpoint. Figure 7-11 illustrates the message.

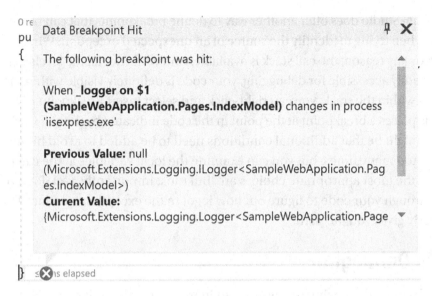

Figure 7-11. Message that appears for a data breakpoint

At this point, your execution has been paused and you have access to all of the typical debugging information and functionality.

Note   As a word of caution, the data breakpoint is fired when the value of a variable changes. If you associate the breakpoint with an object, that works just fine. But setting a breakpoint on an object won't pause execution when a property within that object is modified. To do that, you would need to expand the object within the Locals/Auto/Watch window and select the property within that object that you want to watch. And, just to emphasize the point, the data breakpoint is instance sensitive. If you have two instances of the same class, then a data breakpoint set on the property of one will not cause execution to pause if the same property on the second is modified.

Using the Call Stack to Define Breakpoints

For large applications, one of the challenges of debugging is getting the breakpoint set at the right place. Set it too early in the execution and you will spend a long time using the Step Into and Step Over functions. Set it too late and, well, it's too late to be any good. This was actually one of the reasons why judicial use of conditional breakpoints can be so valuable.

But Visual Studio does offer another way to define breakpoints that can be quite useful, especially when trying to identify the source of an unexpected exception. When execution is paused for any reason, the call stack is available. And while not all the levels in the call stack are readily accessible for debugging, your code is definitely visible within the stack. At any level within the stack, you can right-click and select Insert Breakpoint in the context menu. This places a breakpoint at the point in the code indicated by the call stack.

Now it might be that additional conditions need to be added to avoid hitting the breakpoint too many times, but you can examine the local variables at the call point to see what the most appropriate choices are. But most importantly, you don't need to navigate through your code to figure out how it got to the exception location. The call stack already gives you the path.

Remote Debugging

The lure of remote debugging is ever-present in troublesome production applications. How many times have you developed and tested an application locally, and even in a staging environment, only to have it encounter brand-new issues once it has been deployed into production.

Through the use of a small executable, it is possible for you to debug a remote application in the same manner as a local one, which is to say that breakpoint and step-through functionality are available, as is the ability to view the value of variables. The key to this is that small executable and the details behind exactly which one to use.

The first step is to download the appropriate executable. The starting point is to download the Remote Tools for Visual Studio 2019. You can find the link to download it at `https://visualstudio.microsoft.com/downloads/#remote-tools-for-visual-studio-2019`. A portion of the page itself can be seen in Figure 7-12.

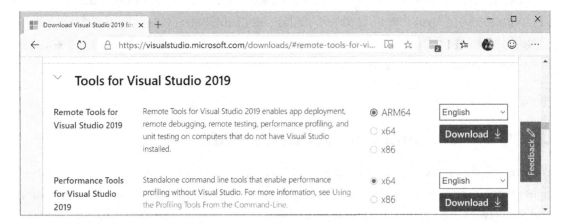

Figure 7-12. *Download page for Remote Tools for Visual Studio 2019*

The trick is to download the correct set of tools. There is a set of radio buttons to the right of the description for ARM64, x64, and X86. This option should be set to the architecture of the target machine, not the one on which you'll be running Visual Studio.

The Remote Tools consist of the Remote Debugging Monitor and the Remote Debugger Configuration wizard. At the simplest deployment, you can just copy the Remote Debugging Monitor (msvsmon.exe) to the target machine and execute it. Realize that the monitor needs to be executed each time that you want to initialize a debugging session. The purpose of the configuration wizard is to help you set up the Remote Debugging Monitor as a Windows Service, allowing remote debugging on a more regular basis without additional effort required by the developer or IT personnel.

When you execute the Remote Debugging Monitor, it's important that you have administrator access to the machine. This can be down by either logging in as an administrator or using the Run As Administrator option in the context menu for the application. When the application launches, the interface can be seen in Figure 7-13.

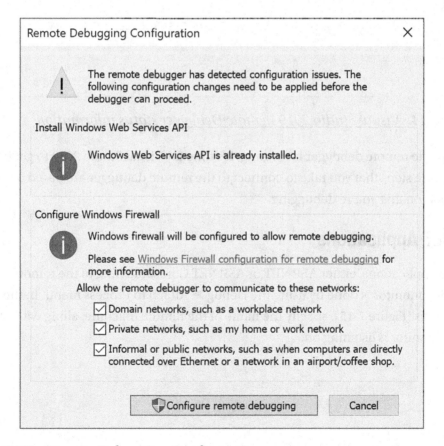

Figure 7-13. Remote Debugging Configuration

The Remote Debugging Monitor requires both the Window Web Services API to be installed and the Windows Firewall configured to allow remote access to the port that is used by Visual Studio to communicate with the monitor. The necessary options to configure the remote machine are available through this dialog, which appears only if your current configuration doesn't allow for remoted debugging. The only options you have are which networks should be allowed to remotely debug. As a standard security practice, it is recommended to choose only those options that you really need. While checking all of them works, it does have the potential to open up an attack vector for the machine on which it is running.

When the monitor starts, it displays a screen that contains status information. Figure 7-14 shows the dialog when it starts.

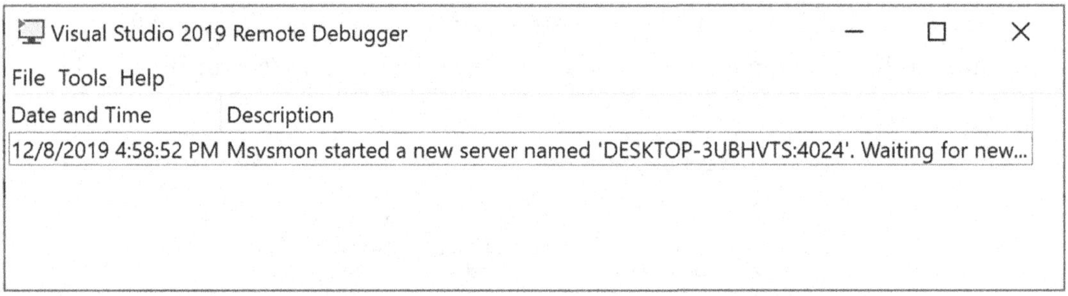

Figure 7-14. *Visual Studio 2019 Remote Debugger status information*

Once the remote debugger is running, it's time for Visual Studio 2019 to get into the act. Now the steps that you take to connect to the remote debugger are based on the type of application that you're debugging.

ASP.NET Applications

For Web applications, either ASP.NET or ASP.NET Core, attaching to the remote debugging monitor is done by using the Debug ➤ Attach to Process menu. In the dialog that appears (Figure 7-15), specify the name of the remote machine, along with the port that the monitor is listening on.

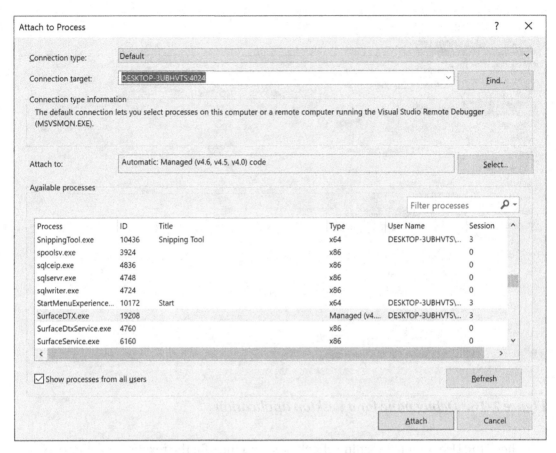

Figure 7-15. *Attaching to a remote process for debugging*

By default, for Visual Studio 2019, that port is 4024. The list might already include the process that you're looking for, but if not, check the Show processes from all users to get every running process into the list. Attach to the desired process (which would typically be a w3wp.exe process) and the debugging session begins.

Desktop Applications

For desktop applications, the configuration of remote debugging takes place within the properties for the project. Open the Properties pane (by right-clicking the project and selecting Properties) and navigate to the Debug section, shown in Figure 7-16.

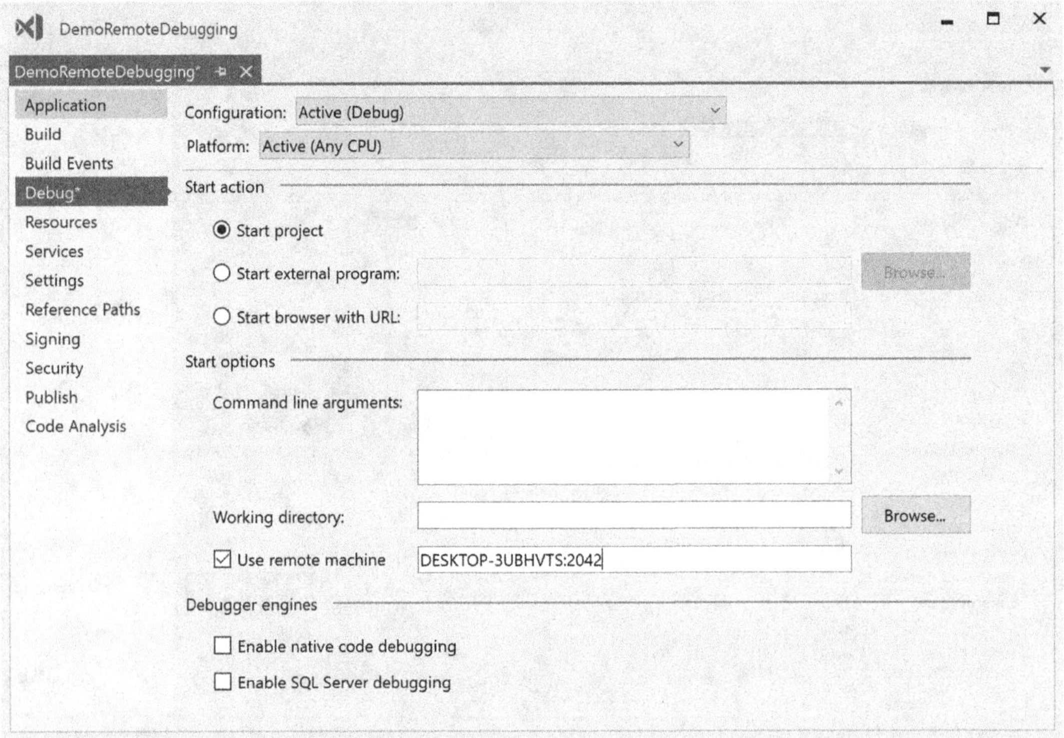

Figure 7-16. *Debug pane for a desktop application*

Check the Use remote machine check box, and then fill the text box that appears to the right with the name and port number of the remote machine. A couple of other conditions need to be met before you can start debugging. First, the Working directory field needs to be empty, and the Enable native code debugging check box must be unchecked. The working directory needs to be empty because you'll be running the application on the remote machine, so having a working directory specified locally isn't going to be effective. And native code debugging is not currently supported for remote debugging.

The last major requirement is that the debug version of the application that you want to debug needs to be on the remote machine in the same path where the debug instance of the application would be found locally. That is to say that everything folder in the path needs to match up, including the .../bin/Debug folders (by default). Typically, the workflow would be to build the application, then copy it to the remote machine using your favorite method, and then launch the debug session.

Azure Applications

If you have deployed your application into Azure, you still have the ability to debug it remotely. Again, the path depends on the type of deployment. If you loaded your application into a virtual machine (VM), the steps to remotely debug are the same as for an ASP.NET or a desktop application, depending on the application you have running on the VM. However, if you deployed into an Azure App Service, the steps are a little different. Start by opening the Server Explorer and expanding the Azure node (Figure 7-17).

Figure 7-17.   *Azure node in Server Explorer*

When you click the Open Cloud Explorer option, found under the App Service node, it launches the Cloud Explorer. The tree found in that pane includes all of the Azure subscriptions that you have access to using the current credentials used in Visual Studio. If you haven't logged in, you'll be prompted to provide credentials for Azure before continuing. Figure 7-18 illustrates the Cloud Explorer with the App Services node expanded.

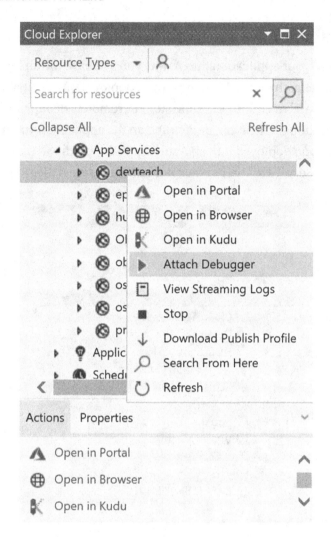

Figure 7-18. *App Services node in Cloud Explorer*

Right-click the App Service that you want to debug. In the context menu that appears (and it might take a few seconds), select Attach Debugger. This connects to you to remote debugger in the same manner as the ASP.NET application section described earlier.

Snapshot Debugging

The other holy grail for debugging applications is working to address issues that arise in production. It's a rare developer that hasn't encountered that "but it's working on my machine" feeling. And while the increasing use of testing and staging environments that mimic production has reduced the frequency, there are still instances where applications that work in earlier environment have issues in production. And the idea of setting breakpoints and stepping through code, with the associated halting of all other threads, while people are really using a website is a nonstarter.

The aim of the Snapshot Debugger is to help to address this situation. At appropriate points during the execution of the application, a snapshot of the state of the application is taken. This process takes about 10–20 milliseconds, so there is a moderate impact on performance. But the overall impact should be negligible to the overall user experience.

In Visual Studio 2019, you need to have the Snapshot Debugger component installed. This is part of the ASP.NET and web development workload. As well, your application needs to be running in one of a number of different environments: Azure App Service, an Azure virtual machine, or an ASP.NET app running in a Kubernetes service, in all cases, an ASP.NET app running on at least .NET Framework 4.6.1 or .NET Core 2.0.

In general, the flow for performing snapshot debugging is to open the solution that you want to debug. Then attach to the snapshot debugger by specifying the endpoint for the application. At this point you are debugging the application, but not in the usual way. Instead of specifying breakpoints, you specify snappoints. The process is similar to setting breakpoints. However instead of pausing execution and allowing you to view local state, a copy of local state is made and execution continues. You can still view local state, but the application is not paused... something that is pretty critical when you're dealing with production.

Now let's walk through the steps in a little more detail. To start, open up the solution for the deployed application. It's important that the source matches the deployed version. If not, you'll run into the same problem that you get when you debug a local project using outdated source code, which is to say that your snappoints would be hit. In fact, mismatched source code is the leading cause for issues when attempting snapshot debugging, so if you find yourself not able to follow along, that should be the first place you look.

Once the solution is read, select the Debug ➤ Attach Snapshot Debugger menu item. The dialog seen in Figure 7-19 appears.

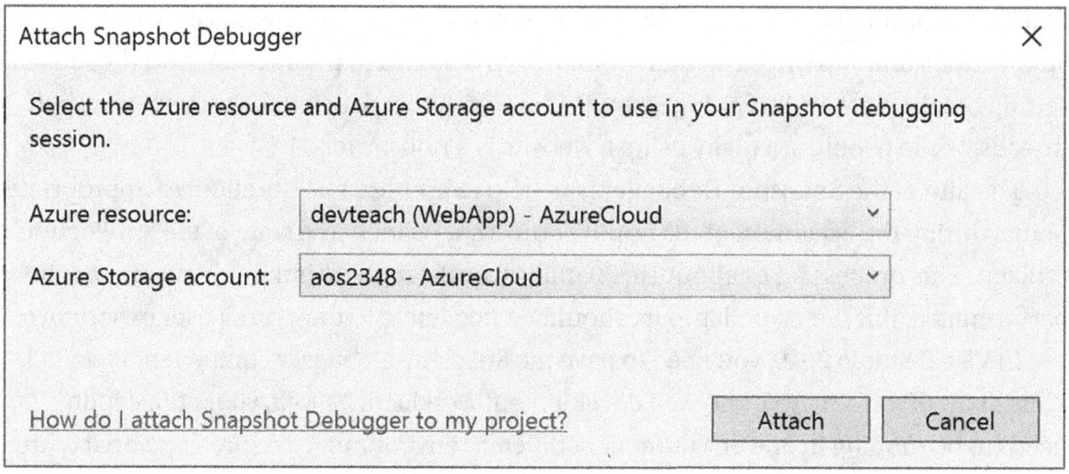

Figure 7-19.. *Attaching to a Snapshot Debugger*

This dialog remembers the last entries that you made, so the first time you attach, both the dropdowns will be empty. In both cases, the dropdown brings up a dialog like the one seen in Figure 7-20.

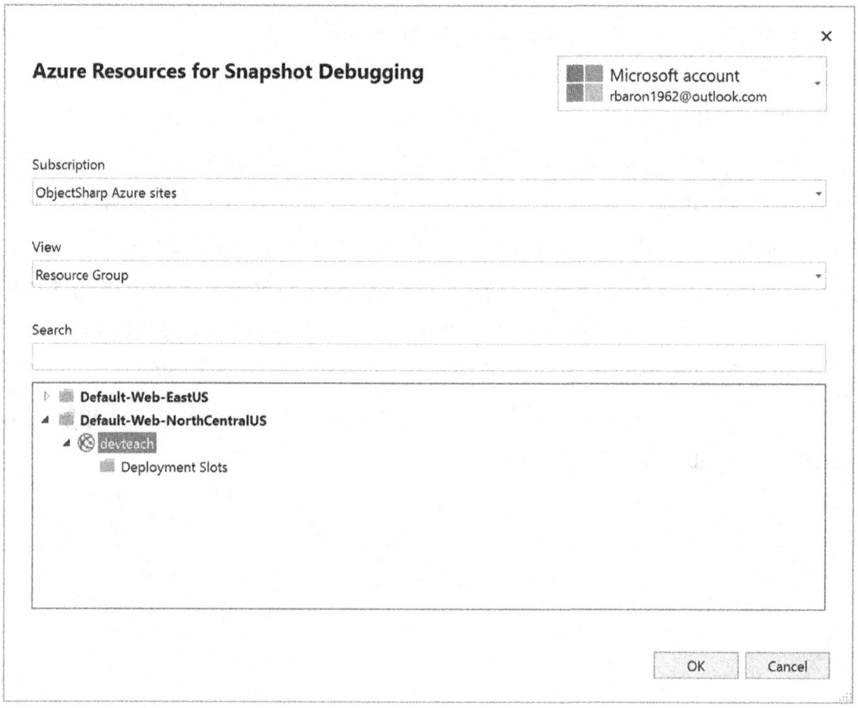

Figure 7-20. *Choosing an Azure Resource*

The purpose of the dropdown values is to let you identify the azure resource that you want to debug and the storage account that will be used to contain the snapshot information. For both dropdowns, you select the Azure subscription and then the App Service, virtual machine or Kubernetes service (for the Azure Resource value) or the storage account (for the Store Account value).

When both values have been specified, click the Attach button in Figure 7-19 and wait while the debugging session begins. If this is the first time you have used Snapshot debugging on chosen resource, you will see a dialog like Figure 7-21 asking for your permission to install a couple of extensions.

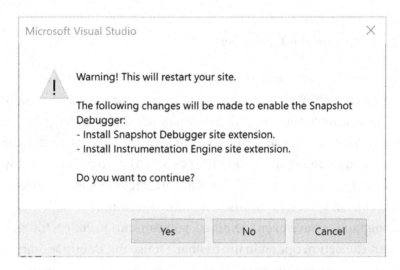

Figure 7-21. *Giving permission to install extensions*

While the extensions are necessary to run the Snapshot Debugger, please be aware that installing the extensions will restart your site. And restarting might have ramifications for your application's state. And once the extensions are installed, you'll need to go through the steps to attach to the Snapshot Debugger again. After all, the target resource has been restarted.

Once you have attached to the Snapshot Debugger, the next step is to set snappoints. Click in the gutter to the left of the line of code where you'd like the snappoint to be placed. There is a hexagonal indicator displayed to show the location of the snappoint. Once the snappoint is in place, you can right-click it to provide additional details, such as the conditions for taking the snappoint. Figure 7-22 illustrates not only the snappoint indicator but also the options that are available.

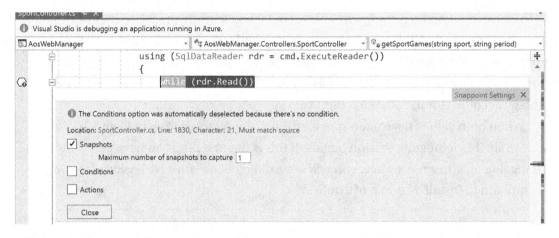

Figure 7-22. *A snappoint has been set*

Along with the Conditions and Actions that were available within Breakpoints, there is also a Snapshots option. You can determine the maximum number of snapshots that get captured. The reason for limiting this information is that each snapshot takes up resources in your Azure storage account. The more snappoints you create, the large the storage used and therefore the greater the costs that could be incurred. By limiting the number of snapshots, you ensure that having hundreds of users or placing your snappoint in a loop isn't going to overuse the storage account.

Once the snappoints have been identified, you can start to collect the snapshots by clicking the Start Collection option in the toolbar. Or use the Debug ➤ Start Collection menu item. Visual Studio will deploy the snappoints to the resource. In order to generate a snapshot, either you need to arrange for the line of code where the snapshot was placed through the web application or wait for a user to do so. Once the snapshot has been hit, you'll see details about the snapshot appear in the Snapshot Debugger pane in the Diagnostic Tools window (Figure 7-23).

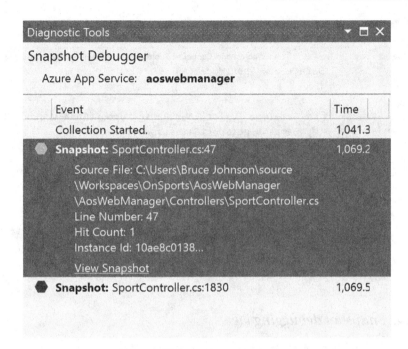

Figure 7-23. *Snapshots taken while attached to the Snapshot Debugger*

Details about the snapshot can be seen by clicking the snapshot. But if you want to view the details of the snapshot, including the state, click the View Snapshot link at the bottom of the corresponding snapshot. Or you can just double-click the snapshot.

At this point, the contents of the snapshot are downloaded to your local machine. How long this takes depends on the speed of your network, but it's possible that there could be a delay of a couple of minutes.

Once the snapshot is available, you will be placed at the location in your code where the snapshot was taken. The view at this point looks very much like a typical debugging session (see Figure 7-24).

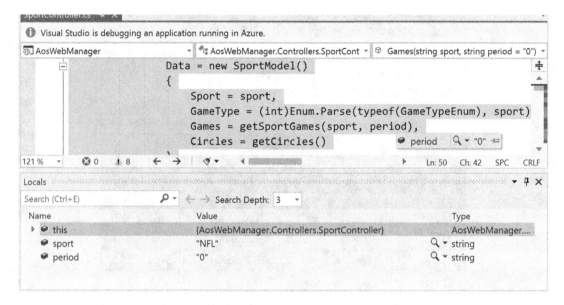

Figure 7-24. *Snapshot debugging view*

What you are looking at is something called historical debugging within Visual Studio. You have access to the values that were in scope at the time the snapshot was taking. For instance, the Locals window contains the values for all of the local variables. And you can expand any objects to see the values of the properties, along with any other related objects. The Call Stack window is available to show the path taken through your code to get to this point. And you can view the value of variables by hovering over them.

Of course, what you can't do is step through the code to see what happens next, or change the value of variables so as to impact the program flow. This is historical information you're seeing and the request that generated the snapshot is already long since completed. But keep in mind that the purpose of snapshot debugging is for you to see the state of the application while in production. And the Snapshot Debugger definitely meets that criterion.

By default, only one snapshot is taken for any snappoint that you set. As has already been mentioned, you can change the number of snapshots through the snappoint settings pane (Figure 7-22). But the snapshot will only contain the information from the first time the snappoint was hit. If you want to collect another snapshot of data for the snapshot, then click the Update Collection button that appears in the toolbar, or use the Debug ➤ Update Collection menu item.

IntelliTrace

The challenge associated with getting debugging information from a production environment was already mentioned in the section on the Snapshot Debugger. And in that section, a technique that works for ASP.NET applications deployed into a variety of Azure environments was described. But as a shock to no one, Azure is not the only environment into which .NET applications are deployed. IntelliTrace was intended at least in part, to allow the state of an application to be captured on a server (production or not) and then reviewed by a developer looking at the original source code.

And IntelliTrace is not limited in its usage to production environments. It can be quite handy when a bug identified by a tester cannot be reproduced in the development environment. The information captured through IntelliTrace can be attached to the bug and then opened up by the developer at a later time.

To start with, the IntelliTrace collector needs to be installed in the environment where the application is running. IntelliTrace works for ASP.NET applications running under Internet Information Services (IIS) from versions 7.0 to 16.0. But it can also be used to capture information from SharePoint 2010 and 2013 applications, Windows Presentation Foundation (WPF) applications, and Windows Forms (WinForms) applications. The collector can be found in the Microsoft Download Center (`https://visualstudio.microsoft.com/downloads/#intellitrace-standalone-collector-for-visual-studio-2019`). This download is an executable file. This file needs to be executed on the machine from which information is being collected. That would be the web server for an ASP.NET application or a SharePoint application, or the user's machine for a WPF or WinForms applications. When it is executed, it creates the `IntelliTraceCollection.cab` file. Once the .cab file is available, the command `expand /f:* <pathToCabFile>/IntelliTraceCollection.cab` will populate the directory with the necessary files. The `<pathToCabFile>` is the path to where the `.cab` file was generated, either relative to the current directory or as a fully qualified path.

You also need to create a directory into which the IntelliTrace files can be created. There is nothing wrong with it being the same directory where the `IntelliTraceCollection.cab` file was expanded, but that's not a requirement. Then you need to ensure that the user running the application has full permissions to the IntelliTrace file directory.

If you are planning on using IntelliTrace on a web or SharePoint application, there are some PowerShell scripts that are useful. Use the Install-Module cmdlet to install the `Microsoft.VisualStudio.IntelliTrace.PowerShell.dll` file that was expanded. The command to do this is as follows:

```
Install-Module -Name Microsoft.VisualStudio.IntelliTrace.PowerShell
```

Now you're ready to capture the IntelliTrace files. Whether you are working with web applications or client-side executables, the concepts are the same. You will specify a location into which the trace files will be placed and identify a collection plan to be used by IntelliTrace. The collection plan is an XML file that specifies the events to be captured while IntelliTrace is running. There are a number of standard collection plans found among the expanded files that can be used.

For a WPF or WinForms application, the IntelliTrace collector can be used to not only start capturing the trace files but also launch the application itself. The basic structure of the command line is as follows:

```
IntelliTraceSC.exe launch
    /cp:<collectionPath>
    /f:<pathToTraceFileDirectory>
    <pathToExecutableBeingTested>
```

It's important to note that the path to the location for the trace files needs to be a fully qualified path. A relative path won't work.

For a web or SharePoint application, there is a PowerShell cmdlet, although the information provided is basically the same.

```
Start-IntelliTraceCollection "<applicationPool>"
    <collectionPath> <pathToTraceFileDirectory>
```

The application pool is the name of the application pool where the web application is running.

Now replicate the problem that you've been having. While you're running the application, trace information is being generated, but you won't necessarily be able to see the trace file (which has a .itrace extension) increase in size. The application you're tracing needs to be completed before the .itrace file is generated. For the WPF or WinForms application, that's just a matter of terminating the application. For a web or SharePoint application, run the following command to stop collecting information:

```
Stop-IntelliTraceCollection "<applicationPool>"
```

The result from all of this activity is a .itrace file. For a developer to use it, it needs to be moved to a machine where Visual Studio 2019 Enterprise has been installed. And once it is there, it can be opened to provide the developer a historical debugging experience similar to what the Snapshot Debugger provided, with a one major twist.

Both IntelliTrace and Snapshot Debugger provide functionality that is known as historical debugging. This means that information about the debugging session is available to Visual Studio even though it was executed in a different environment. The difference is that while Snapshot Debugging is the information captured at a single snappoint, the information captured through IntelliTrace allows you to continue what feels like a more traditional debugging session.

When you open up a `.itrace` file, you are presented with an overview that looks similar to Figure 7-25.

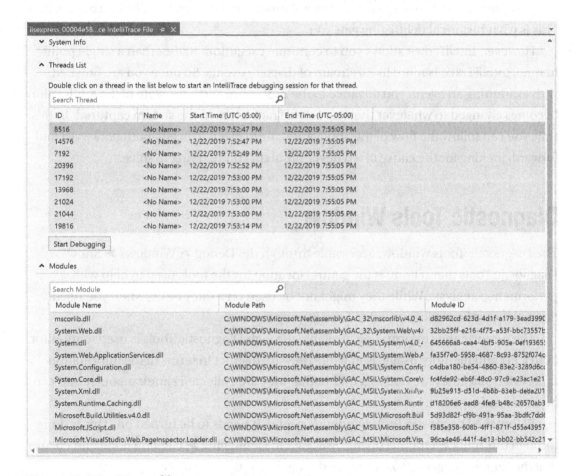

Figure 7-25. iTrace file summary pane

There are a number of expandable sections visible. And you might have a couple of others visible as well. For instance, if there were exceptions raised within the application or the performance of certain parts of the application took too long, then there will be sections visible for those. For each one of the sections, you have the ability to select an item and click a button to start debugging. This will open the details for the IntelliTrace event or item.

What happens when you debug an event depends on the event. If you debug an exception or a performance violation, and the triggering event was raised within your code, you will be taken to the point in the code where that happened. From this point, you can use the Call Stack, Locals, or Autos windows to see the current value of variables. This is what historical debugging gets you.

However, IntelliTrace allows you to continue execution. Rather than a single point in time, IntelliTrace is more like a stream of discrete events. So once you are finished with examining an event, you advance to the next event. Now the state of the application becomes changed to whatever the next IntelliTrace event in the stream captured. In this way, you can follow the flow of the application, from event to event, both backward and forward, looking for the cause of whatever problem you're trying to solve.

Diagnostic Tools Window

The Diagnostic Tools window, accessible through the Debug ➤ Windows ➤ Show Diagnostic Tools menu item, is the central location for the tools used to help with performance analysis. While they might not be used on a daily basis, when you need them, they are incredibly useful to have in your toolbox.

The performance information available through Diagnostic Tools is used to monitor both CPU and memory usage. And while they are distinct in terms of the information that is viewable, they are tied together in that they are collected simultaneously and can be visualized together.

Before the Diagnostic Tools window is useful, it needs to be turned on. This is done through the Tools ➤ Options dialog. Navigate to Debugging ➤ General node and ensure that the Enable Diagnostic Tools while debugging option is checked.

Once Diagnostic Tools has been enabled, when you debug your application, the Diagnostic Tools window opens and starts to collect and display information. Figure 7-26 is a sample of what this window looks like after an application has been running for a period of time.

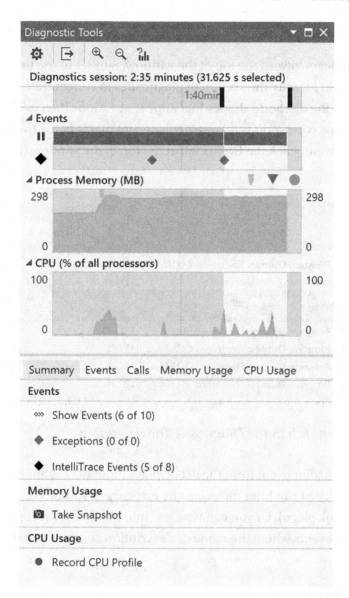

Figure 7-26. *Diagnostic Tools window*

There are three expandable sections at the top of the window in Figure 7-26. They are for Events (specifically, IntelliTrace events), the amount of memory being used by the running process, and the CPU usage for all the processes that are part of the solution. At the very top, there is a timeline of the debugging session. You can use this timeline to selected subsets of the session when it comes to drilling into some of the details.

Events

The Events tab appears toward the top of the window. Similar to the timeline, it's intended to help you identity the section of diagnostics to concentrate on. The main feature of Events is the diamond shapes that appear at various intervals along the timeline. Each shape corresponds to a particular event that is being tracked. To see details about the events, click the Events tab at the top of the window (Figure 7-27).

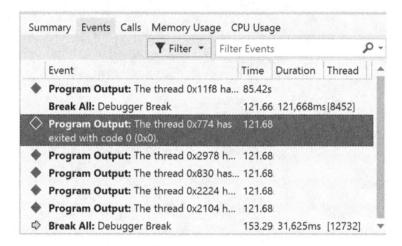

Figure 7-27. *Events tab in the Diagnostic Tools window*

Selecting a particular event from the list displays more details about the event. And at the top of the list, you can filter the events by category or source (i.e., the thread on which the event took place). Or you can type text into the box at the right and it will display only those events where the name or description contains a match.

Memory Usage

The chart seen in the middle of Figure 7-26 tracks the memory usage of the application over time. There are two indicators that mark when certain events related to memory take place. The first is a smaller orange arrow. This indicates, within the timeline, when a garbage collection took place. The second, a blue triangle, indicates when a snapshot was taken.

While the chart of memory usage is nice, it's not overly useful when it comes to identify the source of any memory issues that you might have in your application. At the bottom of the Diagnostic Tools window, there is a Memory Usage tab. Figure 7-28 is an example of this tab.

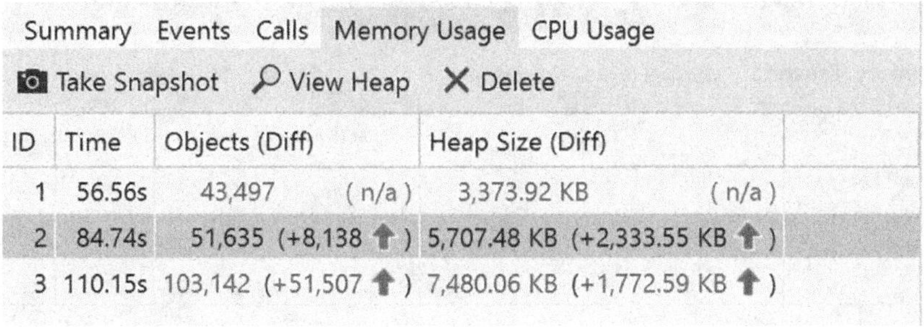

		Summary	Events	Calls	**Memory Usage**	CPU Usage		

◉ Take Snapshot   🔍 View Heap   ✕ Delete

ID	Time	Objects (Diff)		Heap Size (Diff)	
1	56.56s	43,497	(n/a)	3,373.92 KB	(n/a)
2	84.74s	51,635	(+8,138 ↑)	5,707.48 KB	(+2,333.55 KB ↑)
3	110.15s	103,142	(+51,507 ↑)	7,480.06 KB	(+1,772.59 KB ↑)

Figure 7-28. *Memory Usage tab*

Initially, this tab is pretty empty. The key to using it is the Take Snapshot button. The purpose of this button is to take a snapshot of the memory being used by the application at a particular point in time. It collects all of the information found in the heap and displays a count of the objects and the size of the heap. And you can take multiple snapshots over the running of the application. This allows you to compare the size and contents of memory over time, which is frequently the heart of identifying the source of memory over usage.

As you might imagine, it does take a little time to gather up the information. And you might even be a little surprised at the number of objects that exist within your application. In the case of a web application (which is the type of application used to generate the figures), it includes not only all of the objects that you've created but also the objects necessary to serve up the web page. So, for an MVC application, it includes session information, routing information, and the objects used to build up the rendered page. In other words, there are a lot of objects that, while they are created in service of the application, you didn't create explicitly.

In Figure 7-28, you can see that there are three snapshots that have been taken, at different points in the process. With each one, you can see the point at the timeline when the snapshot was taken. And there is a visual representation of how the count of object and heap size has changed from snapshot to snapshot. To drill into the contents of a particular snapshot, click the object count or heap size value. Or select a snapshot and click the View Heap icon in the toolbar. The details are found in a window like Figure 7-29.

Object Type ▲	Count	Size (Bytes)	Inclusive Size (Bytes)
ApplicationStartPage+<>c	1	12	12
ApplicationTrust	1	36	132
AppSettingsSection	2	172	6,144
ArrayList	683	52,924	297,520
ArrayList[,]	1	316	364
ArrayModelBinderProvider	1	12	12

Paths to Root | Referenced Types

Object Type	Reference Count ▼
▲ ArrayList	
▷ ConfigurationValues	268
▷ HttpApplication+AsyncAppEventHandler	75
▷ ConfigurationPropertyCollection	32
▷ StringCollection	32
▷ Hashtable	18
▷ PropertyInformationCollection	16
▷ ConfigurationLockCollection	16
▷ AggregateCacheDependency	15
▷ BuildResultCompiledType	15

Figure 7-29. Contents of a memory snapshot

The details of a snapshot are seen in two sections. At the top is a list of the type of objects that make up the snapshot. Each type of object is included in the list. For each type, you can see how many objects exist and the cumulative size of the objects. There are actually two Size columns. The difference between the values is that the Size column is the size in bytes of the specific object. The Inclusive Size column is not only the number of the bytes in the object, but also all of the bytes in the children referred to by the object.

The lower half of Figure 7-29 breaks the count for a selected object type into different derived types. Figure 7-29 shows that the bulk of the ArrayList objects in the application are actually ConfigurationValue objects.

If you want to see more details about the individual objects for a particular type, click the icon that appears to the right of the object type name when you hover over a particular line. The icon is visible in Figure 7-29, next to the ArrayList type. The details are shown in Figure 7-30.

Snapshot #2 Heap iisexpress.exe (105.96s)   ▾ ☐ ✕

🔙 **Instances of ArrayList**

ℹ️ Snapshot does not reflect current program state. Values not available.

Instance	Size (Bytes)	Inclusive Size (Bytes) ▾	
<0xE977158>	164	27,896	
<0xE9ADCE8>	180	26,296	
<0xE9772C8>	704	12,604	
<0xE9B26F4>	704	12,092	
<0xE97BC90>	740	10,924	
<0xA969FA0>	544	10,196	
<0xE99A3EC>	68	8,048	
<0xE9B6B20>	52	7,292	
<0x169AD6B0>	116	5,732	
<0xE9AF64C>	216	5,264	
<0xE9D5750>	276	5,068	
<0xE988050>	280	4,916	
<0x169AD9C4>	268	4,644	

Paths to Root | Referenced Objects

Instance
▲ArrayList   <0xE977158>
▲ConfigurationValues   <0xE9770D4>
▲CompilationSection   <0xE977078>
▲SectionRecord   <0x16963F88>
▲Hashtable   <0x16962A00>
▲RuntimeConfigurationRecord   <0x16962570>
▲RuntimeConfigurationRecord   <0xA9652FC>

Figure 7-30. *Examining the instances of a specific object type*

In Figure 7-30, you can see a list of the different instances of the selected object type. For each instance, you have the size and the inclusive size, in bytes. At the bottom of the screen, you have the same expansion of derived types that were visible in Figure 7-29.

One of the purposes of taking snapshots is to compare the growth of memory over time. Okay, it's possible that memory could decrease over time. But what's the likelihood of that happening?

At the top of the original window used to view the different object types, there is a dropdown containing the other snapshots for the current process. By selecting one of the snapshots, you can compare the change in objects between the two. The visualization of this information is similar to Figure 7-29 but also includes the changes. This can be seen in Figure 7-31.

Snapshot #2 Heap iisexpress.exe (105.96s)			▼ □ ×

Managed M...   Compare to: Snapshot #3 ☑ | ▼ | Search type names

Object Type	Count Diff.	Size Diff. (Bytes)	Inclusiv
RuntimeType	-11,893	-333,004	^
RuntimeMethodHandle	-16	-552	
ArrayList	-48	-2,360	
ConfigurationValue	-3	-60	
Signature	-68	-3,924	
Hashtable	-17	-10,180	
ListDictionary+DictionaryNode	+533	+12,376	
FileMonitorTarget	-5	-140	
CacheDependency+DepFileInfo	-4	+2,240	
Action<Object, EventArgs>	-10	-320	
CacheDependency	-9	-4,116	
FileChangeEventHandler	-5	-160	∨
ConfigurationProperty	+359	+26.648	
‹		›	

Paths to Root | Referenced Types

Object Type	Reference Count Diff.	Reference Count ▼	
▲ ArrayList			^
▷ ConfigurationValues	-4	268	
▷ HttpApplication+AsyncAppEventHandler	-30	60	
▷ ConfigurationPropertyCollection	0	32	
▷ StringCollection	0	32	
▷ Hashtable	-10	18	
▷ TraceListenerCollection	-5	17	∨

Figure 7-31. *Comparison of two snapshots*

Now the columns show the difference between the snapshots, for count, size, and inclusive size. And the lower half of the screen includes the same breakdown of the object type and its derived types, with a column to show the difference in the reference count between the snapshots, as well as the absolute count.

CPU Usage

The lower graph in Figure 7-26 tracks the CPU usage as a percentage, again over the time that the application is running. If you have multiple CPUs, the percentage is calculated across all of the available CPUs. For more details about the CPU usage, click the CPU Usage tab to reveal an area similar to the one shown in Figure 7-32, without the functional information.

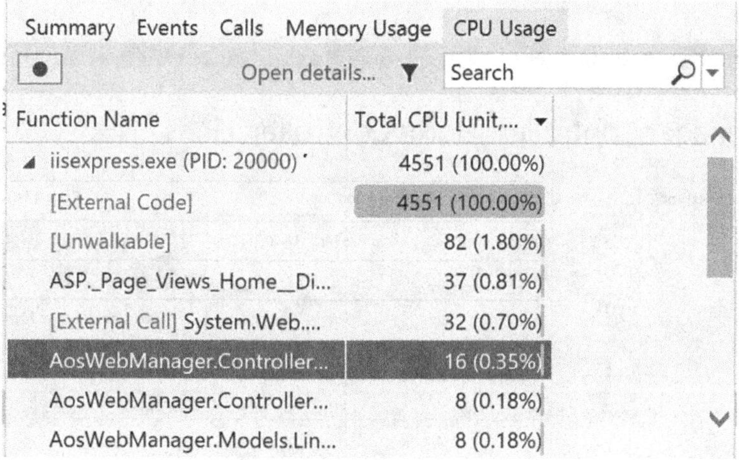

Figure 7-32. *CPU Usage tab in Diagnostic Tools*

In order to see the information visible in Figure 7-32, the application must be paused. The initial state of the pane includes a Break All link that can be clicked to pause all the threads. Or the application can be paused by any breakpoint that you place. When the application breaks, the CPU usage information to that point is collected and, after a few moments, is displayed as shown in Figure 7-32.

There are two other elements in the Diagnostics Tools window that impact the display of the CPU usage information. The first is on the CPU Usage tab. On the left of the toolbar is a circle that is either black or red. This icon is used to start or stop the collection of CPU information. You won't be able to see any of the detailed information unless the collection process has been turned on.

The second element is actually something that runs across all the grids, and was actually mentioned earlier in this section. It's possible to select a time range by holding the mouse down and dragging it along the CPU usage graph found in the top portion of the window. The select time range then becomes the boundary over which the CPU usage information is generated. If the CPU information has not been collected within the specified time range, then a message appears on the CPU Usage tab to that effect. Otherwise, the usage information is calculated and displayed.

271

The usage information, as seen in Figure 7-32, illustrates the amount of CPU used by the different components in your application. From the figure, you can see that most of the time is spent in external code, which for a web application is not unusual. But you can also see a couple of controllers and a model that utilize CPU.

But that information isn't sufficiently detailed to act on it. To get more details about CPU usage within a particular component, double-click it. This displays the details in a form seen in Figure 7-33.

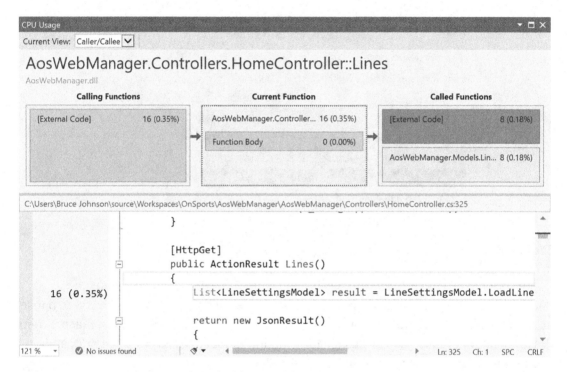

Figure 7-33. CPU Usage details

At the top of Figure 7-33, you can see three areas. On the left are the functions that call into the selected class. On the right are the functions that are called from within the selected class. The middle area contains the functions in the selected class that have used CPU. For each function, you can see the CPU usage percentage. The bottom of Figure 7-33 breaks the CPU usage for the current class down to the line level.

Keep in mind that the goal of this area is to allow you to navigate through your application, searching for the sources of CPU usage. Navigation is accomplished by double-clicking the desired section of the areas. For instance, if you wanted to see the usage for the AosWebManager.Models.Lines class, you could double-click the lower half of the Called Functions area. This will modify the data shown in the CPU usage details window so that the Current Function is AosWebManager.Models.Lines. And the other two areas (Calling Functions and Called Functions) are adjusted to match. This technique gives you the ability to quickly move up and down the call tree looking for potential issues.

Summary

Debugging is where many developers spend the bulk of their day. So any help provided by their development environment is welcomed. For years Visual Studio has been at the forefront of debugging assistance technology and the latest version is no different. The tools that are available not only help with some of the more mundane situations, they are also ready to let developers tackle more challenging scenarios, like identifying issues in production environments, all of which goes a long way toward making Visual Studio as popular as it is.

But diagnostics and debugging are not the sole interest for developers. And indeed Visual Studio works hard to ensure that developers, regardless of the language they use, get improvements. In the next chapter, we look at the additional functionality available to programmers who work with ASP.NET, Node.js, C++, and other languages and platforms.

CHAPTER 8

Language-Specific Improvements

While many of the improvements made in Visual Studio 2019 are useful across different languages and platforms, there are always those changes made that are specific to individual languages. They fulfill a particular need for a particular subset of developers. Or, perhaps, the underlying structure of the language makes replication of the feature on different platforms too difficult to implement smoothly. Over time, these improvements might find their way into other environments, but, initially, they are available only in certain workloads.

A good prior example of this is the data breakpoints discussed in Chapter 7, "Debugging and Profiling." Data breakpoints have been available for C++ developers creating native code applications for a number of versions. The capability to support data breakpoints was never implemented in the .NET Framework. It was only in Visual Studio 2019 that they became accessible to C# applications, and even then only in the .NET Core platform.

With that mindset, this chapter looks at some of the enhancements found in Visual Studio 2019 that are more tightly focused on a language or platform. Even if you don't develop using the environments, sometimes knowing they exist is useful. At a minimum, it might compel you to make a suggestion to Microsoft that they expend the resources needed to bring the feature to a larger audience.

General Improvements

Before we start on the functionality added to support individual languages, let's spend a couple of moments taking about features that cut across languages, but also don't fit neatly into any of the other chapters.

© Bruce Johnson 2020
B. Johnson, *Essential Visual Studio 2019*, https://doi.org/10.1007/978-1-4842-5719-7_8

DPI Awareness

It has long been known that developers using multiple monitors are more productive than those wishing with just a single monitor. The ability to view code, run the application, and browse without needing to switch applications is surprisingly powerful. However, in the real world, it is not without headaches. Having identical monitors is great, but not always possible.

The difference in resolution, scaling settings, or just being above 100% is frequently enough to reduce the clarity of the text. It is common to experience blurry or fuzzy text under these situations. The typical scenario involves text looking great on one monitor, but not as clear on the second. Or maybe it just looks bad across all the monitors.

Visual Studio has been a DPI (dots per inch) aware application for a number of versions. It was set to a mode known as system aware. This means that Visual Studio would use the system-level resolution information when determining how to render the various visual elements, including text. This was a problem when dealing with multiple monitors, as previously described. Immediately, it is also an issue when remoting into a machine with different display configurations.

Visual Studio 2019 introduces per-monitor DPI awareness (PMA). It requires that .NET Framework 4.8 be installed, along with running on Windows 10 (April 2018 update or later). If available, it is automatically activated. The difference is that instead of having a single setting (the system setting) be applied to all the monitors, it uses the settings for each monitor to determine how elements are rendered.

While it's unlikely that you would ever want to disable this functionality, there is an option available to you. As shown in Figure 8-1, there is a setting in the Environment ➤ General section of the Options dialog.

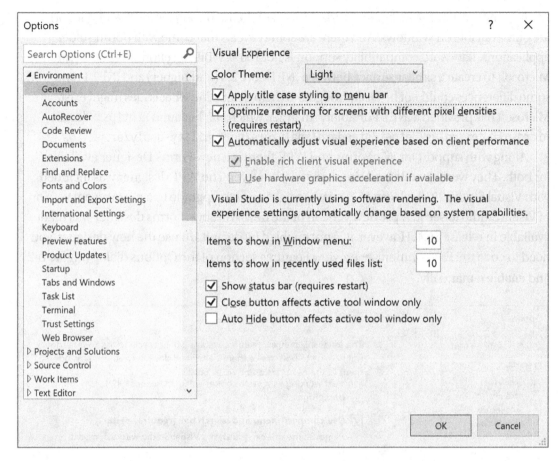

Figure 8-1. *Environment settings used for PMA support*

Probably the main benefit of looking at this setting comes if you are noticing that the text or icons in Visual Studio are blurry when looking at different monitors. If the associated option (it's labeled with the obvious name of Optimize rendering for screens with different pixel densities) is grayed out, it means that your system doesn't meet the .NET Framework 4.8 or Windows 10 requirements. Upgrading to both of those should address the issue.

.NET Core 3.0 Support

In 2019, Microsoft announced the release of .NET Core 3.0. While the name doesn't appear to be significant, it terms of the functionality that was provided, it's a watershed moment for .NET developers. For the first time, .NET Core supports many older technologies, including Windows Forms (WinForms) and Windows Presentation Foundation (WPF). What this means to developers is that you can port older applications to .NET Core and have it work using the latest set of APIs.

Now not all platforms are supported for all of the technologies. WPF and WinForms are only available on Windows. And there are some caveats that come with porting older applications. Backward compatibility support is not 100%. While an effort was made within Microsoft to create a similar surface between .NET Core 2.0 (and higher) and .NET Framework, some differences could not be easily bridged. To help determine what issues might exist, Microsoft has provided a .NET Portability Analyzer, which can be found at `https://docs.microsoft.com/en-us/dotnet/standard/analyzers/portability-analyzer`.

Along with support for WinForms and WPF, there is a new Forms Designer available for both. They were not released simultaneous, however. The WPF designer was included with Visual Studio 2019 release 16.3, so you might need to upgrade to a more recent version of Visual Studio to see it. A preview version of the new Windows Forms designer was made available in release 16.4. However, it is not enabled by default. To use the new designer, you need to go to the Environment ➤ Preview Features section of the Options dialog (Figure 8-2) and enable it manually.

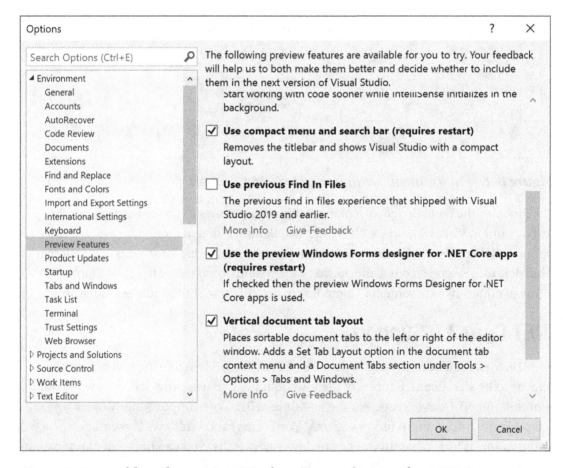

Figure 8-2. *Enabling the preview Windows Forms designer for .NET Core*

C++ Improvements

In Visual Studio 2019, the C++ space has a number of incremental improvements aimed at helping developers update and debug their applications. What's interesting about the improvements is that they illustrate the cross-pollination that takes place between the languages. For example, data breakpoints, which are new to C# developers, have been available in C++ for a while. On the other hand, C# has had a Quick Action that adds references to missing packages for a couple of versions. This is the equivalent in C++ of adding missing packages to CMake.

CMake Support

CMake is an open source tool that manages the build process. It has been supported by Visual Studio since Visual Studio 2017 and the latest version adds to that in a number of ways.

The first change you notice, however, might be a little disturbing. The CMake menu is no longer a top-level menu in Visual Studio 2019. But have no fear. It's not that the menu items have disappeared. It's just that with integration with Visual Studio, the items have moved into the more appropriate Project, Build, Debug, and Test menus. This reorganization makes it easier for the average Visual Studio user to find the functionality they are looking for. It makes more sense, intuitively, to find the CMake Build option under the Build menu than under a CMake menu.

CMake Settings Editor

The CMake process is controlled by the CMakeSettings.json file. This is just a text file in a JSON format that contains the properties used to control how a CMake build functions. As it is just a JSON file, it can be edited using any text editor, including within Visual Studio. However, based on feedback from developers, Visual Studio 2019 includes a new editor for CMake settings, as seen in Figure 8-3.

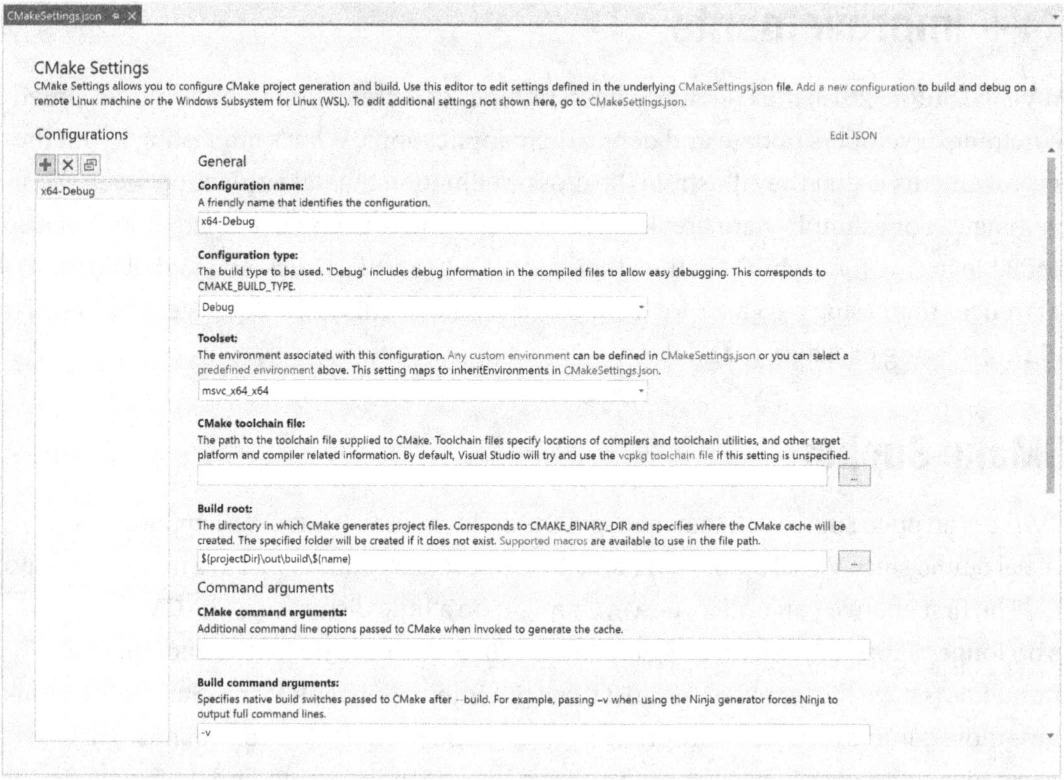

Figure 8-3 shows the CMake Settings editor.

Figure 8-3. *CMake Settings editor*

The editor is available through the Manage Configurations option that appears at the bottom of the list of existing configurations (see Figure 8-4).

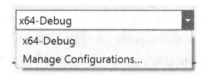

Figure 8-4. *Accessing the CMake Settings editor*

On the left of the editor is a list of the configurations that have been defined for your project. The buttons at the top of the list are used to add, delete, and clone configurations. When you add a configuration, you are presented with a list of the CMake configuration templates that are installed on your machine (Figure 8-5, although your list might be different).

Figure 8-5. *Adding a CMake configuration*

The right side of the screen is where the actual settings are managed. There are four main sections: General, Command Arguments, CMake Variables and Cache, and Advanced. The actual values that are provided are context dependent (and way beyond the scope of this book). For instance, the Linux settings are different than the Windows settings. But the mechanism provided to edit the values should be familiar to any developer. Also, the Advanced section is hidden by default. To view and modify the Advanced values, click the Show advanced settings link at the bottom of the editor. Finally, if you would prefer to modify the JSON file directly, at the top right of the editor, there is an Edit JSON link that will open the settings file in a text editor.

CMake Warning Integration

Visual Studio 2019 includes a couple of different integration points when it comes to warnings generated in conjunction with CMake. Some are aimed at helping developers identify issues that might previously have been difficult to catch. For example, inconsistent or incompatible CMake settings (such as using a 32-bit generator with a 64-bit configuration) generate warnings that are available in the Error List window.

Along with this integration, you can also configure the level of error messages that are generated. By default, only errors are displayed. Warnings end up being suppressed. However, in Visual Studio 2019, you have a bit more control over that behavior. Figure 8-6 shows the CMake settings page available through the Tools ➤ Options menu.

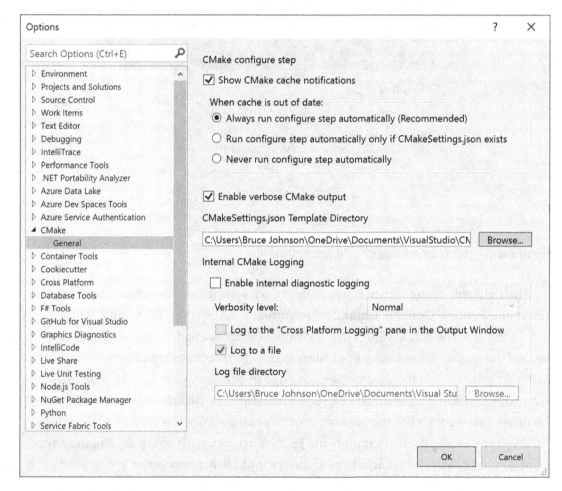

Figure 8-6. *CMake settings through the Options dialog*

In the middle of the right side of Figure 8-6, there is an option to enable verbose CMake output. If this option is enabled, warnings will not be suppressed. And if you need to drill even more deeply into CMake issues, there is an option to enable internal diagnostic logging for debugging. This causes messages that are generated by CMake itself to optionally be logged to a file or displayed on a separate pane in the Output window.

Just My Code Support

Just My Code is a debugging feature that has been part of Visual Studio in C# and Visual Basic for a number of versions. The premise is that, while stepping through code, the debugger will skip over code you didn't write. This would include system calls or certain types of generated code. The idea is that the automatic stepping performed while debugging your application would only stop at code you've written.

One of the interesting things about adding a feature like Just My Code as the default is that there will always be a group of people who need to be able to turn it off. As you might expect (or just consider it a fortunate coincidence), there is a setting that can do just this. In Figure 8-7, you can see the Debugging tab.

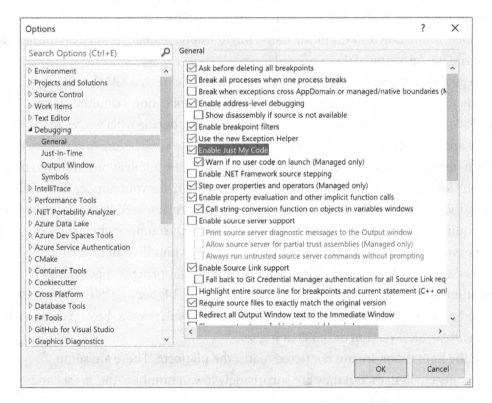

Figure 8-7. *Enable Just My Code setting*

The highlighted setting is used to enable or disable Just My Code. As a word of warning, this setting is not language specific. If you disable Just My Code and start debugging a C# application, you might find yourself stepping into functions that you didn't expect to.

XAML

If you work with XAML, whether as WPF developer or because you're writing UWP (Universal Windows Platform) apps, then the additions and improvements found in Visual Studio 2019 are very exciting. The main focus is on improving how you create and debug XAML, but there are other tidbits that you'll find very useful.

Hot Reload

You might know this feature as XAML Edit and Continue, but it has been renamed to XAML Hot Reload with this version of Visual Studio. The rationale for the name change is that the name more closely mimics the hot reloading functionality frequently found in web applications. With XAML, there is no pausing of the application when the reload takes place, as the Edit and Continue name might imply. Instead, it's just an immediate and automatic updating of the rendered form.

The goal of Hot Reload is to address a long-running issue that XAML designers have – debugging the look of an application using the application's runtime context. Prior to Hot Reload, you would need to look at the application, decide what you want to change, stop the application, make the change, and then rerun the application. And if there were multiple steps needed to get back to the desired point in the applications, well, too bad.

With Hot Reload, you can make changes to the XAML for your application while running the application in debug mode. The changes are detected immediately, without even requiring that the file be saved. The rendering for the component is then triggered for the new XAML and your application's appearance is modified immediately.

There are some limitations to Hot Reload. From a platform perspective, WPF applications need to be running .NET Framework 4.6 or higher and .NET Core 3. And you need to be on Windows 7 or above. For UWP apps, you need to be on Windows 10 or above, with an SKD version of 14393 or higher.

But the limitations are not restricted to just the platform. There are some functionality challenges, but they are surprisingly few in number. And most can be corrected by pausing the application.

For example, you can't modify an event handler attribute within the Hot Reload. Nor can you add controls, classes, or other files to your application while it's running. This includes any managing of NuGet packages. And, while it applies only to UWP apps, you can't modify the x:Uid directive.

Now all of this makes sense, conceptually. In each case, you're not actually changing the look of the application, but some of the components of the application executable. So if you need to make changes like those, pausing or restarting the application is necessary.

There is one powerful feature that is supported starting with Visual Studio 2019. That's the ability to adjust the value of the x:Bind markup extension. This means that you can change where the value of an attribute in XAML comes from as part of Hot Reload.

Since there are some potential impediments to having Hot Reload available, Microsoft added a notice in the In-App toolbar that is available while debugging XAML applications. Figure 8-8 shows what the toolbar looks like when Hot Reload is available.

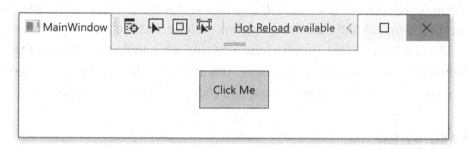

Figure 8-8. *In-App XAML toolbar*

You can show or hide the message by clicking the chevron at the right side of the toolbar.

One final consideration – Hot Reload is only available when you launch the application in debug mode from within Visual Studio (or Visual Studio Code, as it turns out). If you use the Attach to Process functionality to attach the debugger to an already running application, the Hot Reload functionality will not be available.

In-App Toolbar

Since we're already looking at the In-App toolbar, there are a couple of minor tweaks that improve its usability.

You now have the ability to reposition the toolbar within the top section of your application. The left side of the toolbar includes a gripper that lets you drag the toolbar across the top of your window, as illustrated in Figure 8-9.

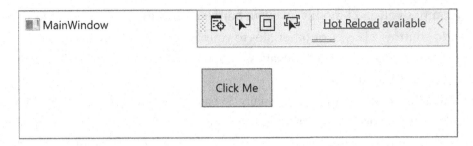

Figure 8-9. *In-App toolbar repositioned*

Also, you might notice that the styling in the In-App toolbar is a little different. In previous versions of Visual Studio, the toolbar was always dark in color. It has been modified so that it picks up the theme that you're using within Visual Studio.

From a functional perspective, there is one change that might take some getting used to. The second icon from the left is used to select an element in the application and have the corresponding element selected in the Live Visual Tree pane. Previously, you could keep selecting elements and have that behavior continue (i.e., each selected element modifies the Live Visual Tree). However, that was confusing, in that it's different than how the developer tools in various browsers work. The In-App toolbar has been changed so that once you have selected an element, subsequent clicks won't select other elements.

Just My XAML

Visual Studio 2019 has a window available during a debugging session named the Live Visual Tree. It contains the entire visual tree for the application, allowing you to drill into even the individual controls to see how the functionality and visual effects are achieved. While there is no question that the Live Visual Tree has a lot of value, it has been plagued by one significant issue. It can get very cluttered, very quickly. Consider the Live Visual Tree seen in Figure 8-10.

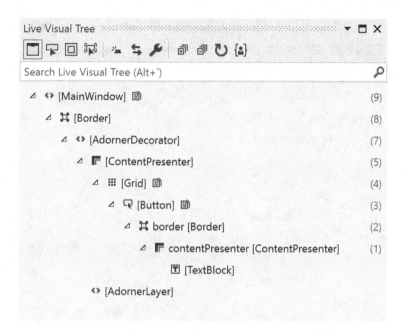

Figure 8-10. *Live Visual Tree for a form with a single button*

This tree is generated from a form that contains a single button on it (the one seen in Figure 8-9). The problem with the tree is that it doesn't represent how a developer visualizes the form. They think it's a form with a button, not an adorner with a content presenter with a grid and so on. From most developer's perspective, the Live Visual Tree should contain only the components that they added. The additional elements, while completely accurate, get in the way of working with the tree.

To improve this situation, Visual Studio 2019 introduces the Just My XAML feature. Similar to Just My Code in debugging, when Just My XAML is turned on (which is the default), the Live Visual Tree only shows the components that were added by the developer. Figure 8-11 illustrates the Live Visual Tree for the same form when Just My XAML is enabled.

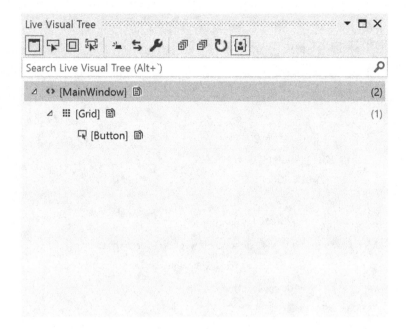

Figure 8-11. *Live Visual Tree with Just My XAML turned on*

While there are definitely benefits from the less cluttered view, there are times when you may want all the details. You can toggle between enabling and disabling Just My XAML using the rightmost icon in the toolbar in the Live Visual Tree pane. Or if you would prefer to just always have it turned off, there is a setting in the Debugging pane of the Tools ➤ Options dialog (see Figure 8-12) that can be used to disable it.

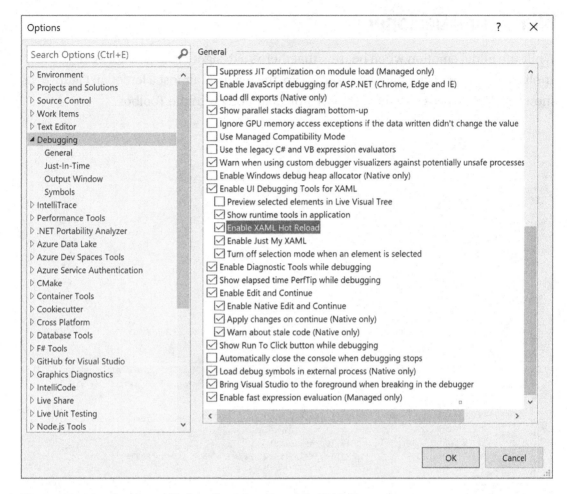

Figure 8-12. *Options dialog showing Just My XAML setting*

.NET Core

.NET Core 3.0 is a big deal for developers of Windows applications, and not just because the version number is bigger than 2.0. Version 3.0 completes a journey that has been going on for the past 5 years. You can now build server applications to run on Windows, naturally. But also those applications will run on MacOS, numerous versions of Linux, iPhone, and IoT devices.

The client-side support for .NET Core 3.0 is just as impressive. You can use .NET Core 3.0 (only running on Windows platforms, not Linux or MacOS) to build Windows Forms and WPF applications. This means you can move your old desktop applications into the present and know that they will be supported into the future as well. Alongside support for the venerable, there is also support for cutting edge. .NET Code 3.0 provides the ability to write client-side web applications using Blazor.

WPF Forms Designer

While the initial emotion when hearing that there's a designer available for WPF application in .NET Core might be skepticism, the reality is almost a letdown. Figure 8-12 shows the WPF Forms designer for .NET Core 3.0, along with the Toolbox.

Figure 8-13. *WPF Forms Designer in .NET Core 3.0*

The reason for the letdown? The Forms Designer looks and acts pretty much exactly like the WPF Forms Designer has looked for the last few versions of Visual Studio, which is to say that it's going to be comfortable and familiar for WPF developers.

To get to the designer, there is a project template for WPF apps that targets .NET Core. When you create a new project that way, the WPF Forms Designer is available as the default designer. So you can double-click a XAML file and open the designer, just as you have been doing.

The more interesting piece to WPF support in .NET Core is migrating from existing WPF applications to .NET Core. There are some fundamental differences that need to be addressed, but the steps to do so are well documented and there is a sample project available on GitHub (Bean Trader, found at *https://github.com/dotnet/windows-desktop/tree/master/Samples/BeanTrader*).

In general, the migration issues break down into two main categories. First, the method for adding referenced packages needs to be changed to use NuGet. Even more, instead of having a separate `packages.config` file, the NuGet references need to be included as `<PackageReference>` elements within the `.csproj` file. And while it's not a requirement, it's a good idea to use NuGet packages that target .NET Standard, as opposed to .NET Framework. The reason that it's not a requirement is that .NET Framework development efforts have been directed toward targeting .NET Standard. As a result, .NET Framework 4.7.2 has solid .NET Standard 2.0 support. And that support includes sufficient overlap between the .NET Core and .NET Framework surface that many packages will work without change. However, if there is a problem, you won't find it until a runtime exception is encountered.

The second category also relates to the difference between .NET Core and .NET Framework. It's possible that your application is using functionality that isn't available across any or all of the platforms that .NET Core supports. As mentioned earlier, Microsoft has provided a .NET Portability Analyzer (*https://docs.microsoft.com/en-us/dotnet/standard/analyzers/portability-analyzer*). This tool helps you identify areas where compatibility issues might arise, as well as being able to identify the parts of .NET Core that your application uses. That can be useful as you determine the platforms that are capable of supporting your application.

Windows Forms Designer

The flow for using the Windows Forms .NET Core Designer is almost identical to WPF applications. The difference is that, while the designer is installed, it is still in preview mode. As such, it is not enabled by default. Instead, the first time you launch the designer by double-clicking a Windows Forms component, you will see a yellow notification bar at the top asking you to enable the designer. Enabling the designer is done through the Preview Features tab in the Tools ➤ Options dialog (see Figure 8-14). And be aware that you need to restart Visual Studio before the designer is available.

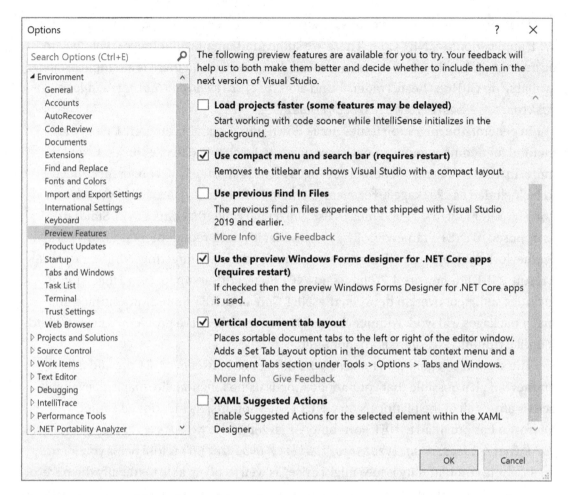

Figure 8-14. *Enabling the Windows Forms .NET Core Designer*

Note   Earlier versions of Visual Studio 2019 (before 16.5) had the Windows Forms .NET Core Designer as a separate VSIX (Visual Studio Extension) package that needed to be downloaded and installed before use. It is likely that, in future versions of Visual Studio 2019, after the designer is no longer in preview, that the Windows Forms designer will be enabled by default.

But once the designer is enabled, you'll find that the experience is pretty much the same as you're used to. Figure 8-15 shows the Windows Forms .NET Core Designer.

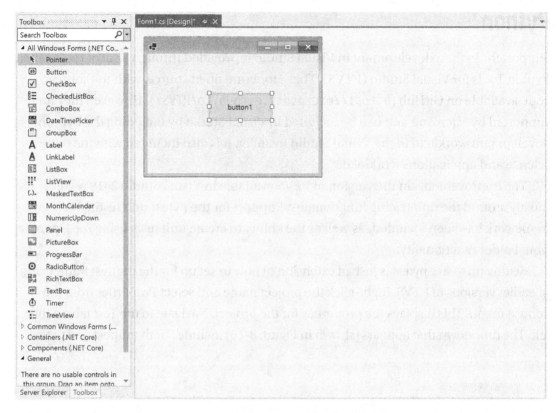

Figure 8-15. *Windows Forms .NET Core Designer*

The process of converting to the .NET Core version of Windows Forms is similar to WPF. The same .NET Portability Analyzer tool as described in the WPF section is useful for identifying potential issues. And if you are using NuGet packages, so it's a good idea to upgrade those to ones that target .NET Standard instead of .NET Framework.

One area that Windows Forms applications is more likely to have issues with is the surface of the .NET API. That's just a result of the age of Windows Forms. To help alleviate some of these situations, Microsoft has provided a Windows Compatibility Pack. This is a library that adds many of the APIs that are available to Windows Forms applications that are not found in .NET Core. And when you consider that there are about 20,000 APIs in the package, you quickly realize how useful it can be when porting from Windows Forms. You can find more information about the package, including how to add it to your application, at *https://docs.microsoft.com/en-us/dotnet/core/ porting/windows-compat-pack*.

Python

Support for Python development in Visual Studio is provided through a set of tools called Python Tools for Visual Studio (PTVS). These tools are open source, with the source code available on GitHub (`https://microsoft.github.io/PTVS/`). However, they are supported by Microsoft and can be included in Visual Studio by including the Python development workload in the Visual Studio Installer. It is also included with the data science and applications workload.

The improvements in the version of PTVS available in Visual Studio 2019 revolve mostly around the unit testing functionality. Support for the pytest unit testing framework has been included, as well as the ability to create unit tests using the Open from Folder functionality.

Setting up to use pytest is just an extension of how to set up for the unittest framework in earlier versions of PTVS. Right-click the project name and select Properties from the context menu. This displays the properties for the project. Navigate to the Test tab on the left. The dropdown that appears (shown in Figure 8-16) includes both unittest and pytest.

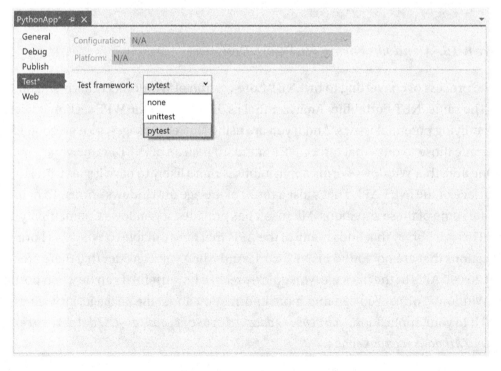

Figure 8-16. *Setting the unittest framework for a Python project*

Now the .ini configuration that is part of pytest will be used when the test discovery process is performed. If you open the Test Explorer window, you will see the list of tests determined by using the patterns that are part of the configuration file. Keep in mind that it can take up to a minute for the discovery process to complete.

Visual Studio 2019 supports the Open Folder scenario for Python development. In this scenario, instead of opening a project file, you are using the contents of a directory as the entire Python project. This is a very popular way to use Visual Studio to work with existing Python projects that weren't originally created in Visual Studio.

When using the Open Folder approach, you can still identify the testing framework to use. In the PythonSettings.json file, you can add a number of attributes that Visual Studio will use to configure the test discovery and execution. The following is an example of the PythonSettings.json file that works with pytest:

```
{
    "TestFramework": "pytest",
    "UnitTestRootDirectory": "tests",
    "UnitTestPattern": "test_*.py",
    "SearchPaths": [ ".\\src" ]
}
```

The `TestFramework` property identifies the unit testing framework. The `UnitTestRootDirectory` specifies the name of the directory containing the tests. This directory will be scanned for files matching the `UnitTestPattern` pattern. Finally, if your source code files are not in the same folder that contains the `tests` directory, you need to specify the path that contains the source code.

Summary

The architecture of Visual Studio is such that many different teams, both from inside and outside of Microsoft, are able to contribute to the improvements made to the environment. The change to a more modular structure also allows the different teams to release functionality on their own cadence instead of being dependent on when new versions of Visual Studio were made public. As such, you will find that the list of features that are being added to Visual Studio is challenging to keep up with. This chapter focused on the changes that are major in scope, but it is not an extensive list, as the different tooling teams continue to release new functionality even as this book is being published.

Areas that were intentionally left out of this chapter were the changes to Visual Studio 2019 related to cloud computer and containers. That's because each of them is significant enough to warrant its own chapter. And those changes are covered in the next two chapters.

CHAPTER 9

Azure Tooling

In one way or another, the cloud has moved to the center of most software development. Whether you are writing desktop applications, creating websites, or working with mobile devices, there is likely a component that utilizes the cloud, or could utilize the cloud, under the right circumstances.

Visual Studio has evolved to embrace this trend. You can see some of that in the Live Share functionality described earlier in this book. But it also wholeheartedly supports the use of Microsoft Azure as the foundation for your cloud development efforts. The focus of this chapter is to describe how this support is provided.

One thing that this chapter is not going to do is spend time describing what Microsoft Azure is in any detail. It contains too many different pieces for a couple of paragraphs to do it justice. And odds are pretty good that between the writing of the paragraphs and your reading them, things will have changed. Such is the pace of development in the cloud world. So instead, any details of Azure will only be mentioned in the context of the Visual Studio components that are covered.

Cloud Explorer

The heart of the Azure experience within Visual Studio is the Azure Cloud Explorer. Through the Cloud Explorer, you are able to view your Azure resources across different resource groups and subscriptions. As well as viewing their properties, there are also actions (the list depends on the resources) which can be performed against them, including the kind of diagnostics that developers require to identify and solve problems.

The Cloud Explorer is available by default when you install the Azure workload through the Visual Studio Installer. Once installed, it appears as the Cloud Explorer option on the View menu. When the option is selected, the Cloud Explorer window appears, as shown in Figure 9-1.

© Bruce Johnson 2020
B. Johnson, *Essential Visual Studio 2019*, https://doi.org/10.1007/978-1-4842-5719-7_9

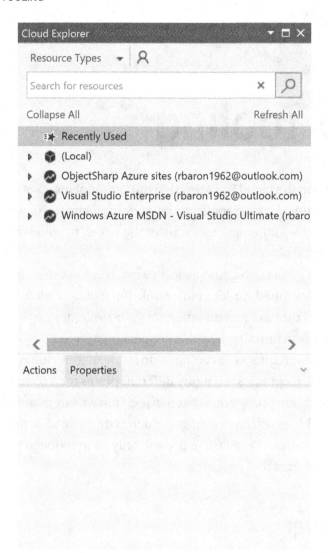

Figure 9-1. *The Cloud Explorer*

Figure 9-1 shows the bare-bones look for the Cloud Explorer. In the top portion of the window is a list of the Azure subscriptions that are available for the current user. The bottom port of the window, which is currently empty, is used to view and modify the properties of the individual resources, as well as initiate different actions against the resources.

By default, the credentials you used to sign into Visual Studio are used to retrieve the Azure resources. But you are not limited to using that account, or are even limited to using a single account. To add an account, click the Account icon (the one shaped like the head and shoulders of a person) in the toolbar at the top of the pane. This opens up an area where you can see the different Microsoft accounts that have been associated with Azure for your instance of Visual Studio (see Figure 9-2).

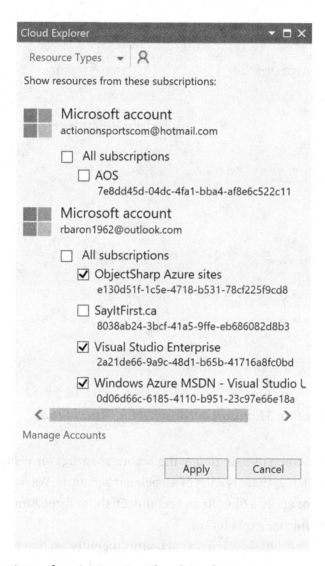

Figure 9-2. *Selecting subscriptions in Cloud Explorer*

For each account, you can see the different subscriptions with which they are associated. By checking and unchecking the corresponding check boxes, you specify whether the resources for those subscriptions are available within Cloud Explorer. At the bottom of the list, there is a link that is used to manage the accounts visible through this pane. If you want to add or remove accounts, click the link to display the dialog shown in Figure 9-3.

Figure 9-3. *Associating Microsoft accounts with Visual Studio*

This is the same screen used to define the account settings for Visual Studio. At the bottom right of the dialog, there is a list of associated accounts. You can add an account, remove an account, or apply a filter to an account. Of those three functions, only the Apply filter requires further explanation.

It's possible to link multiple Microsoft accounts together, so that even though there are different email addresses being used, they are treated as a single login. That way you can sign in once, yet have the access granted to each of the linked accounts. By applying a filter, you can see the list of linked accounts and select the ones you want to use when accessing Azure. Figure 9-4 illustrates the dialog that appears when you click Apply filter.

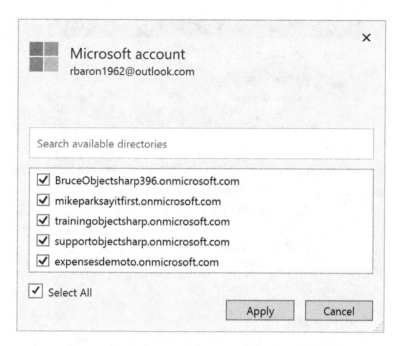

Figure 9-4. *Applying a filter to a Microsoft account*

If there are Azure subscriptions associated with any of the checked Microsoft accounts, they will appear in the list seen in Figure 9-2. Unchecking an email address will remove any associated subscriptions from the list.

Resources

Once the accounts have been identified and the desired subscriptions selected, you go back to the basic Cloud Explorer in Figure 9-1. Each of the subscriptions is available in a tree view. By expanding a subscription, you can see the resources, collected into groups by Resource Type or Resource Group. Figures 9-5 and 9-6 illustrate the two views for the same subscription.

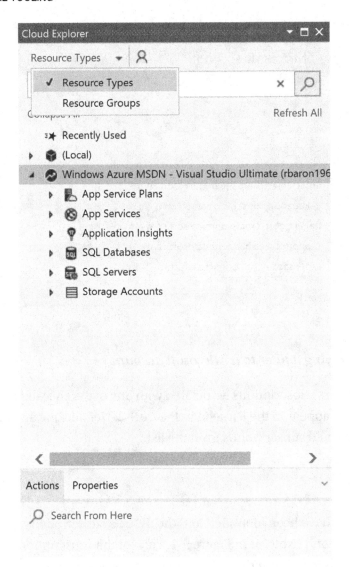

Figure 9-5. *Resource Type view in Cloud Explorer*

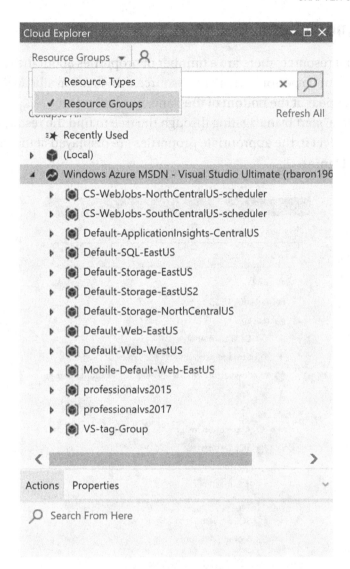

Figure 9-6. *Resource Group view of Cloud Explorer*

The Resource Type view breaks the resources in the subscription down into predefined grouping based on the type of resource. If you want to see all of the databases or virtual machines in your subscription, they will appear when you expand the appropriate node.

The Resource Group view breaks the resources into groups that you have defined. The idea of a resource group in Azure is a collection of resources that are placed into a bucket by the administrator. Maybe the resources are grouped by department or project or location. The choice is left up to the administrator.

303

Properties and Actions

For any individual resource, there are a number of properties about the resource, along with actions that can be performed on the resource, which are available through Cloud Explorer. These appear at the bottom of the pane, in a tabbed area.

To use this area, start by navigating through the tree to find the resource you want to view. When you select it, the appropriate properties are displayed at the bottom of the pane, as seen in Figure 9-7.

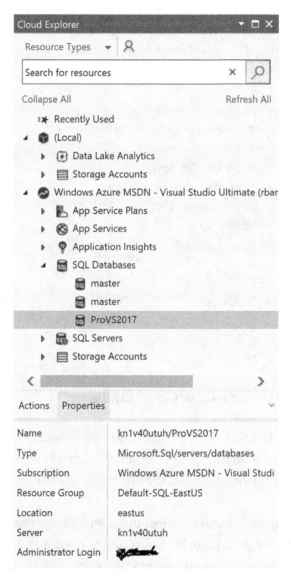

Figure 9-7. *Properties pane in Cloud Explorer*

The properties displayed are read-only. If you want to make changes to them, then you have to go into the Azure portal to do so. And the list of properties depends on the type of resource. Some have little more than the name and type. Others provide more detail.

The same is true on the Actions pane, as seen in Figure 9-8.

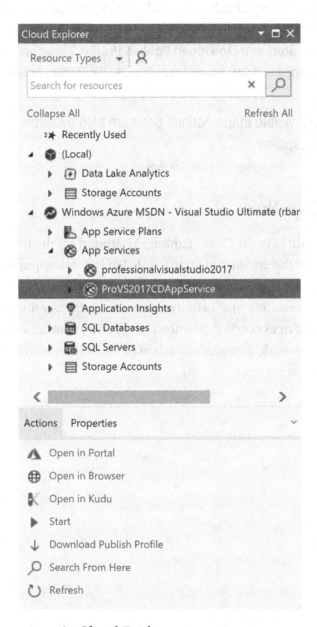

Figure 9-8. *Actions pane in Cloud Explorer*

In the Actions pane, there are a list of actions that can be performed against the selected resource. Even more so than the Properties, the list of possible actions varies based on the selected resource. At a minimum, every resource supports the Open in Portal action. This will launch the Azure Portal website, placing you in the selected resource automatically. As well, if the selected resource has any child resources, there is a Search From Here and a Refresh action. All of these are visible in Figure 9-8, which are the actions related to an App Service. From Figure 9-8, however, you can also see other actions, such as Start and Download Publish Profile. These are very specific to App Services and will disappear if you move to resources of different types.

Note   The choices visible in the Actions pane are also available if you right-click a resource in Cloud Explorer.

Internet of Things Hub

One of the newer features in the Cloud Explorer is support for the Internet of Things or IoT. Azure supports the creation of an IoT Hub. For IoT development, the IoT Hub is the central service through which communication, authentication, and monitoring can be performed. If you visualize your IoT environment as a factory floor (see Figure 9-9) having hundreds of devices sending telemetry and performing actions, then the IoT Hub is the center of that network, connecting each of those devices with both one another (if needed) and with other services.

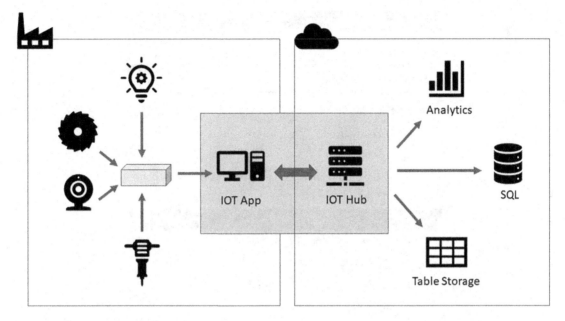

Figure 9-9. *IoT in a factory*

In many regards, the IoT Hub is just like any other Azure resource, when it comes to the Cloud Explorer. It is visible within the tree of resources and has both properties and actions available to it. Figure 9-10 illustrates its position within the tree and the list of actions.

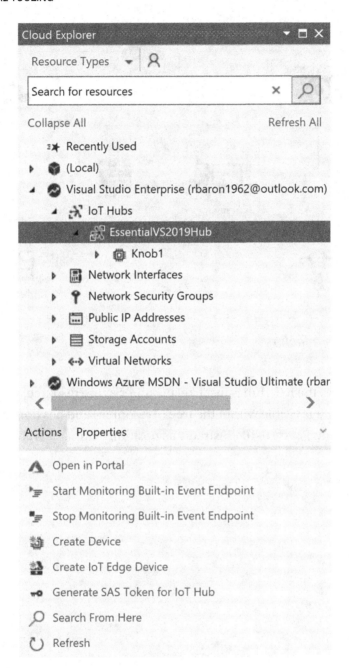

Figure 9-10. IoT Hub Actions in Cloud Explorer

The actions in the list start to give an idea about the capabilities that Cloud Explorer has, related to IoT devices. You have the ability to create a device within a hub, either a regular device or an edge device. The difference between the two devices is found in their capabilities. A regular IoT device is a nontraditional computer (i.e., not a laptop, desktop, tablet, or phone) that is connected to a wireless network and is able to send data and sometimes receive commands and perform actions.

An edge device is a device that has capabilities allowing it to act in a supervisory capacity for regular devices. It communicates with regular devices, collecting data and then passing that data back to the hub. Frequently, it has the ability to run programs (typically deployed using a container infrastructure such as Docker) that allow it to be semiautonomous.

Along with creating devices through Cloud Explorer, you also have the ability to generate a shared access signature (SAS) token for the IoT Hub. This token is used by the IoT Hub and devices to provide a claims-based authentication mechanism.

One of the more interesting features provided by Cloud Explorer and IoT devices starts with the ability to monitor the event endpoint that is part of the IoT Hub. The event endpoint is where the related devices (both regular and edge) send any data. By starting to monitor the event endpoint, you can see all of the incoming messages displayed in the Output window.

This monitoring functionality is useful, but it doesn't stop there. If you select a device in Cloud Explorer, the list of actions changes, as can be seen in Figure 9-11.

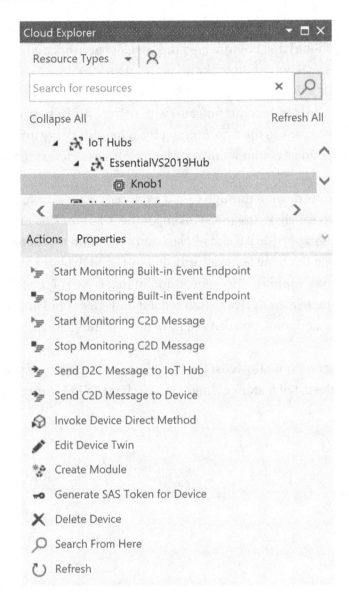

Figure 9-11. *Actions for a regular IoT device*

As with the IoT Hub, you can monitor the incoming events for a particular device. This option is available because it's possible for a regular IoT device to have related subdevices. So this option monitors any incoming requests from those subdevices.

When it comes to messages passing between the IoT Hub and the device, there are four actions available. You can start or stop monitoring the C2D messages. In this action, the "C" stands for cloud and the "D" stands for "device." So what you are monitoring are the messages passed from the cloud (the IoT Hub) to the device. If you wanted to see the D2C messages (i.e., device to cloud), you would monitor the event endpoint messages for the IoT Hub.

But monitoring is not the limit of the functionality offered by Cloud Explorer. You can also send messages manually between the IoT Hub and the device or vice versa. The Send D2C Message to IoT Hub action opens a dialog allowing you to enter the message that will be sent to the Hub as if it were generated by the device. The Send C2D Message to Device action allows you to enter a message which will be transmitted to the device as if it had come from the IoT Hub. Through all of these different options, you have a great deal of flexibility when it comes to diagnosing or correcting any issues that arise within your IoT infrastructure.

There are a couple of other actions that can help with any diagnostic efforts you might need to take regarding an IoT device. There is an action (Invoke Device Direct Method) that allows you to send a message directly to a particular device. When the action is triggered, you will be prompted for a method name and a JSON-formatted payload. The idea with a direct method is that a request will be sent to the URL for the device using HTTPS. The request includes the specified method name and payload. It is expected that the device will respond to the request, but there is no requirement that there be any payload. The result of the request appears in the Output window.

The Edit Device Twin action allows you to edit the JSON file in the IoT Hub that describes the device. This JSON file is called the device twin because it describes the attributes and capabilities of the device. It also contains state information for the device, so it's possible that it gets updated on a regular basis using data provided by the device.

The Create Module action allows you to create a module for the selected IoT device. A module in the IoT world is a separate namespace through which the device can be accessed. The namespace can then be given different access rules, so that they can be secured independently of one another. An example might be a vending machine maintained at a remote location. While the vending machine is considered a single device, there could be multiple sensors in the machine. For example, one sensor might indicate the number of items still in the machine while another might indicate the amount of change remaining. Each set of data could be the responsibility of different departments. In that case, the device would contain two modules, one that exposes the messages related to the inventory and another that exposes the message related to the change.

Triggering the Create Module action adds a child item to the IoT device. You enter the name of the module. If you right-click the module (or view its Action pane), you can edit the Module Twin for the module. Similar to a Device Twin, this is a cloud-based JSON file that describes the metadata, state, and capabilities of the module.

Finally, there is a Generate SAS Token for Device action. This is the corresponding operation for creating an SAS token for the IoT Hub. The action generates the SAS token that can be used by the device to communicate with the IoT Hub. The input from you that's needed to complete the generation is the lifetime (in hours) of the token. This value determines how long the token will continue to be valid before another token would need to be generated.

Azure Function

The official (reworded from the Azure documentation) definition of an Azure Function is a serverless compute service that runs event-triggered code without the need to provision the supporting infrastructure. There are a lot of concepts in that definition, so let's take a couple of paragraphs to break apart the details.

The underlying goal of an Azure Function is to run a piece of code. What makes it different from other code you might run is that it's designed to execute this code without the need to deploy a server beforehand, hence the "serverless" adjective. When you deploy an Azure Function, you are specifying the code being executed, but not the environment in which it will execute. When it needs to run, the environment will be dynamically constructed before the function is executed.

The code itself can be written in one of a number of different languages: C#, Java, JavaScript, Python, or PowerShell. And it's not just the languages that are supported. You can bind different types of resources (queues, database, SendGrid, etc.) to your function declaratively. For C#, attributes are used to connect your function to the resources. For the other languages, the bindings are declared in a `function.json` file.

The execution of the function is initiated through a couple of different mechanisms. One of the more straightforward is a timer. In that situation, the function is executed on a regular, predetermined schedule. But the function can also start running based on external events, such as the arrival of a message in a queue, an HTTP request, or an event being raised in the Azure Event Grid. Through this range of triggers, the number of uses to which an Azure Function can be put is quite large. So let's look at how Visual Studio can be used in this process.

Creating an Azure Function

Visual Studio 2019 provides a project template that can be used as the starting point for your Azure Function. The template is available so long as you have included the Azure development workload in your Visual Studio instance. Also be aware that you're going to need an Azure subscription in order to deploy the Azure Function. And with the exception of Azure Functions that are triggered with an HTTP request, you're also going to need to have blob storage associated with the function. But don't let the requirements be overwhelming, especially as it comes to cost. There are free resources that are sufficient to get your first Azure Function going.

The starting for an Azure Function is to create a new project using the built-in template. Use the File ➤ New ➤ Project menu item to launch the dialog (seen in Figure 9-12).

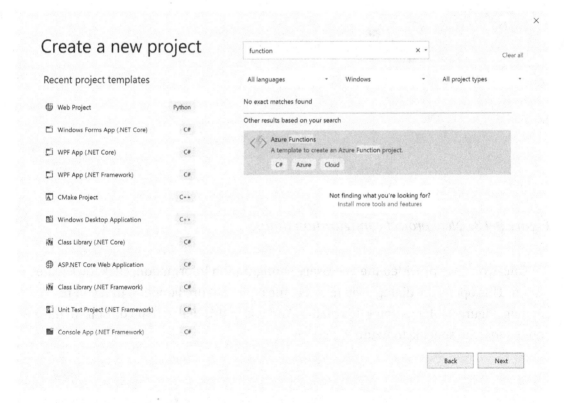

Figure 9-12. *New Project dialog for an Azure Function*

In the list of installed templates that appears on the right of the dialog, find the Azure Functions template. In Figure 9-12, the search box at the top has been used. Select the template and click Next. This opens the dialog used to name the new project and specify the location (Figure 9-13).

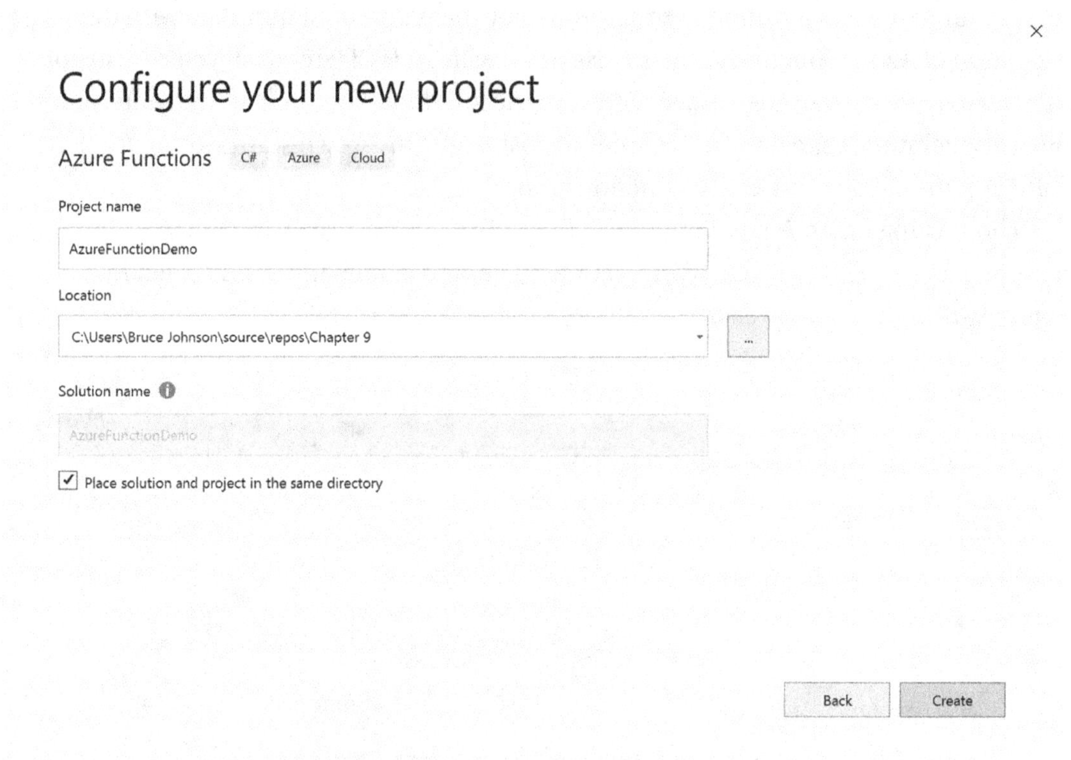

×

Configure your new project

Azure Functions   C#   Azure   Cloud

Project name

AzureFunctionDemo

Location

C:\Users\Bruce Johnson\source\repos\Chapter 9   ▾   ...

Solution name ⓘ

AzureFunctionDemo

☑ Place solution and project in the same directory

Back   Create

Figure 9-13. *New project configuration dialog*

Once you have provided the necessary configuration information, click the Create button. This opens the dialog used to select the type of Azure Function that you're creating. Figure 9-14 illustrates this dialog. And it is in this dialog that you start to have choices that are specific to Azure Functions.

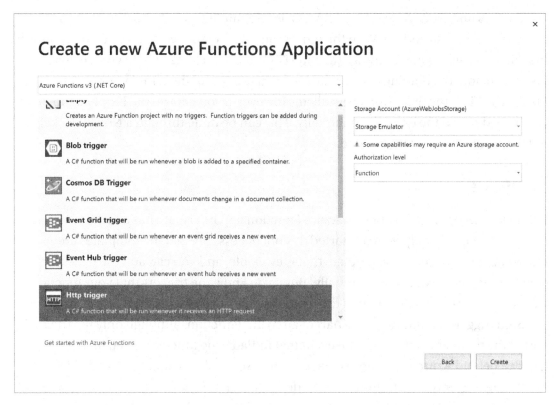

Figure 9-14. *Create new Azure Function application dialog*

There are four different attributes that you need to specify before you create the Azure Function project. They are Platform, Template, Storage Account, and Authorization. The next few sections go into more detail.

Platform

Azure Functions support three different runtime environments that, more or less, correspond to when the different versions were released. The selection is made. For Azure Functions v1, the .NET Framework 4.6 was the supported runtime. For v2, support was added for .NET Core 2.2. With the most recent version, v3, .NET Core 3.0 is supported.

There is also different language support for the different versions. Azure Functions v1.0 supported only C#, F#, and JavaScript. With v2, Java, PowerShell, Python, and TypeScript were added.

There is one other change that impacts development through the different versions of Azure Functions runtime. With the move from .NET Framework to .NET Core, some of the different triggers and bindings (all but HTTP and Timer) need to have an extension installed before the bindings are available. If you use one of the templates described in the next section, the extension is installed. However, if you choose the Empty template, you'll need to add the extension manually. This can be done through a NuGet package, so the mechanism is a familiar one.

Template

One of the strengths of creating an Azure Function app in Visual Studio is the templates that are available to help get you started. It's not necessarily that the templates are required. There is an Empty template that is available, and you can add the necessary configuration and extensions manually. But if you know the triggers that your function will be using before you start, then the template helps to make life easier.

Both triggers and bindings are part of an Azure Function, although only the trigger is part of the template. A trigger is the event that initiates the function. Keep in mind that the idea behind Azure Functions is that they are executed in response to some external event. The trigger type determines the underlying technology that generates the external event. A binding also specifies a technology. The difference is that rather than initiating the event, the binding can be either the input or the output (or both) of the function.

As an example, consider an incoming HTTP request that wants to retrieve the thumbnail for an image. The Azure Function would be triggered by the HTTP request, use a blob storage binding to get the requested image, and then output an HTTP response that contains the thumbnail version of the image. The trigger technology is HTTP. The bindings are blob storage (input) and HTTP (output).

There are a number of built-in templates provided. You can see a partial list in Figure 9-14, underneath the Runtime select. A more complete list, with a description, can be found in the following text. And be aware that the trigger in each template is just a starting point. You can add or remove triggers and bindings through the development process.

Blob Trigger

A Blog Trigger starts the function when a new blob is added or an existing blob is changed. The function is bound to a Blob Storage account, which is the repository that is monitored for the changes. When the trigger is fired, the new or updated blob is provided as a parameter to the function.

Cosmos DB Trigger

Cosmos DB is a NoSQL-style data storage technology. It allows items to be stored in containers, where an "item" is a schema-agnostic piece of data that is similar to a document in MongoDB. The container in Cosmos DB is akin to a database table, although it's more accurately thought of as a namespace in which the document resides.

A Cosmos DB trigger causes the function to be invoked whenever an item within a specific container is modified or added. Included in the trigger is the modified or added item.

Event Grid Trigger

The Azure Event Grid is a service that allows developers to easily build out an event-based messaging application. It works using a publish and subscribe model in the same way that Azure Service Bus does. However, instead of delivering messages, it sends event notifications. Yes, the notification can include data. But that data is just part of the event and is not persisted past the raising of the event. In this way it is different than Azure Service Bus. With the Event Grid, there is no expectation by the sender about who will handle the event or if it will even be handled.

The Event Grid trigger causes the function to be executed whenever an event is raised by the corresponding publisher. In this regard, the Event Grid trigger acts as a subscriber in the publish/subscript model supported by Event Grid.

Event Hub Trigger

The similarity of the name with Event Grid belies just how different it is. Event Hub is an Azure Service that supports the capture and processing of streams of data. It is a big data pipeline, passing along information, such as telemetry or state, potentially from multiple concurrent sources. In this way, it distinguishes itself from the discrete payloads of Event Grid and Service Bus. When you design an Azure Function with an Event Hub trigger, you need to be aware of the possibility that thousands or millions of triggers might occur every second.

The Event Hub trigger is fired as the events are received through the event stream. There is typically data associated with the event, but it's typed as just a string value.

Http Trigger

An Http trigger is fired when a request is received through the HTTP pipeline. This allows an Azure Function to be initiated using any technology capable of submitting an HTTP request, which, to be fair, is just about every technology.

To the sender of the trigger, the response is either an HTTP 200 status code (for Azure Functions v1) or an HTTP 204 status code (for Azure Function v2 and v3). Regardless, there is no indication whether the function triggered by the event succeeded or failed. If that's a requirement of your application, you would need to add an HTTP output binding to the function.

IoT Hub Trigger

An IoT Hub trigger is quite similar to the Event Hub trigger. The IoT Hub is responsible for sending a stream of event data related to one or more IoT devices. With the arrival of each event, the Azure Function is initiated. And any data related to the IoT Hub event is passed to the function as a string data type.

Queue Trigger

Queue Storage is a type of storage in Azure that mimics the functionality of a queue. Messages are received into Queue Storage, having been transmitted by the sender. The messages remain in Queue Storage until they are removed by the receiver of the queue message.

With the Queue Trigger, the execution of the Azure Function becomes the receiver of the queued message. When a message arrives in Queue Storage, the function in invoked. The queued message is provided to the function as a parameter.

Service Bus Trigger

The Azure Service Bus is one of the oldest of the Azure technologies. It supports the traditional concept of an Enterprise service bus. Messages are received and processed in a first-in, first-out manner with guaranteed delivery, transactional support, and filtering capabilities.

The Service Bus trigger initiates the Azure Function upon the arrival of a message into the Service Bus. The trigger can either operate against an entire Service Bus queue or just a topic within that queue. For the latter case, you would choose the Service Bus Topic Trigger, instead of the Service Bus Trigger as the template.

Timer Trigger

While this template is last on the list, alphabetically, it is a very common request across a wide swath of applications. The premise is pretty straightforward. You want to have a function that you want to run on a regular schedule – could be hourly, daily, or even more complicated scenarios. But at the appropriate time, you want the function executed. The Timer trigger enables this capability.

The interesting part about Timer triggers is how the schedule is specified. Azure Functions use a NCRONTAB format for their timings. This format is similar to the CRON format, with an extension that allows for identifying execution time down to the second (CRON limits execution to the minute).

Storage Account

With the exception of the Http Trigger, all of the trigger templates require a storage account. In the creation dialog, there is a dropdown in the top right of the window where you can specify the storage account that you will be using.

There are three choices available in the dropdown: None, Storage Emulator, and Browse. For most triggers (i.e., all but Http), you can choose Storage Emulator as a starting point. This allows you to develop your Azure Function without having to identify the storage account first. Instead, it uses the Storage Emulator functionality within Visual Studio while you are developing your application. You will, however, need to choose a storage account before deploying the completed application. And if you don't choose one, a storage account is created automatically on deployment.

If you already know which storage account you will use on deployment, select the Browse option. This opens a dialog (shown in Figure 9-15) which can be used to select a storage account to use.

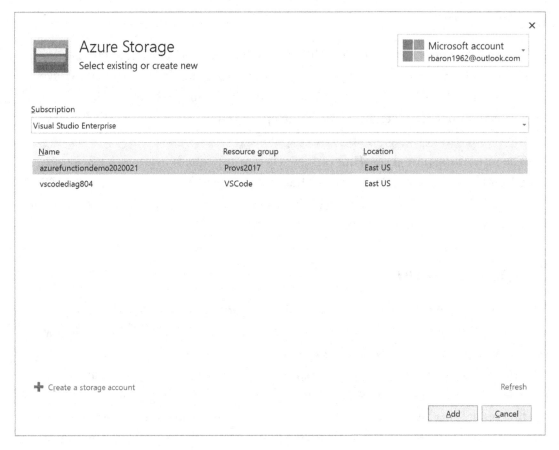

Figure 9-15. Choosing an existing storage account

Authorization

The last option available when creating an Azure Function project is to set the authorization for the Azure Function. The dropdown that is used to set the value is found immediately below the storage account. The available options are Function, Anonymous, and Admin.

The simplest of these options is Anonymous. With that option, there is no authorization performed at all. Any request is accepted, with no further checking being done.

The Function option utilizes a key sent as part of the request to restrict who has access to the Azure function. There are two types of keys available: host and function. A host key is used across all the functions exposed by your Azure Function app. A function key is tied specifically to a single function, the implication being that you would need different function keys, one for each exposed function.

Note   It's very important to realize that the use of a function key is not a completely secure way to access an Azure Function. The key used to access a function is not necessarily encrypted. For example, if you use an Http Trigger, the key can be passed at the end of the URL or in the header as a Bearer cookie. The key is not encrypted, and so, if the request is captured, a malicious user could view and save the key, using it to send requests in the future.

The last option is Admin. This is similar to the Function option, in that a key is required to be passed along with the request. The difference is that the only type of key that is allowed is the host key. If a function key is passed, then an HTTP status 403 (Unauthorized) is returned.

Both the Function and Admin options require that a key be present in any incoming requests. The generation of that key is done through the Azure portal. There is no provision for being able to generate the key using the Cloud Explorer.

Project Files

Once you have specified all of the information that the Azure Function needs, click Create to create the project. There are only a few files that are included as part of the generated project. There is a Function1.cs file that contains a sample Azure function. This is a static class that has a Run method, decorated with various attributes. Typically, this class would be deleted or renamed to provide a more descriptive name for the function.

There are two other significant files in the project. They are both JSON files and contain configuration information used by the function.

> hosts.json – Contains metadata that is applied to all of the functions defined within your function app. This includes details like the instancing model (whether it's a singleton or not), logging details, the triggers used to invoke the functions, and input and output bindings.

> local.settings.json – Contains the settings used by the function when running locally. This includes connection strings, application settings (the typical key/value pairs), and hosting details. This file is only used for local execution. When you deploy the function application, you need to configure the settings contained in this file for use in Azure. This is covered in the next section, "Deploying an Azure Function."

Deploying an Azure Function

Once you have completed development and testing of your function, it becomes time to deploy it to Azure. For Visual Studio, deployment is initiated by using the Publish option. If you right-click the project, there is a Publish menu item that can be clicked. Or you can use the Publish item in the Build menu. Regardless of which way you use, the first time you publish a project, the dialog shown in Figure 9-16 appears.

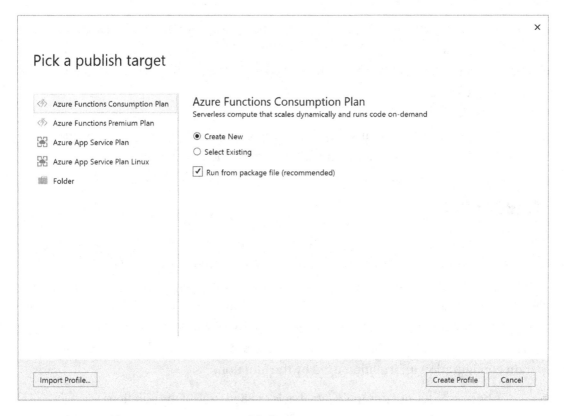

Figure 9-16. *Choosing an Azure publish target*

Before actually deploying the function application, a publish profile needs to be created. The next few dialogs are intended to create the profile. If you already have a profile file available to you, you can use it by clicking the Import Profile button at the bottom left.

Before continuing, you need to be aware that the list of targets that are visible in Figure 9-16 might not all appear when you are choosing a target. The list of possible targets can depend on the profile that you have imported, as well as the template that you used to create your application. For example, if you used a regular .NET Framework application, then the Azure Functions plans described in a couple of paragraphs might not appear.

On the left, you select from one of the five different publish targets. The most straightforward one is the Folder option at the bottom of the list. If you deploy to a Folder, then a ZIP deploy package is created. The package is a ZIP file that is structured in a way that Azure recognizes. It allows you to create a deployment package and give it to someone, who can then deploy it to their own Azure subscription.

The other four options are divided into two separate groups. The first two are Azure Functions Consumption Plan and Azure Functions Premium Plan. For both plans, your function host is dynamically added and removed based on the number of incoming requests. So, from that perspective, your function can scale up and down based on demand. This is what you should expect from the serverless environment of an Azure Function.

The difference has got to do with the ambient readiness of the environment. For the consumption plan, you pay for the resources that are being used, while they are being used. Once your function has finished using them, you stop paying for them. This includes both memory and compute time. But there might be a short lag when a request is made. If the previous function has finished, the memory and compute resources have been deallocated. They need to be reallocated in order to handle the request. This takes a small, but nonzero period of time.

The premium plan, on the other hand, always has a warm instance available on standby. So whenever a request comes in, there are memory and compute resources ready to handle it. Naturally, this comes at a cost. You will pay for the resources that are maintained in standby mode, in addition to the costs incurred when running the function.

In general, the choice you make depends on the demands placed on your function. If there is an almost continual demand for your function, then the premium plan makes sense. It ensures that there the response time for your function will be consistently good for each request. If the demand for your function is spotty or clustered, then the consumption plan makes more sense. The response time might not be as consistent, but you wouldn't be paying for resources that are only occasionally required.

The other two publish targets (Azure App Service Plan and Azure App Service Plan Linux) both involve deploying your function onto an App Service virtual machine (VM). This could be an App Service that is already hosting one or more websites within your subscription. So through this plan, you can choose the size (number of cores and memory) and isolation (shared or dedicated) that you need. And between the two plans, the difference is whether the underlying server operating system is Windows or Linux.

For all the publishing targets except for Folder, you are given the option to create a new App Service or use an existing one. If you choose to use an existing service, clicking Create Profile displays a dialog similar to Figure 9-14 where you can navigate through your subscriptions to select the desired App Service. If you want to create a new App Service for your Azure Functions, clicking Create Profile displays the dialog seen in Figure 9-17.

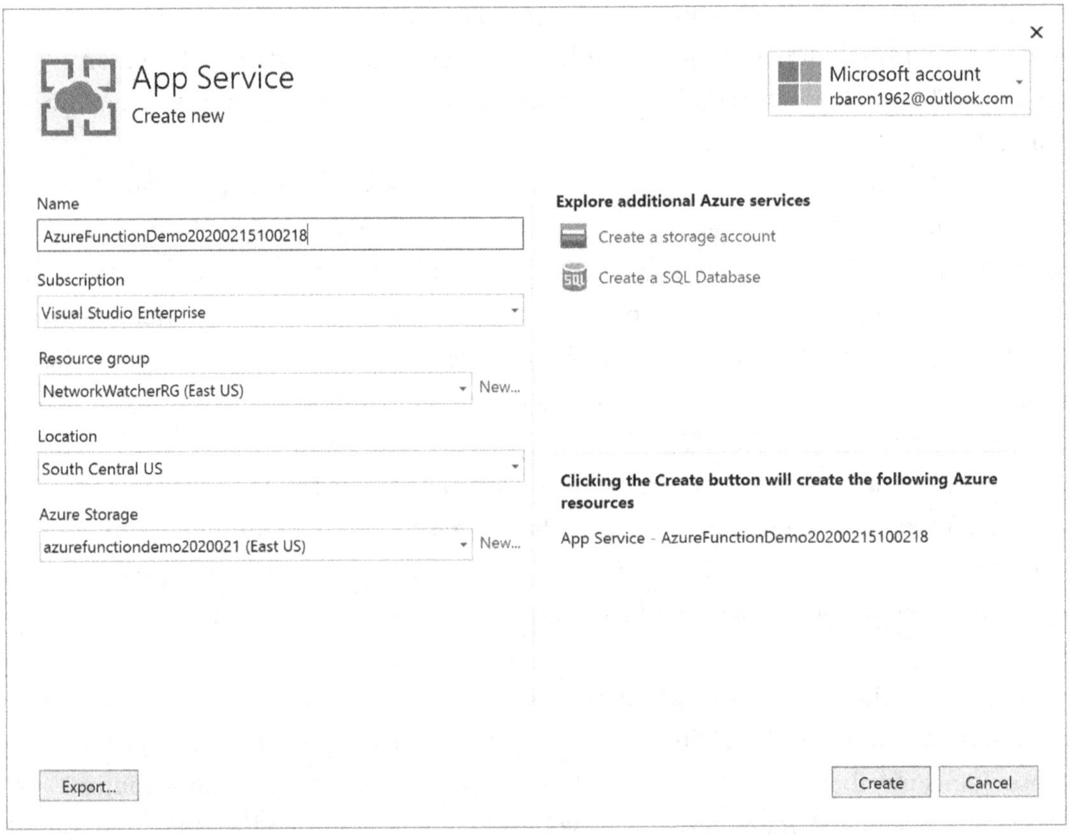

Figure 9-17. *Creating a new App Service for deployment*

The information available on this dialog configures the App Service that will be created. And just to be clear, even though you are currently creating a profile for deployment (as opposed to actually deploying the application), if you click the Create button, a new App Service will be created. In other words, the deployment process doesn't create the App Service. You are actually creating it right then.

Once you have finished creating the profile, or if this is not the first time the function application has been published, the next step is to actually trigger the deployment. Figure 9-18 shows the screen that is used to start deploying to Azure.

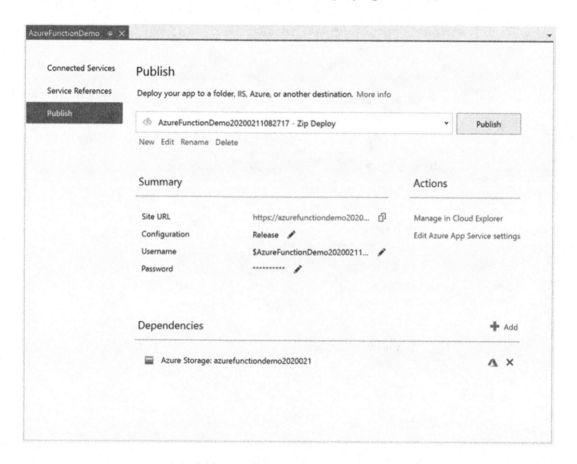

Figure 9-18. *Publishing an Azure Function*

At the top of the dialog is a dropdown containing the list of publication profiles for the project. The steps that you went through earlier in this section created a profile (found in a `.pubxml` file). But there is nothing stopping you from having multiple profiles for a single project. The publication process is as simple as choosing the desired profile and clicking Publish. The area below the dropdown is a summary of the settings for the selected profile, so that you have an idea of what you're doing before triggering the deployment.

On the right of the dialog, there are a couple of links to quick actions that you can take. The top link, Manage in Cloud Explorer, opens the Cloud Explorer pane (Figure 9-19).

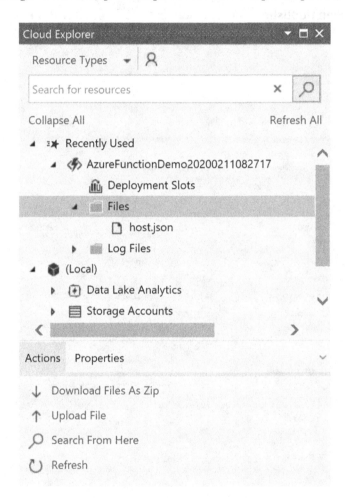

Figure 9-19. *Azure Function App Service in Cloud Explorer*

Within Cloud Explorer, you can view the deployment slots for the App Service, as well as upload and download files (at least, text files like hosts.json and any logging files) associated with the service.

The second option, Edit Azure App Service Settings, was mentioned earlier in this chapter. The `local.settings.json` file contains settings used by the function application when running locally. This click allows you to configure the settings that will be used when your function application is running on Azure. Clicking the link displays the dialog shown in Figure 9-20.

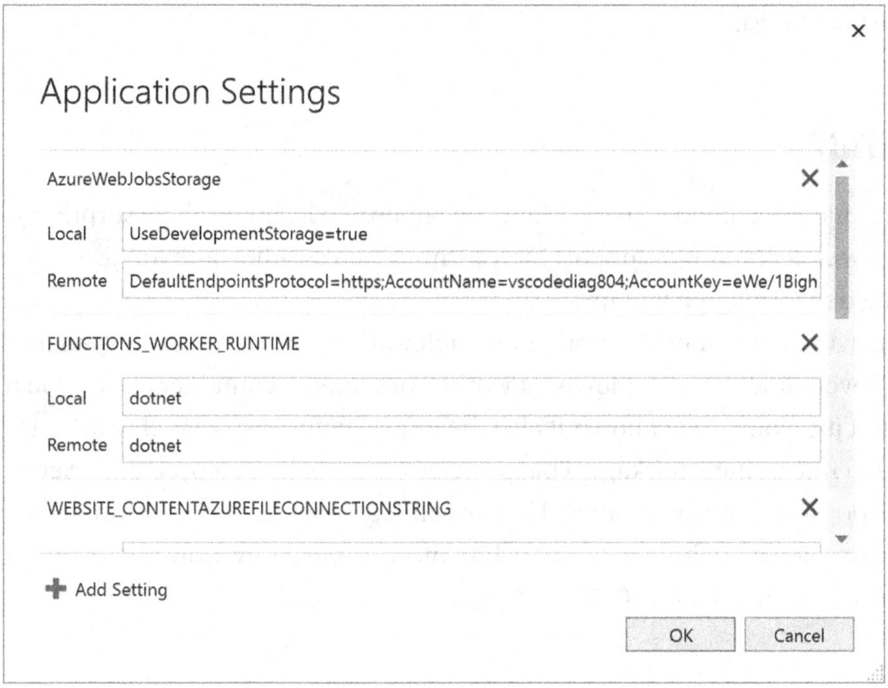

Figure 9-20. *Defining Azure Function app settings*

To get a sense of what the dialog is doing, the pertinent section of the `local.settings.json` file looks like the following:

```
"Values": {
    "AzureWebJobsStorage": "UseDevelopmentStorage=true",
    "FUNCTIONS_WORKER_RUNTIME": "dotnet"
}
```

You can see that there are two settings available for the application. These two settings appear in Figure 9-20, with both the local and remote values available. For the storage setting, the value that indicates that the local storage emulator should be used during development has been replaced by a connection string to the storage specified within the publication profile. For the other setting, the local value has been copied. You can change the value for the defined settings, include additional settings (using the Add Setting) link, and remove settings (use the X to the right of each setting.

As well as the settings that are explicitly defined in the `local.settings.json` file, there are other, ambient values that can be accessed. And since they can be accessed, you can specify the values used when the function application is deployed to Azure using the same mechanism.

Summary

Azure is a major technology in the Microsoft sphere, so it shouldn't be surprising that there is a decent amount of support for it within Visual Studio, both for development and managing deployed applications.

Along with Azure, there is another technology that has been making giant inroads into the development and deployment world: container. A container allows you to bundle not just your application but also the infrastructure associated with your application into a single package. That package can then be deployed and executed on small, disposable virtual machines. The next chapter goes into much more detail about not only the concept behind containers but, more importantly, how Microsoft supports them through Visual Studio 2019.

CHAPTER 10

Containers and Orchestration

It's always fascinating to watch new technologies move through the development ecosystem. If you're old enough, you might remember the move from monolithic desktop applications to client/server architecture. And then everything had to be running on the Web. And then back to a service-oriented architecture. And then onto the Web again.

As you can see, there seems to be a regular cycle of architectural patterns, as the technology catches up to the flaws in the previous iterations. At the moment, the pattern of choice is to deploy applications as a collection of microservices. These microservices can be packaged into containers, which themselves can be deployed into the cloud environment in a scalable matter. The technique of managing the deployment of the containers is called orchestration.

In this chapter, we look at the support that Visual Studio 2019 provides for the creation of containers, and the management of the containers through orchestration. The underlying container technology will be Docker, while the orchestration capabilities of Kubernetes will be covered.

Containers and Docker

One of the best ways to visualize containers used to deploy software is to analogize it with the original containers – containers used to ship goods from place to place. Originally, when shipping goods on a boat, the shipments were packaged up based on the most appropriate box for the goods themselves. Small products were in small boxes. Large products were in large boxes. The problems arose when trying to fit different sets of products onto a single vessel. Imagine the challenge of packing the cargo hold of a

© Bruce Johnson 2020
B. Johnson, *Essential Visual Studio 2019*, https://doi.org/10.1007/978-1-4842-5719-7_10

ship when every single piece of cargo is a different size and shape. It was like playing Tetris in real life. And there tended to be a lot of wasted space.

Shipping containers standardize the process of packing and transporting goods. Instead of accepting individual packages, cargo ships would only take containers. Regularly shaped. Consistently sized. Easy to stack one on top of the other. No wasted space at all. And by adding a couple of standard features, it's even possible to have the same container go from boat to train to truck and never open it once. The development of the shipping container revolutionized the industry completely.

For software deployment, containers play a similar role as shipping containers. If you consider what it takes to deploy an application, you'll begin to see the analogy. Software typically has a collection of dependencies, explicit or not, that must be accounted for when it's deployed – the operating system, database, connection strings, queues, and other resources. The options are many and varied, which is the source of the problem. When you create the package to deploy an application, you need to be aware of all of the different dependencies and how to resolve them. The process of accommodating this is ultimately what makes deployment difficult.

But what if software was deployed in a container that already contained all the dependencies? So the container includes a compatible operating system, a database required by the application, and all of other resources that the application requires. An application delivered like that would just need to be mounted into a network environment. And other application wishing to access the functionality would send a request (typically, although not necessarily, via HTTP) and receive a result.

Naturally, there are other complexities involved in software containers. Issues arise when it comes to how to share data or file systems. But the concept is fleshed out enough to talk about container support within Visual Studio 2019. But there is still a question of what Docker is and how it fits into this world.

What Is Docker?

In the world of containers, Docker has firmly established itself as the technology leader. By working with leading Linux and Windows vendors (which would include Microsoft), they developed the tooling that allows containers to be defined and deployed onto on-premise and cloud platforms.

Docker containers can run natively on Linux, OSX, or Windows, although the restriction is that Windows containers (i.e., containers that use Windows as the underlying operating system) can only be deployed onto Windows machines, running either natively or as a virtual machine (VM) and Linux containers can only be deployed onto Linux machines or a Windows machine that supports a Hyper-V Linux VM.

The process of creating a Docker container involves two steps. The first, creating the application or service, is well understood by developers. In order to create an application in Visual Studio that can be Dockerized (yeah... that's really a word), you are limited to ASP.NET, ASP.NET Core, .NET Framework, and .NET Core applications. This is a broad enough umbrella that most applications fit underneath it. This is not to say that all applications can effectively be containerized, only that the underlying technology is flexible enough to cover most situations.

The second step in creating a Docker container is to package the application. This is equivalent to creating a deployment for the application. The application, along with all its dependencies, is placed into a container image. The image is a static representation of the application's deployment. And the image is what actually gets instantiated when a container is created.

In order to create a Docker container, you need to have the Docker Desktop installed. It can be downloaded from *www.docker.com/products/docker-desktop* and is required in order to take advantage of Docker from within Visual Studio.

There are a couple of additional terms that are useful to understand when working with Docker:

> Dockerfile – To a certain extent, this is the secret sauce of Docker. The Dockerfile is a text file that is like a batch script that describes how to create the image. This includes how to install all the needed programs, which files need to be copied and where, and any other commands that are required to get the runtime environment configured properly.

> Repository – A collection of previously created container images. Generally, there is something that each of the images have in common (belong to the same project, different version of the same image, etc.), but that's not a hard requirement.

> Registry – The registry is a service that allows others to access repositories. There are public registries, the most familiar one being Docker Hub. But it's also possible to host private registries, either within a corporate environment or through a paid service offered by Docker Hub.

Docker Compose – A tool that is used to define a collection of Docker images that make up a more complex application. Compose consists of a command-line interface and a file format based on YAML (YAML Ain't Markup Language). Through the YAML file, you take previously defined container images and describe how the different images should be combined to create a larger application. This file can then be used to instantiate the images through a single command.

Docker and Visual Studio

There are two levels of support available for Docker within Visual Studio. First, if you just want to create a single container, Visual Studio allows you to add support for Docker either as you create the project or afterward. The second level involves orchestrating containers, the term used to describe the use of multiple containers in a single application supported by Docker Compose. Visual Studio supports orchestration using Docker Compose or Kubernetes. The rest of this section covers the first level of support. Support provided for orchestration is in the subsequent sections.

If you are creating a new project, the place to add support for Docker comes when you select the specific template that you want to use. Figure 10-1 shows the dialog that appears after you have selected an ASP.NET Core Web Application template. It is similar in style, and, more importantly, in the location of the Docker option, to the dialog seen for the other application types.

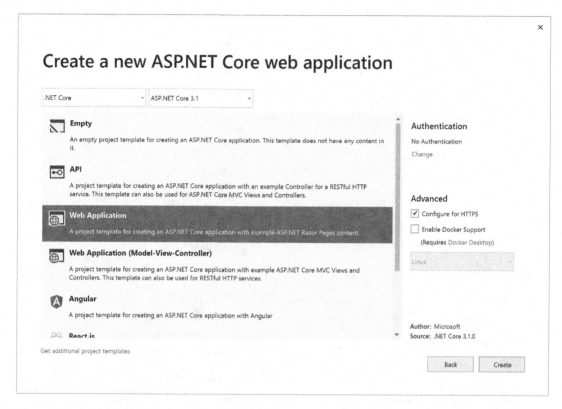

Figure 10-1. *ASP.NET Core Web template selection*

On the right side, in the Advanced section, there is a check box labeled Enable Docker Support. When selected, the generated project will include files necessary to support Docker. As well, the dropdown containing the runtime platform for the Docker files is enabled. The choices are Linux and Windows, and you select the operating system that is most appropriate for your application's deployment plans. It is quite possible to change this choice once the application has been created. And the runtime dropdown doesn't appear if you are creating a .NET Framework, as they are only available to run under Windows.

If you have an existing project that you would like to add Docker support to, right-click the project in Solution Explorer and select Add ➤ Docker Support (shown in Figure 10-2).

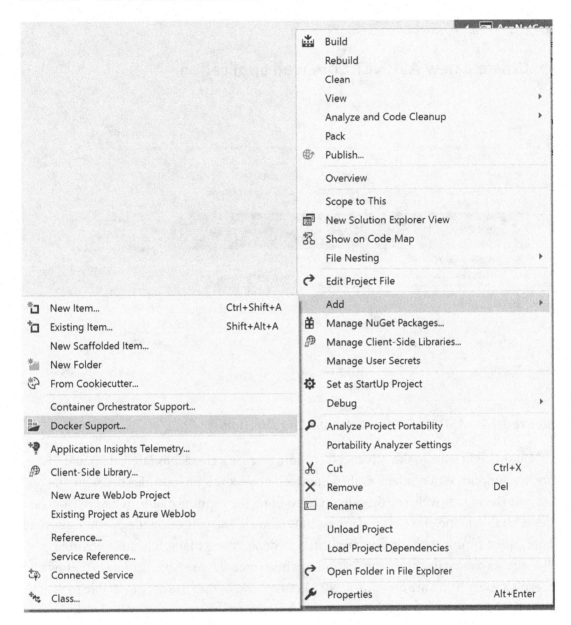

Figure 10-2. *Adding Docker support to an existing project*

If you are adding support to a .NET Core or as ASP.NET Core application, you will be prompted to specify whether the expected runtime is Linux or Windows. For .NET Framework projects, this prompt doesn't appear.

The addition of Docker support results in two files being added to the project, along with a NuGet reference. The NuGet reference is Microsoft.VisualStudio.Azure.Containers.

Tools.Targets. This reference is required for support for containers to be enabled within the project. The two files are a Dockerfile and a .dockerignore file.

The default Dockerfile is a simple one that is used to define the base runtime and then provide instructions on how to build and publish the application. The following is the Dockerfile as it is initially added when you have created an ASP.NET Core project. Different project types will have a different initial Dockerfile, but the basic content and purpose is the same.

```
FROM mcr.microsoft.com/dotnet/core/aspnet:3.1-nanoserver-1903 AS base
WORKDIR /app
EXPOSE 80
EXPOSE 443

FROM mcr.microsoft.com/dotnet/core/sdk:3.1-nanoserver-1903 AS build
WORKDIR /src
COPY ["AspNetCoreSample.csproj", ""]
RUN dotnet restore "./AspNetCoreSample.csproj"
COPY . .
WORKDIR "/src/."
RUN dotnet build "AspNetCoreSample.csproj" -c Release -o /app/build

FROM build AS publish
RUN dotnet publish "AspNetCoreSample.csproj" -c Release -o /app/publish

FROM base AS final
WORKDIR /app
COPY --from=publish /app/publish .
ENTRYPOINT ["dotnet", "AspNetCoreSample.dll"]
```

The base runtime for the application is declared in the first block of statements. The nanoserver-1903 reference specifies that a Windows Server version 1903 will be used. If you want to see the other tags that are available in the public registry, you can find the list at https://hub.docker.com/_/microsoft-windows/ (check the related repositories for Nano Server and Windows Server code instances). Finding the list of Linux servers that can be used as the base for a container is a little more difficult, in that you need to know the variant of Linux you're deploying onto (e.g., Ubuntu, Debian, etc.).

This first block of script also specifies that ports 80 and 443 (HTTP and HTTPS) are to be exposed.

The second block of script defines what happens on build (i.e., when the `dotnet build` command is executed). The steps here include performing a restore, to update any packages used by the project, a copying of the project files to a build location, followed by the build performed against the project directly. The copying step is important in that it uses the `.dockerignore` file to determine which files should or should not be copied.

The third block of script defines the publish functionality for Docker. In this instance, it just invokes the publish command against the project file.

Finally, the fourth block of script performs the final step of creating the static container image using a combination of the base runtime image and the published application.

As mentioned earlier, there is also a `.dockerignore` file that gets added to the project. This file contains a collection of patterns that are used to specify the files that should not be copied as part of the Docker container creation process. By default, this includes folders like `node_modules,` `bin`, and `obj` and files such as `.gitignore` and various settings files. Naturally, the file is completely customizable by you, so that you can make sure only the content required by the Docker container is published.

Running in Docker

When you add Docker support to a project, there is one other element that gets added to Visual Studio. The toolbar at the top of Visual Studio now includes Docker as a possible debugging target (see Figure 10-3).

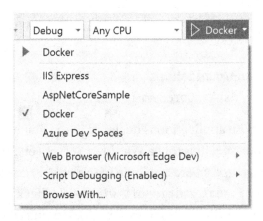

Figure 10-3. *Launching your application in Docker*

The addition of this option means that when you debug your application, you can choose to run the application from within the Docker environment, instead of running it within, for example, local IIS or IIS Express.

With Docker set as the debugging platform, running a debug session starts by creating a Docker container image and the loading the image into Docker for execution.

In order for these steps to take place successfully, a number of criteria need to be met. First, you need to have Docker already running on your machine. Having it installed isn't sufficient. It needs to be running. Now, it's possible to configure Docker to automatically start whenever you boot your machine. But in the absence of that setting, you need to start it manually.

Second, your local Docker needs to be configured to use the correct type of runtime container. Once Docker is running, you can change the container type by right-clicking the icon in the system tray and choosing the appropriate command (Switch to Windows/ Linux containers) as seen in Figure 10-4.

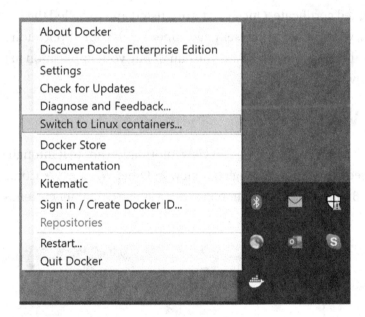

Figure 10-4. *Switching Docker container types*

Once the container type is set correctly (and it does take a few moments to complete the change), you can then run the applications normally.

The first time you run a project through Docker you might be prompted to trust an SSL certification. You'll see a dialog like the one seen in Figure 10-5.

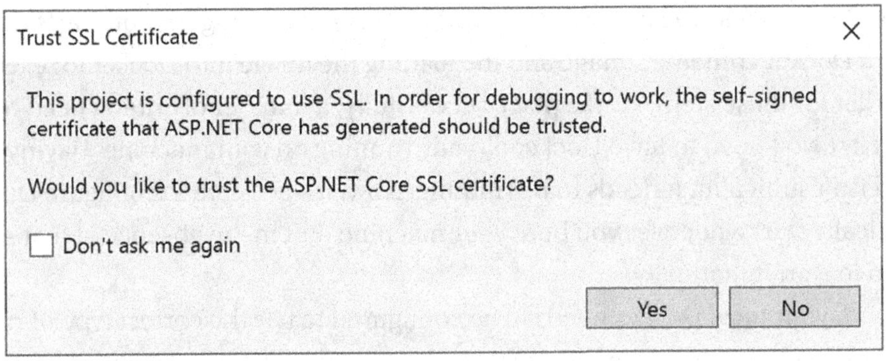

Trust SSL Certificate   ✕

This project is configured to use SSL. In order for debugging to work, the self-signed
certificate that ASP.NET Core has generated should be trusted.

Would you like to trust the ASP.NET Core SSL certificate?

☐ Don't ask me again

                                                        Yes   No

Figure 10-5. *Trusting an SSL certificate*

When you choose to trust the certificate, you will probably also be prompted to
install a self-signed certificate. Once you have trusted and installed the certification, after
a few moments, you will see a browser page appear with your application running within
it (for a web application, anyway). And you can debug your application just as if you were
running it locally.

Containers View

While your container is running, you can view information about it through the Containers
pane. You can see the window through the View ➤ Other Windows ➤ Containers menu
item. Figure 10-6 shows the Container pane with a single container currently running.

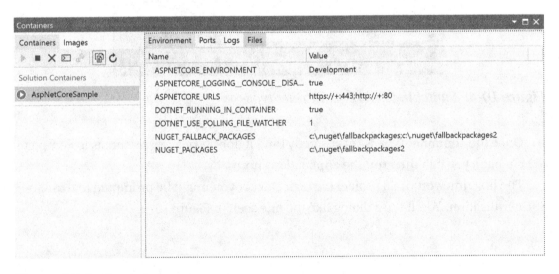

Figure 10-6. *Containers pane*

There are two main functions of the Containers pane. The first is to visualize information about a specific container. In Figure 10-6, there are four tabs of information for the selected container. The tab that appears, Environment, displays the configuration information for the container. The other tabs show the exposed ports, the logs generated by the application, and the files that are part of the container image.

The information should in the tabs is read-only. Yes, the log files are updated as the application running in the container generates message, but you have no control over the execution of the container through the tabs. However, through the Containers pane, you can execute commands that impact the application.

In the toolbar above the list of containers on the left side, you can start and stop the container using the two icons (the triangle and the square) on the left side. There is also an icon that removes a container from Docker (the X). However, if you want to be able to execute commands within the container, the Terminal icon (fourth from the left, looking like a command prompt in a box) fits the bill.

When you click the Terminal icon, a command-line window opens. It looks like any other command-line window, except that this one is connected to the running container. When you execute commands, they are executed against the container instance. And, since it's a command line, you can run a wide range of commands as needed to view the state or modify the image.

Keep in mind, however, that any changes you make are only for the currently executing image. When you shut down and restart the image, the changes made will be gone. If you want to make them permanent, you will need to modify the Dockerfile so that your images are configured correctly.

Orchestration

Now that the concept of a container has been introduced, let's add in how a number of containers can be managed. If you have developed an application that uses a single container, then managing it in terms of deployment, life cycle, and resources is pretty easy. Even if your application consists of three or four services running on a dozen containers, it's still not overly challenging to manage. However, once you get into hundreds of containers running hundreds of services, then dealing with container creation, destruction, and management would be overwhelming to perform manually. For that reason, orchestration tools were created.

The idea of orchestration is to have a tool that deals with the details of containers: when they get created and destroyed, where they are created, what sets of containers should be created in close proximity to each one, what external resources are required and where should the resources be created, and what network connections are required.

In orchestration tools, these details are defined in a separate file, typically JSON or YAML formatted. The definition is processed by the tool to load the images, mount any required resources, and connect them to one another. The definition files are typically version controlled by the team in charge, so that the application can be deployed to different environments, such as staging or quality control, prior to being rolled out into production.

In complex environments, containers are deployed onto hosts. When a new instance of a container is required, typically when the container image has been modified, the orchestration tool looks for the most appropriate host on which to deploy. The criteria used to determine what is "appropriate" are included in the orchestration definition file. It can include criteria such as geographic location, host capabilities (CPU, memory), or administrator-defined tags.

In Visual Studio 2019, there is support for two different orchestration tools: Kubernetes and Docker Compose. In the next sections, we'll look at the nature of the support that is available.

Kubernetes

Kubernetes is tool that came from Google. Google has been running containerized workloads to support its many different features and projects for 15 years. Along the way, it developed a number of tools specifically designed to help manage the different workloads. The internal tool used to manage these workloads is called Borg, and it was the precursor to Kubernetes. Many of the ideas found in Kubernetes have their origin in Borg. But, more importantly, a number of pain points that were in Borg too deeply to be refactored away have been addressed in Kubernetes.

As you might expect, there is some terminology in Kubernetes that is important to be aware of as you use it from within Visual Studio:

> Cluster – A collection of storage resources and compute nodes (hosts) that make up a management unit within Kubernetes. Each cluster has at least one Kubernetes master that is responsible for the scheduling and deployment of application instances across the different nodes.

Pods – The lowest level unit of scheduling in Kubernetes, a pod consists of one or more containers that are deployed onto a single host machine. And each container in the pod has the ability to share resources with the other containers. Each pod is also assigned an IP address, ensuring that the application can define the necessary port numbers for communication without worrying about collisions.

Kubelet – A service agent that runs on each compute node within the Kubernetes environment. The agent is responsible for managing and reporting on the state of the containers running on the node. When the Kubernetes master issues instructions, it is the Kubelet agent that actually performs the actions on the node.

Deployment – As mentioned in the description of orchestration, there is a file that defines the containers that are grouped together. In Kubernetes, that file is YAML formatted and is called a deployment. When a Kubernetes master schedules a deployment, it presents the YAML file to the Kubelet for the actual creation of the various container instances and resources to take place.

Replica – As part of the definition of a pod, you can also declare that a certain number of identical set of containers are used. Each set is called a replica and the intention is that any incoming request can be serviced by any of the individual replicas. The idea of a replica is used to help ensure that uptime is maintained.

StatefulSet – A deployment is intended to be a stateless application. It is this statelessness that allows for the concept of replicas to be implemented easily. However, there are situations where the application needs to be stateful, and for those cases, there is the concept of a StatefulSet in Kubernetes. A database server is a good example of when a StatefulSet might be required.

Support for Kubernetes starts in Visual Studio with adding support for orchestration. In Solution Explorer, right-click the project and choose Add ➤ Container Orchestration Support from the context menu. A dialog appears (Figure 10-7) that lets you identify the type of orchestration tool you would like to include in the project.

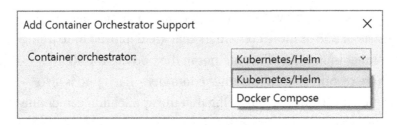

Figure 10-7. *Adding container orchestration support*

To add Kubernetes support, select the Kubernetes/Helm option and click OK. This process adds one or more files and couple of references to your project. If you hadn't previously added support for Docker, then the files and references associated with Docker are added. For Kubernetes, the YAML file that describes the orchestration is added, along with a folder called charts that contains the Helm template files. The name of the file is `azds.yaml` (for Azure Dev Spaces – more on that shortly) and it defines the orchestration in which the project participates. Keep in mind that the default file contains a very simplistic orchestration that consists of a single container (the one defined in the Dockerfile for this project). For more complex application, the YAML orchestration file can get quite large.

You might have noticed that when you added the container orchestration support, the selected option includes Helm along with Kubernetes. Helm is, in a couple of words, a package manager for a Kubernetes cluster. But to be fair, it also goes a lot further than just a package manager. Part of the reason for that is that managing package in Kubernetes can be a complicated endeavor.

Consider the following scenario. You have an application that includes a number of different microservice projects. The application has a YAML configuration that works great to get the application deployed and running on a staging environment. But the production environment is just a little different. The URL used to access the database is not the same in production as in staging (of course). So you write a script that, as part of your continuous deployment process, modifies the URL in the YAML file between the staging and production steps in the pipeline.

This solution works fine. For one application. Or maybe even two or three. But the more applications you deploy, the less effective this do-it-yourself approach will be. It becomes difficult to version the staging and production YAML files, because there is another script that modifies production before it is executed. And there is the longer-term problem of trying to understand the differences between the staging and production environments. It's not sufficient to compare the YAML files. You also need to look at the transformation script to get a complete understanding.

This is where Helm comes into play. Along with managing packages for your deployments, it also provides a single source of truth about the services and configurations that are currently deployed in your environment. And it provides a templating mechanism that addresses the discrepancies between environments.

From an architectural perspective, Helm is just a command-line tool. Now, being a command-line tool, it is easy to develop scripts for it. And the text format of the scripts means it's simple to version the scripts as needed. However, along with the command line, there is also a server component called `tiller`. Tiller runs on each Kubernetes cluster. It accepts commands from Helm and executes them on the cluster. This allows a centralized command window to impact the deployment of software onto remote Kubernetes clusters.

A Helm package is called a chart. And when you added Kubernetes/Helm support to your project, a directory called charts was created. In that folder, a subdirectory with the name of the project was created. Inside that folder, a number of files were created, in a structure recognized by Helm. This includes the following:

- templates – A folder that contains a collection of YAML files which act as templates when creating the Kubernetes manifest. As part of the Helm build process, the templates are combined with values found in the values.yaml file.

- .helmignore – A file containing patterns which are used to identify the files which should be ignored by Helm.

- Chart.yaml – This file contains metadata about the specific chart.

- values.yaml – Contains various values that are used by the templates in order to generate the manifests that are specific to this application.

At this point, you have all that you need to utilize Helm and Kubernetes to package and deploy your application. As you might imagine, these tools are a lot more complex than what we have talked about in this chapter. The details of how to use the tools are well beyond the scope of the book. And, at least for the moment, the generation of the necessary files is the level of support that Visual Studio provides.

Azure Dev Spaces

One of the features offered within Azure is Azure Kubernetes Service (AKS). This is a hosted Kubernetes service that allows you to develop and run complex Kubernetes orchestrations in Azure. The service provides a Kubernetes master and handles the health monitoring and maintenance tasks for you. It's up to you to create the application and deploy them to the nodes.

Azure Dev Spaces is an extension to AKS that allows for fast and iterative development and deployment of Kubernetes clusters. The goal is to help developers create applications for use in Kubernetes and to deploy them to the cluster so that they can be tested in conjunction with the other, already deployed, services.

The purpose of the `azds.yaml` file is to define how the application is deployed into AKS. The format of the file is similar to Python, in that the nesting of the content is determined by the indentation of the lines. The default file is typically sufficient for a single project deployment, so long as the functionality of the project is not overly complex. In other words, the more external resources your project needs, the more likely that the default will not be good enough.

The default file includes both build and install sections. The build section controls the process used to build the project. The install section describes the publication details, including the files containing settings and secrets (like connection strings), the image to use, and details like any exposed endpoints.

In order to take advantage of Helm and Azure Dev Spaces, it requires a bit of command-line scripting. You need to create an instance of AKS in your Azure subscription and then use Helm to install your application onto the AKS cluster. If you need to make changes to your application, you can use the `adzs` command to upload the updated package to the Kubernetes cluster. A detailed description of the steps involved can be found at *https://docs.microsoft.com/en-us/azure/dev-spaces/quickstart-team-development*.

Docker Compose

When you were adding container orchestration support (Figure 10-7), you could have selected Docker Compose instead of Kubernetes as your orchestration technology. Like Kubernetes, Docker Compose is used to define and execute multicontainer applications. There is a YAML file that contains a description of the different containers that are used.

And there is a single command (`docker-compose`) that will launch all the containers described in your YAML file.

So what is the difference between Docker Compose and Kubernetes? Complexity and features. Kubernetes is an enterprise-level container orchestration tool. It handles multiple containers running across multiple hosts. And it provides administrative ability that includes automatic scaling and restarts.

Docker Compose is much, much simpler. Its real purpose is to allow you to start multiple containers on a single host without needing to launch each one individually. You can start and stop services, view the status of the running containers, rebuild and update containers, and display the logs from the different services.

In Visual Studio, you add support for Docker Compose by selecting that option when adding orchestrion support. When selected, Visual Studio adds a `docker-compose.yml` file. And if your project didn't already have Docker support added, those files and references are also added. The following is the content of the Docker Compose file:

```
version: '3.4'

services:
  aspnetcoresample:
    image: ${DOCKER_REGISTRY-}aspnetcoresample
    build:
      context: .
      dockerfile: Dockerfile
```

There is a single service, since this file is related to a single project. There is a description of the base image used for the Docker container. And there is a section that describes how to build the application that will be deployed into the container.

Along with the `docker-compose.yml` file, there is also a `docker-compose.override.yml` file created. The purpose of the file is to allow for additional configuration details to be added. The difference is that the contents of the override file, well, override any of the settings in the base configuration file. And you have different override files, typically with names that are indicative of its purpose (e.g., `docker-compose.test.yml`).

By default, the `docker-compose` command reads the base configuration and then uses the content in the override file to supersede any configuration settings. If you want to use a specific override file, you can include the name of the file in the command line for `docker-compose`.

The first application that you add Docker Compose orchestration support becomes the application that started if you run or debug your application from within Visual Studio. This is the equivalent of specifying the startup project for a solution. You have the ability to change this behavior. If you right-click the docker-compose folder that was added when you added support, and choose the Properties option, the dialog in Figure 10-8 appears.

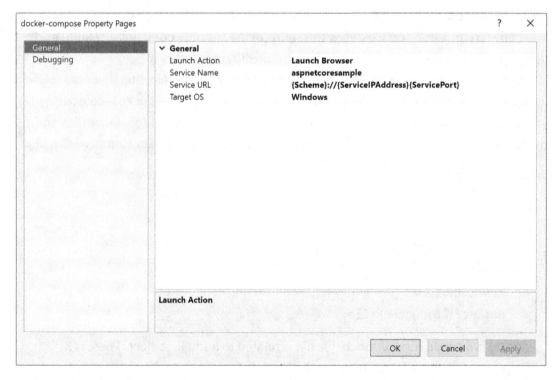

Figure 10-8. *Docker Compose property page*

These are the settings used to run the Docker Compose configuration from within Visual Studio. The meaning for each of the settings is as follows:

- Launch Action – What should Visual Studio do when the application has been successfully compiled and deployed? By default, it will launch a browser, passing in the Service URL. However, you can also have no action take place. In that case, the containers will be running, but will not have a default request to process.

- Service Name – The name of the service that the initial request is sent to on startup. The name is used as part of the next property.

- Service URL – The URL used to access this service. The default value is a template script that includes values that are taken from the configuration file. By default, it will access the service name using port 80 and the HTTP schema.

- Target OS – The operating system that the containers will be running.

Summary

Containers and orchestration will play a major role in developer community over the next 5 years. It has been a focus for companies that are concerned a great deal about scaling issues. And the microservice architecture that takes advantage of containers is useful in a wide variety of situations.

But even if you are not currently using containers, there are benefits to considering their capabilities. Even in the simplest case, the fact that you can create self-contained applications and deploy them to a wide variety of environment with just a couple of scripting commands is incredibly powerful. Not to mention that if you need to rehost your application onto a different server due to an unexpected hardware or software issue, being able to quickly spin up a container is a breath of fresh air for your IT staff.

What's important is that Visual Studio provides a collection of supporting services that can help address this entire range of use cases and, ultimately, the kind of functionality that makes Visual Studio so essential to such a large percentage of the developer community.

Index

A

Action breakpoints, 242, 243
AddOrderLine method, 71, 73, 78, 86
Anonymous types, 114, 115, 143
azds.yaml file, 344
Azure Cloud Explorer, 297, 298
    Actions pane, 305, 306
    Apply filter, 300, 301
    IoT Hub, 306, 307
    Microsoft accounts, 300
    properties pane, 304
    Resource Group view, 301, 303
    Resource Type view, 301–303
    selecting subscriptions, 299
Azure Dev Spaces, 344
Azure function
    authorization, 320, 321
    code, 312
    creation, 313–315
    definition, 312
    deployment (*see* Depolyment)
    execution, 312
    goal, 312
    platform, 315, 316
    project files, 321
    storage account, 319, 320
    templates, 316
    triggers/bindings, 316
Azure Kubernetes Service (AKS), 344
Azure Portal website, 306

B

Blog trigger, 316
Breakpoints
    call stack, 247
    condition (*see* Conditonal breakpoints)
    debugging techniques, 235
    remote (*see* Remote debugging)
Built-in analyzers, 56
    choices, 59
    property sheet, 58
    rule set, 59
    Solution Explorer, 57

C

CMake, 279
    configuration, 281
    editor, 279, 280
    settings, 282
    warning integration, 282
CalculateTotalCost method, 118
Class declarations
    anonymous types, 114, 115
    Change method name, 113
    encapsulate field, 118, 119
    extract Interface, 119, 121
    generate parameter, 124
    Get method *vs.* property, 115–117
    local function method,
        convertion, 117, 118

© Bruce Johnson 2020
B. Johnson, *Essential Visual Studio 2019*, https://doi.org/10.1007/978-1-4842-5719-7

Printed in the United States
By Bookmasters